TEACHING THE HOLOCAUST

SIMONE SCHWEBER
AND DEBBIE FINDLING

 TORAH AURA PRODUCTIONS

Library of Congress Cataloging-in-Publication Data

Schweber, Simone.

   Teaching the Holocaust / by Simone Schweber and Debbie Findling.

       p. cm.

   Includes bibliographical references and index.

   ISBN 13: 978-1-891662-91-1 (pbk.)   ISBN 10: 1-891662-91-0 (pbk.)

   1. Holocaust, Jewish (1939-1945)--Study and teaching--United States.   I. Findling, Debbie. II.
Title.

   D804.33.S353 2007

   940.53'18071073--dc22

                              2006039283

Torah Aura Productions • 4423 Fruitland Avenue, Los Angeles, CA 90058
(800) BE-Torah • (800) 238-6724 • (323) 585-7312 • fax (323) 585-0327
E-MAIL <misrad@torahaura.com> • Visit the Torah Aura website at www.torahaura.com

MANUFACTURED IN THE UNITED STATES

Dedication

This book is dedicated to our fathers, Silvan S. Schweber and Fred S. Findling, whose hardships were honed into wisdom and whose wisdom was shared with love.

"Like the crying blood of Zechariah, which could not be brought to stillness, the blood of our brothers and sisters cry out from under the foundations of Europe. ...These immortals live with us, in us. They will live in us forever. This it is that makes our hearts so heavy—and our luggage still heavier. Let us carry it together." —Simon Rawidowicz, *Studies in Jewish Thought* (1974)

Acknowledgements

In writing this book, we are indebted to more people than we can name. Numerous friends and colleagues read and edited chapters, giving us invaluable feedback and historical insights. Others allowed us to exploit their expertise in other ways, by making dinners, taking care of our children or holding our calls. First and foremost, we thank our husbands, Jonathan and Steven, for their patience and support. We also thank our kids, Talia, Max, and Sara, for teaching us anew about the importance of this project. To Sara Lee and Audrey Friedman Marcus, we owe thanks for setting us on the course of writing this book in the first place. For seeking out countless resources and helping us vet them, we thank Howard Freedman. For sharing her expertise in early childhood Jewish education, we thank Janet Harris. Stephen Feinberg, Director of National Outreach at the U.S. Holocaust Memorial Museum, checked every word of this book on his own time, for which we remain in his debt and will repay him in pastry. Jordan Ottenstein and Jessica Krasnick caringly read an early draft of the book, and Maggie Wunnenberg carefully fact-checked the final draft. We are also grateful to Rachel Brodie, Adrian Schrek, David Shneer, Elias Stahl, Ilan Vitemberg, and Adam Weisberg for helping us fill in gaps and fill out our knowledge. The faults, gaffs and omissions of the book are our own; we thank these people, though, for narrowing the pool of mistakes. Finally, we will always be indebted to this book itself, as it was through the work of writing it that our very real friendship was forged.

CONTENTS

INTRODUCTION

In recent years, the Holocaust has come to occupy a position of tremendous power in the American imagination. It has become a moral reference point not only for American Jews, but for almost all Americans regardless of religion, ethnicity, or political persuasion. Indeed, as Peter Novick has written in his book, *The Holocaust in American Life*, the Holocaust has become such a dominant metaphor for Americans that references to it abound in political life regardless of context. In other words, you are as likely to hear people invoke the Holocaust at a pro-life rally, for example, as you are to hear people invoke it at a pro-choice demonstration, a pro-Israel or anti-Israel event, an anti-hunger campaign, etc. In the U.S., the Holocaust has become so powerful rhetorically that it serves as a rallying cry for almost any cause, even opposite sides of the same cause. And the U.S. is not unique in this regard. In many other countries across Europe and across the world, the Holocaust has become a focal point of attention, in one way or another.

Why has this happened? We'd argue that it's the moral power of the Holocaust which accounts for this magnetism; we'd suggest that the seeming moral clarity of the Holocaust has drawn the attention of the world. This is a history, after all, which people think of as having crucial moral lessons, maybe the most important moral lessons we stand to learn as human beings. Moreover, they are moral lessons that seem to garner agreement across the political spectrum. It is this clarity that draws people from decidedly different political positions to call on the Holocaust in support of their platforms. It is this moral clarity which entices people to use the emotional weight of the Holocaust as a metaphorical bullhorn, amplifying their arguments. As a side note, perhaps, we have often thought that when the immediacy of the losses of September 11 recede further into the past, an analogous kind of political utilization may occur with its events. As the Holocaust has been for most Jews, 9/11 is now for many Americans; though of course radically different in scale, timing and circumstance, both events are emotionally devastating and morally clear cut since the murder of innocents is always, utterly wrong. It is out of this same moral urge that we are drawn to teach about the Holocaust regardless of where we teach: public school, synagogue school, Jewish, Catholic or Christian day school.

In the wake of destructions, large and small, immediate and more distant, we are often moved to draw lessons, perhaps as a vehicle to soften the blows of loss. Learning from loss extends the possibility of hope; it provides the thread from which a silver lining can be sewed. Consider the slogan "Never Again!" While it may have served first as a rallying cry during the 1970s to drum up support for Jews trapped and discriminated against in the former USSR, its psychological staying power may be explained by its redemption of the Holocaust's tragedy. "Never Again!" allows us to make some use of the Holocaust; it allows us some relief from its horrors, allows us at least the temporary conviction that things will be different in the future, that we can make a difference.

Other lessons that people have drawn from this history seem to extend the same analgesic. Such lessons include the imperatives to: defend the rights of minorities, speak out against injustice and oppression in all of its forms, safeguard the freedoms of democracy, question personal participation in bureaucratic systems, support the state of Israel, support an independent Palestine, and fundamentally preserve the dignity and uphold the sacredness of all human life. The lessons—whichever ones are embraced—are easy to arrive at. We don't mean that the lessons are easy to enact in our lives or to teach to students, but they're usually easy for people to identify with and to connect to the events of the Holocaust.

The seeming moral clarity of the Holocaust stems not only from its overarching wrongness, however, but also from the clarity of its actors' roles. In other words, we know that the Nazis and their collaborators were the bad guys; the rescuers and resisters were good; the bystanders allowed and perpetuated atrocity. And the victims were victimized; they were thus innocents to be remembered as martyrs, heroes and heroines.

As Americans and as Brits, Australians, and Canadians, we're usually positioned as rescuers. In fact, some have argued persuasively that one of the reasons the Holocaust has become so popular in the American imagination is that it is our last good war, the last moment in our collective memory as a nation that we were rescuers, heroes, unreservedly good. In contrast with our role in Vietnam and in a host of other, more recent events (some might add as a force of cultural imperialism), as regards the Holocaust, we were the ones who liberated the concentration camps, who fought and defeated fascism, who finally ended World War II. You need only imagine the entry points for visitors to the United States Holocaust Memorial Museum to understand the power of this conception; as visitors travel to the main exhibit areas, the elevators show films taken during the liberation of the concentration camps. Visitors are therefore positioned as

American liberators. They are, in effect, introduced to the Holocaust museum through the "eyes" of liberators. The role we played during the Holocaust epitomizes how we'd like to perceive ourselves as a country more generally; we like to see ourselves as defenders of democracy, a nation which is selfless and heroic, triumphant and good.

The Myth of Moral Clarity

Unfortunately, this kind of thinking is a trap. While it may be alluring to think of Holocaust history as morally simple, it isn't. The large categories and the broad lessons may be simple, but when you really start to investigate their historical realities and more specifically, their implications, they become very, very complex, not only for American Jews, but for all Americans, for all Jews and for all thinking people. It may be tempting to think that as public school, Jewish or Christian educators, we serve our students best by simplifying history, by glossing over its considerable complexities, by clarifying its moral messages. The premise of this book is that the opposite is true. Following the arguments articulated in Katherine Simon's groundbreaking research, *Moral Questions in the Classroom*, we are fully convinced that, as she writes, "The moral, existential and intellectual are intertwined [in education]; exploration in one realm often augments the others."[1] In other words, delving deeply into the complicated moral terrain of the Holocaust not only serves our students intellectually, but morally and spiritually as well, and ultimately, religiously. If we want our students to be empowered to make hard decisions in the complicated world they will inherit, we would do best to help them illuminate the complexities of history. This means that we cannot teach stereotyped roles or simplified lessons.

An example of what we mean here may help to concretize our point. Consider the category of victims. Ask yourself what words come to mind when you hear the phrase, "Holocaust victim." (Think specifically about "Holocaust victim" as the word, "victim" alone may carry quite different associations.) Do you find on the list of associated words a notion of martyrdom, of *Kiddush HaShem* (sanctification of God's name), of innocence, of heroism? We would be surprised if somewhere in your associations these themes didn't appear.

And yet, the approach to Holocaust education that we are advocating in this book would have you bear in mind as you plan your Holocaust unit the ugly reality that not all victims behaved heroically (although those are the accounts we most like to read). There were, among the victims, parents who sacrificed

---

[1]Katherine Simon, *Moral Questions in the Classroom* (New Haven: Yale University Press, 2001), 13.

children, sisters who stole from brothers, children who betrayed parents, people who within the concentration camp system occupied the liminal status of the [moral] "grey zone" in Primo Levi's magnificent wording. Of course it is vitally important to recall that the systems of Nazi terror forced people into roles they wouldn't otherwise occupy; nonetheless, the idea that Holocaust victimization yielded a huge range of human behavior among victims should make it into your curriculum.

Likewise, the idea that not all perpetrators were cruel should be represented in your teaching. The vast majority of perpetrators, in all probability, were not the animalistic killers portrayed by Ralph Fiennes in *Schindler's List* but people we would recognize, indeed people with traits we need to recognize in ourselves. The perpetrators of this atrocity were people, fully human; they had aspirations, families, careers and foibles. (In this line of argument, we are closer to adherents of Christopher Browning's claims in his book, *Ordinary Men*, than to Daniel Jonah Goldhagen's position in his, *Hitler's Willing Executioners*. Ultimately, though, we consider both works useful in teaching about the Holocaust, which we discuss in greater depth below.) To teach about the perpetrators as a morally complicated group is exceedingly challenging, but utterly necessary. Were bystanders perpetrators? By doing nothing and allowing evil to flourish, were they culpable for the tragedies of the Holocaust? And, if so, to what degree, and how do you decide? Even the question of who constitutes the category of perpetrators, therefore, is morally complex.

Finally, not all rescuers were wholly altruistic or uncomplicatedly good. There were rescuers who exploited those they hid, extracting money, and labor, in some cases even sexual favors. Regarding Americans, while we were rescuers, liberators, fighters against Nazism, White Americans were also simultaneously racists and bystanders (at least most of us) to home-front injustices. Our immigration quotas severely restricted those who could find refuge on our shores. Our Black soldiers were fighting on two fronts. And our Japanese American neighbors were sequestered in internment camps. So, even rescue, the most valorized role associated with Holocaust history, must be recognized, at least in some senses, as a morally complicated category.

While working as an educator on the March of the Living program, Debbie learned an important lesson about not viewing Holocaust survivors as one-dimensional figurines of heroic icons.

Debbie: Bella, a Holocaust survivor who was liberated from Auschwitz, traveled with the teenagers to Poland and Israel. Bella had moved to Berkeley, California after the war and was a former hippie who was active in Berkeley's liberal political scene. On the trip, I became increasingly frustrated with Bella because she would encourage the teenagers to sneak out of their rooms after their curfew to smoke cigarettes with her, publicly defying the rules of the trip. That experience helped me readjust my stereotypical image of Holocaust survivors. In short, because Bella was a survivor did not mean she was necessarily a role model (even if the students on that trip will likely remember smoking with Bella fondly). Throughout your teaching, we encourage you to present survivors and perpetrators and bystanders in the fullness of their humanity, rather than as personifications of stereotypes.

It may sound from this introduction that we are advocating a kind of cynicism in teaching about the Holocaust that we are recommending that all heroism be diminished, that only the bleakest truths be taught. That is not what we are suggesting at all. Instead, what we believe and what forms the basic premise for this book is that in teaching about historical actors in the fullness of their humanity, we are more likely to treat each other humanely, whether victims, perpetrators, bystanders, collaborators, resisters or rescuers. For aren't all of us at one time or another (indeed sometimes simultaneously) in all of these roles?

The Challenges of Teaching: One Example Not to Follow

What does it mean to teach about historical actors in the fullness of their humanity? On the one hand, as mentioned above, it means that we avoid valorizing, ennobling and condemning so much that we forget that the Holocaust involved real people in truly complex situations. In other words, we need to do our utmost to understand the moral complexities of the situations in which people found themselves. We don't pretend for a minute that we can know how it might have felt to be Anne Frank hiding in the annex, Elie Wiesel traveling in a boxcar, or Primo Levi reciting poetry to himself in Auschwitz. But what we can understand is something of how complicated it was to live in that time, in those places, and specifically, how morally complicated. The real question at the heart of the endeavor, then, is: How do we do that? How do we teach our students to gain an appreciation for moral complexity rather than to diminish it, especially given the kinds of mythologies that shroud this history? We'll begin by giving an example from Simone's teaching of what not to do.

Simone: By the time you read this, I will have taught Holocaust history for almost 18 years, to students in grades four all the way through college. For the first 10 years, when I taught mostly middle and high school students, I did what a lot of good history teachers do. I taught the informational content: the names, dates, places, what happened where and why. I don't mean that my teaching wasn't interactive; it was. But I would purposely hold off engaging the tough moral questions until the close of the unit, when we would spend one or sometimes two class sessions on the implications of this history. "Now that you understand what happened during the Holocaust and have some sense of why," I'd ask my students, "What is it you think we're supposed to learn from the Holocaust?" The students and I would come up with a list of moral lessons, profound ones even, and then we'd move on to the next unit or the next course.

When I think back about why I structured my unit that way for so long, I do have justifications—good ones even. Foremost among them was my dedication to content coverage. I firmly believed then that in order to draw lessons and make moral judgments, you needed to have the historical information under your belt, so I structured the two sequentially: have the students learn the information first, then they'll be prepared to make sound judgments. Over time, this conviction changed. While I still believe that students need rich wells of information in order to draw up meaningful lessons, I came to think that the best way to teach about the Holocaust was to do both in tandem: to have students muddle through the thick mud of moral issues as a way to examine the historical information itself. The moral issues, when fully explored, help students understand the historical circumstances and vice versa; the historical circumstances, when fully explored, necessitate discussion and exploration of the complex moral issues at play.

When I sat down to think about it, I came to realize that my own insecurities and inexperience as a teacher were preventing me from engaging kids in tough moral questions throughout studying the Holocaust. I think I was afraid of looking stupid. As teachers, we're trained to have answers. We serve as role models because of our knowledge, because of our competence, because of our abilities to guide students. Engaging students in discussions of tough moral questions in class, in some sense, is to compromise all three, at least it can feel like that. You don't know what will happen in a discussion of thorny moral problems, and engaging tough moral questions is to admit publicly to our students how little we understand, how little we know, how much we have yet to learn or figure out. I didn't know how to do that. I wasn't trained to lead conversations about morally complex events for which there can be no right answers. (As a side note, perhaps, I think it's fair to say that we have very few models for that kind of discussion in our public spheres. Think of a presidential debate, where in order to appear competent, you must condense the moral complexities of a question rather than explore them. In order to model leadership, you must appear utterly convinced of a particular side rather than appear to understand multiple angles on an issue.) To facilitate a discussion of a morally complex issue, by contrast, requires teachers to hold their own answers in check, to fully expose the values underlying students' opinions, and to weigh moral issues critically.

According to Katherine Simon's research, I was not alone in my proclivities for avoidance; it is common for both public and religious school teachers to avoid raising such issues and to close down such questions when they do surface in classrooms. Consider the brief exchange Simon observed in a Jewish day school where the students were studying Elie Wiesel's famous memoir, *Night*:

Gary [a student, asks]: How can Wiesel still believe? How is it possible for anyone to believe in God after the Holocaust?

Ms. Sherman [the teacher, replies]: That's an important question. You really should bring it up with the rabbi in your religion class.[2]

While I understand Ms. Sherman's unwillingness to engage Gary's question, the reasonableness of deflecting Gary's inquiry to a rabbi's expertise, I can also attest to the greater power of that kind of teaching which delves students into such questions fully and consistently, whether they bring up the questions or you do. I know from my own practice that once my philosophy shifted to structure those kinds of discussions throughout the curriculum, my impact on students increased tremendously. They learned more, more deeply, and more enduringly.

As learners, we all have a natural tendency to connect what is foreign to what is known to create understanding and make meaning. That is, we compare what we don't know to what we do. Consider for a moment a time when you traveled to a new city, state or country. Oftentimes, travelers will say things like, "This French cafe reminds me of the coffee house near my house." Or, "The balmy weather in Florida is so different from the cold climate at home." The process of comparing what is not known to what is known enables us to make sense of new information. Debbie witnessed this natural tendency repeatedly over nearly a decade of traveling with teenagers to Poland and Israel on the March of the Living program.

Debbie: Depending on current world events at the time, students would naturally compare the Holocaust to other genocides. During the early 1990s, for example, students would say things like, "The Holocaust is being repeated again today in Bosnia." In the late 1990s, I heard students compare the Holocaust to

---

[2]Ibid, 86.

the genocide taking place in Kosovo. My initial inclination was to discount those comparisons for fear that comparing other genocides to the Holocaust would somehow diminish its severity or distinctiveness. I would respond emphatically with statements like, "Six million people aren't being systematically murdered in Bosnia like they were in the Holocaust." My reluctance to have my students make these comparisons is understandable, but ultimately was not beneficial to their learning. Rather than shut down students' natural inclinations to compare events, I learned not only to encourage those comparisons, but also to help students contrast current events with the Holocaust to better inform their learning. As the events of the Holocaust recede deeper into history, this process becomes even more important. As educators, we need to find ways to help students grapple with and comprehend a history that most students will have an increasingly more distant relationship to as the years pass.

A Guide to this Guide: What it is and What it is Not

We have designed this book to help you avoid many of the mistakes that we and all teachers make in teaching about the Holocaust. Throughout this book we include lessons learned from our own teaching experience and disclose some of our own family histories in the hopes that doing so will engender deeper learning and will enable you to teach about the Holocaust with more integrity. We want you to be able to guide your students through its complicated moral terrain from the first day of your unit through the last one, and we want you to enter your classroom unafraid of engaging students' queries. We're not discouraging your students from bringing their questions up with their rabbis, grown ups, priests or parents, too; we simply want to make sure that the questions don't get shut down in your classroom. We hope that you will encourage inquiry and discussion and caution you not to confuse students' questions or doubts with disrespect. Towards that end, each chapter in this book contains ethical dilemmas and pivotal, moral questions, issues and scenarios to encourage student questioning and to help focus the discussions you have with your students.

The chapters in this book are organized by theme, which creates a vaguely, but not wholly, chronological architecture. As a result, certain ideas, topics or events may appear in more than one chapter. For example, the Wannsee Conference appears in the chapters entitled, *Naming the Holocaust*, *The War*, *Perpetrators*, and *Aftermath*. To ease your reading of the chapters, we decided not to reference these overlaps in the chapter text. In other words, we don't include references like "See Chapter 12 for more information about…." Instead, we encourage you to use the index to aid you in your searches.

Each chapter begins with an introduction, followed by *big ideas* and *key terms*. The *big ideas* are the main, overarching concepts that we hope your students will learn. The *key terms* are the words, phrases and names associated with those *big ideas*. Scientists ask "robust questions" as part of scientific inquiry; they look at the big picture while probing the details. We have designed the *big ideas* and *key terms* sections to mirror that approach; the *big ideas* relate to the big picture of the chapter and the *key terms* relate to the details. For example, one big idea related to resistance during the Holocaust is that acts of resistance were heroic, regardless of their outcomes. A *key term* of this big idea is the Warsaw Ghetto Uprising. In deciding what to teach, we suggest you first read the *big ideas* section of each chapter. Depending on whether you are teaching a single class, a short unit, a semester or entire year on the topic of the Holocaust, the *big ideas* sections will help you determine what you want your students to learn and to focus your curriculum accordingly.

Please bear in mind as you use this text that we have specifically avoided writing a history of the Holocaust. In other words, this book does not cover everything that is now known about the Holocaust. Instead, each chapter provides an overview of the teaching issues pertinent to its theme, a significant overview of content in that area, teaching ideas, and resources for classroom use and for further study for you and your students. Almost regardless of the reasons you're teaching about the Holocaust, we think that the issues outlined in the following chapters are integral to a coherent, thorough and meaningful education on the topic. Whether, for example, you're teaching about the Holocaust because it is one of the major historic events of the 20th century, because it continues to shape the world stage today, because it illuminates the tragic powers of antisemitism and racism, because it can aid in understanding the psychological processes by which victimizers oppress and the victimized respond, or whether because you know that study of the Holocaust can enrich your students' senses of what it means to be a Jew, a Christian or indeed a human being, the chapters in this guide can be used to form a unit of study.

As you'll see, with the exception of the first chapter, (*Teaching Young Children About the Holocaust*) all the teaching ideas and resources are designed for middle and high school students, not for students in lower grades. This reflects our conviction that the Holocaust should not be part of the formal school curriculum for young children, except in exceptional circumstances. To accommodate such circumstances (*Yom HaShoah* commemorations, communities with large populations of survivors and their families, etc.), we have included a number of single-session activities for teachers of young children. The bulk of this book, however, is dedicated to the teaching of much older students—students who we feel are mature enough to begin tackling this subject with the seriousness it deserves.

Closing Thoughts

Teaching about the Holocaust is necessarily an act of shaping memory, of forging the consciousness our students have. In creating our students' links to this past, we are helping to define their understandings of the present, and we are helping orient them towards particular futures. Of course as teachers, we are not alone in influencing their memory of the Holocaust; they will learn from their families, their friends, from the movies, from television, books, magazines and websites. They will hear urban myths about the Holocaust ("Wasn't Hitler part Jewish?"), contested rumors, even deniers' insults, the detritus of an information age and an ever-expanding politic. In our classrooms, by contrast, we have the unique opportunity to shape our students' memory of the Holocaust in carefully thought-through ways, to structure their learning caringly, with serious regard for the nature of the subject matter, for the needs of our students individually and the demands of our religious communities as collectives. We thereby stand in a position of special responsibility: to aid in fashioning the collective memory of future generations. We hope that this book helps you in accomplishing that formidable job by helping you navigate the incredibly complex moral terrain of teaching about the Holocaust.

TEACHING YOUNG CHILDREN
ABOUT THE HOLOCAUST

A group of Roma prisoners congrgate in the Rivesaltes internment camp in France, 1936–1942. USHMM, courtesy of Elizabeth Eidenben.

To date, there have been very few studies on how old kids should be before they learn about the Holocaust as part of their formal school studies. Nonetheless, there are lots of opinions people hold about the subject of how old is old enough, and people often hold their opinions passionately, basing their ideas on their personal convictions, experiences or dispositions. Roughly speaking, there are three schools of thought on the issue.

In the first are those who argue that early childhood should be a protected time, a time when adults need to shield the curious minds of children from the harsher aspects of the world they inhabit. This group tends to argue that teaching the Holocaust to youngsters is also developmentally inappropriate; young minds are simply not sophisticated enough to comprehend the complexities of the Holocaust, and young hearts are not well equipped to tackle the enormity of this tragedy. This group asks, "Why risk giving children nightmares needlessly? When the students are old enough and more mature, they will be ready to learn, and until then, we shouldn't teach about it."

In the second group are those who claim that it is the duty of adults to teach children, even young children, about the Holocaust. While children cannot fully comprehend its complexities, they can nonetheless begin to learn about it in a simplistic fashion. This group's proponents tend to agree with Jerome Bruner, the educational theorist who believed that "there is an appropriate version of any skill or knowledge that may be imparted at whatever age one wishes to begin teaching—however preparatory the version may be."[3] Kids can be taught what racism is, for example, or how important it is to speak up when someone is being hurt. In other words, kids can be taught about the social dynamics at play during the Holocaust as a way to prepare them for learning about its specific history in greater depth later. These proponents consider it better for students to be ushered into Holocaust knowledge slowly than not to be exposed to it at all; otherwise kids will be utterly unprepared for its horrors when they do encounter the Holocaust later.

In a third group are those who advocate teaching young children about the Holocaust without intellectually simplifying or emotionally minimizing its tragic content. According to this argument, it is the unenviable role of teachers sometimes to confront their students with the horrors of the world, the Holocaust among them. And it is better for kids to learn about the Holocaust for the first time from adults who can shape the experience carefully and caringly than for kids to learn about the Holocaust for the first time randomly, from a television show, older kids' insensitive renderings or widely circulated rumors. As the Holocaust survivor Batsheva Dagan puts it, "Today's children grow up in a

---

[3]Jerome S. Bruner, *Toward a Theory of Instruction.* (Cambridge, MA: Belknap Press of Harvard University, 1966), 35.

world without secrets"[4]—better then to help them navigate what they will learn about anyway.

Most people can find some claim in each of these orientations to agree with. In fact, there is a way in which all three orientations are compatible if the age barriers between the orientations are left unexplicated. The question at the heart of all three, though, is still "how old is old enough?" or, put differently, "how young is too young?" What could we take as a sign that a child is ready to move from the protected zone of early childhood to a later stage of gentle exposure to the Holocaust, and then again, from gentle exposure to full confrontation? At what age or grade should we teach kids formally about the Holocaust or some preparatory version of it? And, more importantly, if we *are* going to teach young kids about the Holocaust, what should that preparatory version look like?

Although far from conclusive, Simone ran one of the only studies of what happens to young kids when they learn about the Holocaust as part of the formal school curriculum. She found that students in the third grade were too young to learn this material in any depth. While the parents and teachers in that study thought the kids were old enough to confront these horrors, the kids themselves wished they had been older before learning about it in school. If we are serious about listening to kids' voices and valuing their opinions, the results of this study seem pretty persuasive. (It's also clear that more studies need to be done.)

We base our recommendations in part on this empirical research, which is why we advocate strongly that kids in Kindergarten through third grade not be exposed to the Holocaust as part of their formal school curriculum. That is, we don't advocate that you teach about the Holocaust to this age child. While you ought to teach preparatory Holocaust education to young kids—teaching them the importance of accepting difference, caring for the hurt, not judging others superficially, thinking critically, Jewish *mitzvot*, etc.—we don't advocate that you teach about the Holocaust directly until fifth or sixth grade at the earliest. And, even then, we hope you'll make accommodations by teaching kids in those grades about the Holocaust's more redemptive aspects only—rescue, resistance, and stories that soften the harder blows of this history. We think that the earliest young people ought to be taught about the Holocaust in depth is when they are older, when as a group, they are mature enough to be appropriately staggered by its enormity and developed enough to discuss its implications. Some communi-

---

[4]Batsheva Dagan, "Heutige Kinder wachsen auf in einer Welt ohne Geheimnisse" 6 Wie können wir Kindern helfen, über den Holocaust zu lernen? Ein psychologische-pädagogischer Zugang. Warum, was, wie und wann?, in Jürgen Moysich and Matthias Heyl (ed.), *Der Holocaust: Ein Thema für Kindergarten und Grundschule?*, (Hamburg: Krämer, 1998,) 36–50.

ties insist that students become *bar* or *bat mitzvah*, seventh grade before studying about the Holocaust in-depth; others put off study until even later.

As conservative as it may sound, this means that we advise you to keep younger students out of school-wide Holocaust commemoration activities if the ceremonies are to be overly explicit; in other words, if you are planning to commemorate the Holocaust in your school, plan to have separate arenas running simultaneously so that the K-third kids can have their own program separate from the older kids. This will allow you to help both groups commemorate an important part of Jewish history in an age-appropriate manner. Below are some ideas to help you plan such single-session educational commemorations.

Teaching Ideas
Pre-Kindergarten (ages three/four/five)–Kindergarten

1. **Candles:** Bring to class an array of different types of candles—Sabbath candles, a *havdalah* candle (braided candle used in the service that marks the end of Sabbath), birthday cake candles, decorative candles, and a *yahrzeit* (memorial) candle. Ask the students to describe what they know about each kind of candle and if they've used each kind in their home, and when. (This is an important step since it may let you know if your students have lost a family member.) Then, explain that some candles we light to celebrate happy events (birthdays); some we light to mark special times (Sabbath); and some we light to mark sad events, to remember people we love who are no longer with us.[5]

2. **Happy/Sad Holidays:** Ask your students to move around the room with their bodies showing that they feel happy. Then ask your students to move around the room with their bodies showing that they feel sad. Then ask, what did you do to show that you felt happy? What did you do to show that you felt sad? How did you feel doing each? Explain that in the Jewish tradition, we have some holidays that are happy (*Simhat Torah, Purim, Tu B'Shevat*) and some that are sad (*Yom HaShoah* or the 10th of the Hebrew month of *Tevet*). Just as people sometimes feel happy and sometimes feel sad, so we have holidays that either celebrate happy times or help people remember sad times. Use an artistic medium to have students render happy holiday feelings and sad holiday feelings. (For example, they may make paper plate faces, paintings, drawings, collages, body tracings of both feelings, etc.)

---

[5] Thanks to Janet Harris, Berkeley, California-based early childhood educator, for this activity idea.

3. **In God's Image:** Sitting together, explain to your students that it says in the Hebrew Bible that people are made "in the image of God" (Genesis 1: 26). That means that people are made to be like God, not the same as God, but like God in some way. Ask what your students think is like God in each of them. What do they think is "Godly" in them? What do they like about themselves? What do they like about each other? Then ask if we're all of us made to be like God, what does that mean we're doing to God when we hurt each other?

4. **Losing Things:** Ask the students to imagine for a moment that they've lost something they love—maybe a stuffed animal, a pet or a special toy; what do they think would make them feel better if they knew they wouldn't find it again? What might they do to make someone else feel better when they've lost something (or someone) they won't see again? (There are a number of sweet children's books that could help you talk about this issue further. **Flora's Blanket** is about a little bunny at bed-time who has lost her special blanket. She finds it in the end, but you could talk about how she felt before she found it; the same goes for **Laney's Lost Mama**, which is about a little girl getting separated from her mother in a department store. While this story has a happy ending, too, it is more conducive to talking about losing people and the feelings you might have in that situation.)

5. **Jewish Life Before the Holocaust:** Another appropriate way to introduce this age child to what they will later learn about the Holocaust is to acquaint them with stories about Jewish life before the Holocaust. (Because *shtetl* life is often imbued with a kind of nostalgia, these books tend to be utterly charming. These are good texts for educators wary of any explicit Holocaust content.) A few recommendations include: **Joseph Had a Little Overcoat**, which is graphically interesting, playfully ironic, fun for parents and kids from birth on up and even includes Yiddish song lyrics and music. Although **Hannah's Sabbath Dress** is set in a non-specific time period, it has a sweet "old-world" feel about it and is appropriate for ages three and up. **You Never Know: A Legend of the Lamed-Vavniks** has a specific European setting and is appropriate for slightly older kids, four to eight. **The Feather Merchants & Other Tales of the Fools of Chelm** is good for slightly older kids, five to eight, since the younger ones don't understand its kind of silliness.

First–Third Grades

Many of the activities in the above section can be adapted for use in the older grades. For example, you may use the same candles activity for older kids, explaining more specifically who lights a *yahrzeit* candle, when, and why, etc.

1. *Kaddish Yitom*—**Mourner's Prayer:** Sing or play a recording of the song, "Whenever I feel afraid, I hold my head up high, and whistle a happy tune, and no one knows that I am afraid…." Make sure everyone understands the words of this song before asking the question, "Why would someone who felt afraid whistle a happy tune?" (The kids will come up with good explanations.) Then, ask why someone who felt sad might say a happy prayer? Explain that there's a prayer called the Mourner's Prayer that makes people feel better when they're mourning, when they miss someone they love who's no longer there. The words of the Mourner's Prayer express our belief in the greatness of God, and when people who are in mourning say that prayer, they feel better (maybe not all at once, but after saying the prayer every day for a while they do). Explain that in some synagogues, when someone is mourning, everyone in the congregation says the Mourner's Prayer with that person while in other congregations; just the people who are mourning recite the prayer. (Your kids may know how it's done in their congregation. They may also have someone in their family who has said that prayer.) What's nice about saying a prayer with other people at the same time? What's helpful about saying the prayer alone? Brainstorm together what your kids could do to make a mourner in their community feel supported. (As a follow-up, in one synagogue school, for example, the second graders researched how many mourners their congregation had in a typical year and then produced that number of cards to be sent on behalf of the congregation at the appropriate time.) If you know of someone in your community who has lost someone in their family, observed the practice of saying *Kaddish* and who would be a sensitive and engaging speaker, invite them to come in and discuss what it was like to observe this ritual. (Make sure they know, though, that it's not appropriate to lecture. Instead, invite them to tell stories about the person they lost, how it makes them feel and what it was like to say *Kaddish*.)

2. **The Sneetches:** This Dr. Seuss book is a wonderful way to expose kids to the ideas of prejudice, discrimination, conformity (and commodification). Read this book aloud and talk carefully about what's going on in it both as you read and after. Kids will often listen, but they may not always

understand the story. What do your kids think happens after the book ends? We like following up this book with a "stand-and-smile" exercise meant to show ways that the kids in your class are alike and different from each other. Ask the kids to stand up, smile and thumb their chests when you say a statement that applies to them. ("I have brown hair."; "I'm seven years old."; "I'm wearing white shoes."; "I have a star on my belly.") The kids themselves can take turns supplying statements once the pattern is set up.

3. **Holocaust Picture Books:** There are an increasing number of picture books about the Holocaust targeted for young children. Many of them are very good: sweetly storied, rich in Jewish culture, enfolding loss within continuity, emotionally moving. All of them may evoke complex questions, though, which you should think about how you'll engage before beginning, questions like: "Why do people go to war?" "Why did people blame Jews?" "What happens when people die?" Don't be afraid of asking the kids to elaborate their own thoughts about each of these issues. Don't feel, in other words, that it's your job to answer questions. It is worth reiterating, too, that we suggest the titles below for single class period readings. We don't recommend that you read more than one of these to your students as this age child is simply too young for a mini-unit.

A few of the titles we especially like include: **Grandma Esther Remembers** is great for younger grades and includes beautiful photographs. It is not too graphic of a story, but it is still honest with a great layout and perfect for activity extension ideas (a good recipe for *tsimmes* too). **The Tattooed Torah** follows the story of a Torah through the war (and after,) and in that way shields readers from thinking too much about people. The subtitle of **One Yellow Daffodil** claims that it is a *Hanukkah* story, but it is really a Holocaust story, and a good one to read on *Yom HaShoah* rather than *Hanukkah*. **The Feather-Bed Journey** is a gorgeous book about a family's (and a mattress') transformations from generation to generation. Because the storyteller's family is killed, it's better for older children. **The Never-Ending Greenness** has Van Gogh-ish illustrations, and follows a young boy's childhood in Poland as the Germans take-over. It follows his subsequent move to a ghetto, his escape and his life planting trees in Israel after the war. **The Terrible Things** is marketed as an "allegory of the Holocaust," and tells a version of Pastor Martin Niemoller's famous quotation, "First they came for the communists, but I wasn't a communist, so I didn't speak up..." through the use of animals. If you use the book, it's important to talk about why the "terrible things" did what they did. For a nice follow-up activity, Simone once saw a teacher have his students break up into animal groups shown in the book, and each group had to think up what they would do if the "terrible things" were trying to catch them. What could they have done if they had known what was coming? How could the animal groups have organized a resistance? Have them brainstorm and act out their resistance plans.

Fourth–Fifth Grades

It's worth noting that, except for the first two, all of the picture books in the section above work beautifully with fourth and fifth graders, too.

1. **More Picture Books:** These picture books are more explicit, more depressing, more graphic or more evocative than the preceding ones, which is why it's worth reading them aloud to the whole class or a small group and discussing them together.

   The Yanov Torah is Simone's favorite Holocaust book for fourth/fifth graders since it reveals glimpses of human atrocity but through the lens of the holiness of Torah. It's the true story of a Torah smuggled into a labor camp one scroll at a time. We suggest you edit out the last section of the book which focuses on the Torah's being smuggled out of the former Soviet Union, not because it isn't interesting reading, but because it takes about 45 minutes to read the whole book in total without that section. In **Nine Spoons** a grandmother explains to her grandchildren the origins of a very unusual *Hanukkiah* that she lights every year. The *Hanukkiah* was crafted from spoons in a children's barracks of a slave labor camp. The illustrations are not great, but the story is very moving—uplifting, but still provocative, and centered on Jewish survival and continuity. You may want to not show the pictures and have students design the *Hanukkiah* themselves, based on their imaginations. **Rose Blanche** is told from the perspective of a young, non-Jewish German girl who smuggles food to a group of children in a nearby concentration camp. This story requires some explanation as fourth graders often don't understand the last few pages of the book where Rose Blanche herself is killed since it's only implied. The pictures are riveting, and the bleakness of the story is tremendously powerful. You can have students write letters to Rose Blanche's mother, pretending that they survived their stay in the concentration camp thanks to Rose Blanche's food. **Passage to Freedom: The Sugihara Story** discusses the amazing rescue activities of Sugihara, the Japanese diplomat in Kovno who was able to save thousands of Jews during the Holocaust. It is told from the perspective of his young son. Make it a point to read aloud the Afterward to your students, too; written by Sugihara's actual son, Hiroki, which discusses the repercussions post-war of Sugihara's rescue activities. **Luba: The Angel of Bergen-Belsen** is based on the actual rescue activities of a Dutch heroine. This book contains a marvelous Epilogue, which you should read aloud. **The Grey Striped Shirt** is a little longer than the others and will take more than a single class period to read aloud. It is about a little girl who finds a grandparent's concentration camp uniform in the closet. The story discusses the Holocaust in very simple terms as the grandparents explain their experiences to her. There are no graphic images.

2. **Family Book Groups:** There are a number of good chapter books for kids of this age, too. If your students are strong readers, you can assign them to read these books aloud to their parents at home, chapter by chapter, and you can discuss the chapters in class. It's a great opportunity for family education, too. For example, you can organize "book groups": kids in one, parents in another, then 2-3 families in each group, etc. You can have one family session at the mid-point of a book and another at its conclusion. The kids might put on a skit of a powerful scene for the parents and vice versa, to serve as launching points for the discussions. The three best chapter books, interestingly, all focus on girls' experiences: **Number the Stars, The Devil's Arithmetic**, and **The Upstairs Room**.

3. **Films:** There are not many good films for this age child, but there are two that are both excellent in different ways. If you can find a copy, **Daniel's Story** is the video accompaniment to the U.S. Holocaust Memorial Museum's exhibit for young children. It takes about 14 minutes and brings up many questions specifically about the Holocaust, and yet it is not graphic or scary. It's a great video that sadly went out of print, but lots of Jewish institutions own it and would likely loan it out. Another good one is the Frontline film, **A Class Divided** (sometimes referred to as the "brown-eye/blue-eye" experiment). Students are very adept at analyzing why the kids acted the ways they did, what they should learn from the simulation, and how antisemitism works as a form of racism. We recommend that students watch the video and talk about how they think they would have reacted rather than having teachers perform this kind of simulation.

Resources for Teaching

(Please see the section above for detailed summaries or highpoints of the books listed below.)

A Class Divided. Website: http://www.pbs.org/wgbh/pages/frontline/shows/ divided/. *This website houses the Frontline film in which Jane Eliot divides her kids into blue-eyed and brown-eyed kids. It's moving and fascinating, and despite the fact that it looks somewhat dated (made in 1968), all kids get involved in it quickly.*

Daniel's Story. Produced by the U.S. Holocaust Memorial Museum, 1993, 14 minutes. *This short video, though now out of print, was distributed to Jewish institutions as part of the Jewish Heritage Video Collection.*

The Devil's Arithmetic. Written by Jane Yolen and published by Puffin Books, London, 1990.

The Feather-Bed Journey. Written by Paula Kruzband Feder and published by Albert Whitman & Co., Morton Grove, IL, 1995.

The Feather Merchants & Other Tales of the Fools of Chelm. Written by Steve Sanfield and published by Scholastic Books, New York, 1991.

Flora's Blanket. Written by Debi Gliori and published by Orchard Books, London, 2001.

Grandma Esther Remembers. Written by Ann Morris and published by Millbrook Press, Brookfield, CT, 2002.

The Grey Striped Shirt. Written by Jacqueline Jules and published by Alef Design Group, Los Angeles, 1997.

Hannah's Sabbath Dress. Written by Itzhak Schweiger-Dmi'El and published by Simon & Schuster, New York, 1996.

Joseph Had a Little Overcoat. Written by Simms Tabak and published by Viking Children's Books, New York, 1999. *This version of the book won a Caldecott Medal.*

Luba: The Angel of Bergen-Belsen. As told to Michelle R. McCann by Luba Tryszynska-Frederick and published by Tricycle Press, Berkeley, 2003.

The Never-Ending Greenness. Written by Neil Waldman and published by Morrow Junior Books, New York, 1997.

Nine Spoons. Written by Marci Stillerman and published by Hachai Publishing, Brooklyn, 2002.

Number the Stars. Written by Lois Lowry and published by Houghton Mifflin, New York, 1998.

One Yellow Daffodil. Written by David Adler and published by Harcourt Brace, Orlando, 1995.

Passage to Freedom: The Sugihara Story. Written by Ken Mochizuki and published by Lee & Low Books, New York, 1997.

Rose Blanche. Written by Roberto Innocenti and published by Harcourt Brace, New York, 2003.

The Sneetches. Written by Dr. Seuss and published by Random House, New York, 1961.

The Tattooed Torah. Written by Marvell Ginsburg and published by UAHC Press, New York, 1983.

The Terrible Things. Written by Eve Bunting and published by the Jewish Publication Society, New York, 1989.

The Upstairs Room. Written by Johanna Reiss and published by Harper Trophy, New York, 1990.

The Yanov Torah. Written by Erwin Herman, published by Kar-Ben Publishing, Toronto, 1985.

You Never Know: A Legend of The Lamed-Vavniks. Written by Francine Prose and published by Greenwillow, New York, 1998.

Resources for Further Learning

Auschwitz Explained to my Child. Written by Annette Wieviorka and published by Marlowe and Company, New York, 2002. *This is an excellent introduction to the Holocaust, written as a series of common questions children have and the kinds of answers we as parents wish we could supply. Not suitable for young children, though, given its graphic content.*

Incorporating Holocaust Education into K-4 Curriculum and Teaching in the United States. Written by Harriett Seppinwall. The full text is available at: http://www.chgs.umn.edu/Educational_Resources /Curriculum /Incorporating_ Holocaust_Educat/incorporating_holocaust_educat.html. *The website is produced by the Center for Holocaust and Genocide Studies at the University of Minnesota and the full texts of responses to her article are posted there as well.*

Should there be Holocaust education for K-4 students? The answer is "No." Written by Samuel Totten. The full text is available at: http://www.chgs.umn. edu/Educational_Resources/Curriculum/Curriculum_Concerns/curriculum_concerns.html.*The website is produced by the Center for Holocaust and Genocide Studies at the University of Minnesota.*

Should There Be Holocaust Education for K–4 Students? A Reply to Dr. Samuel Totten. Written by Heike Deckert Peaceman. *This article is one of a series which addresses the question of how old is old enough for students to learn about the Holocaust. It was written in response to Samuel Totten's arguments (cited below).*

NAMING THE HOLOCAUST

Warsaw ghetto residents attend a memorial service for a relative buried in the Warsaw cemetery. August, 1940.
USHMM, courtesy of Gene Berkowicz.

In teaching about the Holocaust, we often start with a lecture/discussion of the very terms people have used to describe its events. This is both a useful and a necessary preface to actually teaching about the Holocaust. While many (if not all?) of your students will have heard of the Holocaust, they may or may not have heard the terms, 'Final Solution,' or *Churb'n*. But teaching these terms isn't only about enriching your students' vocabulary. Teaching these terms, focusing your students' attention on the language they use to describe the Holocaust, is one way for them to begin the difficult project of learning to think critically. After all, each of these terms casts the meaning of the Holocaust differently. Certain terms imply Jewish perspectives (*Churb'n/Shoah*) or Nazi perspectives ('Final Solution'); other terms have decidedly political consequences (genocide). Even the ways that we write these terms or speak them have political overtones. What does it mean, for example, to capitalize the "H" in Holocaust vs. writing it with a lower-case "h"? Is there only one Holocaust, or are there holocausts? Does the distinction matter? In Simone's years of teaching, her eighth grade students were as adept as her college students at discussing the issues and implications involved in using different terms.

When teaching these terms, we usually lecture about their meanings first since we assume that most students don't know their derivations, even when they have heard the terms themselves. We think of teaching in this instance as providing a kind of baseline or platform of understanding that enables everyone to participate in discussions afterwards. We like to teach about each term and then pause to ask the following questions: What does this term imply? What's good about this term? What are the problems this term raises? Who do you think uses this term now, and how? And, how is it different to use this term now than it was when the term first appeared? After we have discussed each term's pros and cons, we ask students to consider which terms are most popular now, why they think that is, and which of the terms they prefer to use and why. We encourage you to make sure that your students know how you'll be using these terms, too, as those decisions will elucidate how you've structured their learning this content. In the following section, the names for the Holocaust are listed in approximate chronological order of their appearance, and some implications of each name are included.

The big ideas of this chapter are that:

- There are many terms used to refer to the Holocaust, all of which carry particular implications.

- Your students should learn the terms and discuss their implications, which should expose you, as their teacher, to their orientations towards this history and vice versa (expose them to your orientation).

The key terms of this chapter include: 'Final Solution', Adolf Hitler, *Wermacht, Einsatzgruppen*, Wannsee Conference, *Churb'n*, genocide, Rafael Lemkin, Auschwitz, Theodore Adorno, Holocaust, *Shoah, Gezerot tash-tashah*, and *Poreimas*.

Terms for the Event

'Final Solution' (1941): This term was used originally by the upper echelons of the Nazi hierarchy to describe the mass murder of Jews, or, in Nazi terminology, the 'Final Solution' to the so-called 'Jewish Question.' Though it was used within the Nazi government to mean other, preliminary steps in the process of annihilation, this was the term which ultimately referred to the plan to murder all of European (and eventually all of world) Jewry.

Hermann Goering was one of the original members of Hitler's party, one of the few who supported him even before **Adolf Hitler** was elected to office in 1933. As such, he became an exceedingly important member of Hitler's cabinet, overseeing and coordinating armament agencies. On July 13, 1941, Goering sent out the following order, which referred (only obliquely) to the planned mass murder of Jews:

> I hereby commission you to carry out all necessary preparations with regard to organizational, substantive and financial viewpoints for a total solution of the Jewish question in the German sphere of influence in Europe.
>
> Insofar as the competencies of other central organizations are hereby affected, these are to be involved.
>
> I further commission you to submit to me promptly an overall plan showing the preliminary organizational, substantive, and financial measures for the execution of the intended final solution of the Jewish question.

Although this order was sent to a subordinate of Goering's in July, which one might assume meant that the mass murder of Jews was not yet in place, the opposite is the case. Though there is some disagreement among scholars, most now believe that the plan to murder European Jews as an entire group was already in place by June 22, 1941, when the German army (the **Wermacht**) advanced into the Soviet Union. Attached to these army units were so-called 'special units,' **Einsatzgruppen**, whose job it was to round up Jews from the areas overtaken and to shoot them *en masse*. By September 1941, the Nazis were already experimenting with Zyklon B gas at Auschwitz to see whether it could be used to kill people; in December, they were experimenting with gas vans at Chelmno to establish exactly how. Clearly, by then, the policy of mass murder had already been established.

On January 20, 1942, the top leaders of the **Third *Reich***, the Nazi German government, gathered to decide how best to implement Goering's orders. They met just outside of Berlin at Wannsee, which is why this conference is referred to (in English) as the **Wannsee Conference**. Commonly associated with the origination of the term, 'Final Solution,' the actual 'Final Solution' was already underway.

Some notes on the term: Like the majority of language used in Nazi talk, policy and documentation, the term 'Final Solution' is euphemistic, that is, it doesn't refer directly to what it means, but shrouds its meaning. The very euphemism, however, illuminates Nazi ideology since mass murder of Jews was seen as a 'solution.' A problem of the term is therefore that it doesn't seem to include non-Jewish victims of Nazi genocide (for example Sinti and Roma, who used to be referred to as 'Gypsies.') As a side note, we never allow students to write the term (or other similar Nazi-generated terminology) without using single or double quotation marks around it, if only to reinforce the notion that it is a Nazi term and that it implies that the mass murder of Jews is positive. (Solution is a positively weighted term.)

Churb'n: This Yiddish term for the Holocaust was used by Eastern European Jews even as early as their being ghettoized, which in the case of Poland began in 1939. From the Hebrew root word, *cherev*, which means sword, the word came to mean warfare. It had been the Yiddish term that Eastern European Jews used to describe the destruction of the Temple, and before the ghettos were established in Poland in 1939, the Yiddish term was used to describe any great catastrophe.

Some notes on the term: There is something especially appropriate about using a Yiddish term—a term in a language whose embedding culture was wiped out—to describe the destruction of European Jewry. That said, Yiddish was not spoken by all Jews targeted by the Nazis. Greek Jews from the upper classes, for example, sometimes spoke Greek at home, *Ladino* for Jewish celebrations, and learned French and German as academic languages. Moreover, the term implies again a kind of exclusion of non-Jewish victims of the Holocaust, since the vast majority of non-Jews did not speak Yiddish.

Genocide: **Rafael Lemkin**, a Polish born Jew, lost 49 members of his family in the Holocaust. He coined the term genocide in his 1944 book, entitled, *Axis Rule in Occupied Europe*. In the text, he describes that he wanted "to denote an old practice in its modern development." He used the term as a lawyer during the Nuremberg Trials. One of the unsung heroes of the fight for universal human rights, Lemkin went on to almost single-handedly draft the Genocide Convention, which he presented at the first meeting of the United Nations in San Francisco in 1945. Leaving a truly historical legacy, he also almost single-handedly lobbied for its passage. On December 9, 1948, the UN approved the Convention on the Prevention and Punishment of Genocide, which meant that nations incurred moral, legal, and military consequences for those instances later deemed to be genocide. By January of 1951, 20 countries had ratified the proposal.

Lemkin's terminology provided an alternative term to 'Final Solution,' providing people with a way to talk about the Holocaust without using Nazi language. The term genocide was also more general than 'Final Solution,' and referred beyond the specific annihilation of Jews. Lemkin invented the prefix from the Greek root, *gen* from *genus*, which refers to birth. This is the same root found in the words: gentleman, genius, genetics. He combined *gen* with the Latin *cide* from the root *cidera*, which means to cut or kill. This is the same suffix as found in the words: homicide, suicide, deicide.

In regular usage, the term has come to mean "the deliberate extermination of an ethnic or national group" (this according to the Oxford English Dictionary definition). When he termed the phrase, though, Lemkin proposed the following definition:

> Generally speaking, genocide does not necessarily mean the immediate destruction of a nation, except when accomplished by mass killings of all members of a nation. It is intended rather to signify a coordinated plan of different actions aiming at the destruction of essential foundations of the life of national groups, with the aim of annihilating the groups themselves. The objectives of such a plan would be the disintegration of the political and social institutions, of culture, language, national feelings, religion, and the economic existence of national groups, and the destruction of the personal security, liberty, health, dignity, and even the lives of the individuals belonging to such groups. Genocide is directed against the national group as an entity, and the actions involved are directed against individuals, not in their individual capacity but as members of a national group.

Notes on the term: Interestingly, there is no mention of political groups being the potential victims of genocide according to this definition. The Russian emissary to the first UN meeting was present when the resolution passed and had wanted to make sure that Stalin could not be considered guilty of genocide. Sadly, as a result of the important moral, legal and economic consequences the term genocide carries with it, governments purposefully avoid using the term in order to avoid intervention. Some people appreciate the clinical or scientific sound of this term, implying as it does a calculated rationality to mass murder. Others dislike the coldness it conveys, as if the term itself denies the humanity of victims of genocide. As a side note, Lemkin believed that the term ought to be capitalized whenever it was used as a way to further emphasize is horrendousness, no matter what the particulars. We do not capitalize it in this book as a way to recognize its tragic everydayness, the fact that at this point in history, it seems to occur frequently, if not constantly.

Auschwitz: Theodore Adorno, the great German-Jewish philosopher, launched many thousands of essays in response to his famous quotation, "After Auschwitz, to write poetry is barbaric." While Adorno modified his claim somewhat after reading the poetry of Paul Celan, what is important for our purposes is his use of Auschwitz to refer to the Holocaust as a whole. In the 1950s, it was quite common for people to refer to the atrocities in general through reference to the largest concentration and death camp, Auschwitz. Though it's uncommon today to speak about the Holocaust as Auschwitz, the use of the term then highlights how little was known in the immediate aftermath of the events.

Notes on the term: It could be said that Auschwitz has become a symbol for the Holocaust and that using the term Auschwitz to refer to the Holocaust highlights the central symbolic image of the gas chambers and crematoria. One problem with this term, though, is that it tends to overshadow other kinds of experiences Holocaust victims and survivors encountered. It used to be the case, for example, that survivor only referred to a survivor of a concentration camp, whereas now we tend to consider Holocaust survivors as those who spent the war years in hiding, in full view with false papers, in ghettos, forests, labor camps, etc. The term is also a little vague since Auschwitz the camp included the camp Birkenau and many smaller satellite camps, and since the name of the concentration camp was also the name of the town (*Oswiecim* in Polish) in which it was located.

Holocaust: Elie Wiesel is said to have fathered this term in the same way that Columbus discovered America; in other words, he was credited with its officiation, but was not in fact its inventor. He was, however, one of the first people to use the term in print in the mid-1950s. That said, the term was not widely used until the 1970s, following the airing of a television mini-series of the same name. This term is now the most widely used, the most widely known, and perhaps as a result, the most widely contested term for the atrocities committed under the Nazi regime.

The term comes from the Greek translation of the Hebrew Bible, which was completed somewhere around 200 BCE. The Hebrew word being translated was *olah*, from Genesis 22: 13: "Abraham went and took the ram and offered him up for a burnt offering in the stead of his son." The wholly burnt offering here is the *olah*, and the Greek translation of the word was holocaust. The prefix, holo-, came from the Greek root, *holos*, which means whole, total, complete. It's the same prefix as in the words holistic or hologram. The suffix of the word *caust* came from the root word *caustos* which means to burn. This is the same root found in the word cauterize.

According to its etymology, then, the word Holocaust links the victimization of Jews under the Third *Reich* to the almost-sacrifice of Isaac in the Hebrew Bible. Many thinkers have objected to this linkage considering its ramifications. The term itself likens the Jews murdered by Nazis and their collaborators to Isaac, which implies that murders under the 'Third *Reich*' served a divine purpose. After all, God commanded Abraham to sacrifice Isaac. In that analogy, too, the Nazis become God's instruments, since they are likened to Abraham. The implication throughout is that God played a role in the perpetration of these events, or at least, that God was included in their universe. The term itself, in short, locates these specific atrocities within a theological terrain, which for many people, is unacceptable. The Holocaust, they might argue, despite this term, was not an example of God's inhumanity to man, but of man's inhumanity to man, or, put in non-sexist language, people's capacity for inhumanity.

Notes on the term: Most of the early debates swirling around use of this term concerned its theological underpinnings. Since the term has become so widely used and widely understood, most of the more recent debates concern its vagueness. Does the Holocaust include only Jewish victims of the Nazis or all victimized groups? Is there only one Holocaust (so that it should be capitalized), or are there many examples of holocausts? And, does the Holocaust refer to all of the anti-Jewish activity in Nazi Germany (which would mean it began in 1933), or does it refer only to those activities that were directed towards mass murder (which would mean that most people date it to 1939, the establishment of ghettos, or to 1941, the year the 'Final Solution' became operationalized)? These days, when people write about the Holocaust, they typically define their terminology along these axes in order to orient their readers. In this book, we capitalize the Holocaust to indicate its special status in history, but we consider the Holocaust to have included not only Jewish victims, but all of it victims, Jewish and non-Jewish.

Shoah: This Hebrew term, like Holocaust, has Biblical origins, but this time, those origins are not connected to the will of God as much as to destruction wrought by human hands. For many, then, the term, *Shoah*, is preferable to the term, Holocaust. The Hebrew word appears in Proverbs 1: 27, "When your fear cometh as desolation (*shoah*) and your destruction comes as a whirlwind." This prophecy references the destruction of the great Jewish Temple, which some have argued is a historic rather than a religious event. The enemies of the Biblical people Israel devastated the great Temple; God did not.

Notes on the term: For some, the fact that this term is in Hebrew is positive. That it is in Hebrew implies that the *Shoah*, unlike the Holocaust, is about an event in Jewish history, as opposed to an event in European or world history, and that it concerns Jewish victimization, rather than the victimization of Soviet prisoners of war, Sinti or Roma (previously known as 'Gypsies'), Jehovah's Witnesses, or other persecuted groups.

Gezerot tash–tashah: It used to be the case that in ultra-Orthodox Jewish communities, the Holocaust was referred to obliquely as "the Decrees of 1939 – 1945." (*Tash-tashah* refers in shorthand to the years 1939-1945 in the Hebrew calendar.) Stated this way, the decrees allow the period to be thought of as either God's work or humans', though *gezerot* were usually considered human decrees. More recently, however, the ubiquity of the term, Holocaust, has meant that it has seeped into ultra-Orthodox Jewish usage.

Poreimas: The group that used to be called 'Gypsies' now refer to themselves as Sinti and Roma, the names of the most prominent family groupings in Germany and Austria respectively. The term Roma often refers to both groups now. 'Gypsy' was not only a term that had become derogatory, but it was originally applied to this group when they were thought to have originated in Egypt. In fact, the Sinti and Roma originated in Northern India and migrated to Europe during the Middle Ages. The Romani term for the Holocaust is *Poreimas*, which translates roughly as "the devouring." Referring to the specific devouring of the Sinti and Roma during the Holocaust, this term is relatively recent and not many Roma use it or recognize it. Almost directly opposite of Jewish tradition, Roma tradition espouses a kind of forgetting, a dismissal of history in favor of "seizing the day." As the historian, Inga Clendinnen puts it, "they have chosen not to bother with history at all, because to forget, with a kind of defiant insouciance…is the Gypsy [sic] way of enduring."[6]

---

6 Inga Clendinnen, *Reading the Holocaust* (Cambridge, UK: Cambridge University Press, 1999), 8.

Teaching Ideas

1. **Your Preference:** Ask your students to simply write for a few minutes about which term they prefer, why, and what it says about them as people. Some teachers refer to this as a "thinking break," an opportunity for each student to collect their thoughts and form opinions individually before discussing them as a group. To begin the discussion, ask each student to go around the room, share their preference, and give one reason for that preference. Make sure your students know that they are entitled to have different opinions about the matter, and that they need not debate which term is right. How would they go about asking others to use the term they think of as the best one?

2. **Word Bubbling:** After hearing this list of terms and their origins, try having your students freely associate words. What do they associate with one of these terms? Go around the room, and encourage the students, as fast as they can, to mention the next word that pops into their minds. You can do this activity in pairs or as a group. You can also do this activity aloud (which is preferable because it's a quicker form) or in writing (which is preferable because it's more private). If the activity gets to silly words, it's a great opportunity to discuss why; why do you think your mind tends towards funny or lightweight associations rather than dwelling in horror? What can that tell us about the endeavor of studying the Holocaust?

3. **Conceptual Mapping:** After distributing blank pieces of colored paper, scissors and tape, ask your students to "map" these words visually. How do they see the relationships between these terms? Which terms are the larger categories or the smaller categories? Which terms are umbrella terms or tree root terms? After the students have had a chance to think and intellectually map, have them explain aloud why they designed their maps as they did.

   The famous Israeli historian of the Holocaust, Yehuda Bauer, for example, puts genocide and Holocaust on the same continuum, but argues that genocide is less extreme than Holocaust. After all, according to Lemkin's definition, genocide can refer to the moral corruption of victims or to the appropriation of economic advantage by the perpetrators, both of which are less extreme than mass murder.

4. **Uses of the Term:** If you or your students have access to the web during school hours, it's a fascinating activity to look at some of the uses of the term, Holocaust. At the time of this writing, for example, there is a slide

show at the website for **People for the Ethical Treatment of Animals** (PETA), which compares the mass murders of victims, not explicitly Jews, during the Holocaust to the slaughter of animals for mass consumption today. The slide show is entitled "Holocaust on Your Plate," and it contains quotations like: "To animals, all people are Nazis," (attributed to Isaac Bashevis Singer, the writer of Yiddish comedic fiction), and "Our grand-children will ask us one day, 'Where were you during the Holocaust of the animals?'" The slides are carefully paired to show, on the left-hand side, images of emaciated or tortured people, and on the right, a visually similar image of emaciated or tortured animals. PETA members would like you to consider the paired images as morally equivalent, not only visually similar. Thus the slide show not only elevates the cause of veganism, but denigrates the sanctity of human life.

In addition, there used to be a record store in San Mateo, California, called 'The Vinyl Solution.' And there's a famous episode of the television show, Seinfeld, called the 'Soup Nazi.' These examples and others, which your students can bring to your attention, can catalyze important discussions around questions like these: When should the word, Holocaust be used for an event other than this Holocaust? When should any of these words be used? What happens to these original meanings when they're used for non-historical purposes? Should the term Holocaust be considered sacred in some way? Why or why not? Why is it people refer to the Holocaust in these ways? How do you feel about these uses, and what do you feel it's important to do about them?

5. **Charting Genocide**: An introduction to names for the Holocaust can help your students begin to identify the axes that are important in under-standing all genocides. As your students listen to your lecture, have them write a list of factors that seem important. Their lists might include, for example, the intention of the perpetrators (to conquer, exploit or murder), the parts annihilated (culture/economy/people), wartime or peace-time, etc. Brainstorm the list together, and then have the students group and sort them. Then, create a chart together that lists the features of all genocides. As your study progresses, you may want students to refer back to this chart, noting how some of these aspects changed. And, when your study of the Holocaust is complete, your students should be able to use these features to compare the Holocaust to other instances of genocide.

Resources for Teaching and Further Learning

Bury Me Standing: The Gypsies and Their Journey. Written by Isabel Fonseca and published by Vintage Books, New York, 1996. *Though relatively little of this book deals with the Sinti and Roma's experiences during the Holocaust, the section that does is, like the rest of the book, beautifully written, personal and fascinating.*

A History of the Holocaust. Written by Yehuda Bauer and published by Scholastic Books, New York 2001. *A fabulous and thorough textbook. Useful as a reference text.*

The Holocaust in American Life. Written by Peter Novick and published by Houghton Mifflin, Boston, 1999. *Crafted by an eminent historian, this book documents public attitudes towards the Holocaust in the U.S.A. in the decades since 1945. Though sometimes his narration is too glib for our taste, the book is excellent. With regards to this chapter's content, it ably documents the political uses to which the Holocaust has been put.*

People for the Ethical Treatment of Animals. Website: http://www.masskilling.com/exhibit.html . *This website contains a gruesome slide show entitled "Holocaust on Your Plate" in which the term, Holocaust, is applied, graphically, to the slaughter of animals for mass consumption.*

A Problem from Hell: America in the Age of Genocide. Written by Samantha Power and published by Basic Books, New York, 2002. *A phenomenal study of U.S. involvement (and non-involvement) in the genocides of the 20th century, this book contains chapters on Lemkin, the Holocaust, Iraq, Bosnia, Rwanda and other genocides.*

Reading the Holocaust. Written by Inga Clendinnen and published by University Press, Cambridge, England, 1999. *A beautifully written set of reflections on Holocaust scholarship, this book weaves the way through various historiographical dilemmas.*

While America Watches: Televising the Holocaust. Written by Jeffrey Shandler and published by Oxford University Press, Oxford, 1999. *This seminal book examines how the Holocaust was transmitted via popular culture to millions of Americans, and how it became a cultural icon as a result.*

JEWISH LIFE IN EUROPE
BEFORE 1933

Shura Mesherowsky sits reading a book, circa 1925, Germany. USHMM,
courtesy of Myriam Abramowicz.

For much of the past 50 years, Holocaust scholarship and education have revolved around the causes, nature and consequences of Jewish death and destruction—antisemitism, ghettos, death marches, the camps, and the like—while frequently omitting remembrance of Jewish life. This is understandably rooted in a need to make meaning from incomprehensible horrors. However, while learning about the atrocities of the Holocaust is essential, it does not offer a complete portrait; it is necessary, but not sufficient. Indeed, perhaps more important than learning about the way Jews died during the Holocaust is remembering the ways they lived.

Debbie was an educator on the March of the Living program in Poland and Israel for 10 years. On her third journey to Poland, Debbie learned a significant lesson in the Warsaw Jewish Cemetery on the importance of teaching about Jewish life as part of a curriculum on the Holocaust.

Debbie: The Warsaw Jewish Cemetery was founded in 1806 and contains an estimated 250,000 graves including those of distinguished Jews from great rabbis such as Rav Chaim Soloveichik—considered one of the most brilliant rabbis of the 19th century—to wealthy bankers, to Esther Rachel Kaminska—the mother of Yiddish theater. I was leading a group of teenagers along the decrepit paths of the cemetery. Pointing to the various broken headstones that had been either wholly destroyed or pilfered by the Nazis to be used to build sidewalks, I commented forlornly that even in death the Nazis robbed Jews of a final resting place. Just then, Rabbi Peretz Wolf Prusan, a remarkable storyteller and teacher, walked by with another group of teens. Like me, he pointed to the broken headstones, but rather than describe the horrific death and destruction that befell the Jews at the hand of the Nazis, he said instead, "See that tombstone in memory of a Polish Jew? Let me tell you about his life…." At that moment I realized that our educational obligation is not merely to teach the literal meaning of the Holocaust—a word which comes from the Greek to mean "burnt whole"—but rather, to illuminate and thereby perpetuate the complex and wondrous Jewish life that existed and was not consumed by it.

Indeed, Jews have lived in Europe for centuries. The first Jews arrived in Poland via the trade routes in the 10th century and the earliest records of Jews in Germany date back to the fourth century. Before the Nazis' rise to power, nearly nine million Jews were living in Europe. Diligence to the vast history of Jewish life in pre-war Europe is unachievable in a brief chapter. In order to provide depth and breadth on the topic, this chapter is narrowed in time—covering roughly 1800 to 1933; in focus—considering cultural, political and religious arenas mostly; and in geography—summarizing these facets of life in Poland and Germany only.

The big ideas of this chapter are that:

- European Jewry responded to the meteoric changes brought on by the Enlightenment in a myriad of forms including assimilating into secular society, rejecting it, and also by creating new forms of Jewish expression.

- Jewish life in pre-war Europe was vibrant, diverse and unique.

- Many aspects of Jewish life today have their roots in pre-war European Jewry.

Key terms of this chapter include: Enlightenment, *Haskalah,* Weimar Republic, Yiddish, Zionist Movement, *He-Halutz,* Bund Party, *Agudat* Israel, Hasidism, *yeshivot,* Moses Mendelssohn, Reform Movement, Rabbi Zechariah Frankel, Conservative Movement, Modern Orthodox Movement, and Rabbi Samson Raphael Hirsch.

Jewish Life in Europe

The 19th and 20th centuries were periods of dramatic development tied to modernization, industrialization and nationalism. The Jews of Europe were deeply affected by the cultural, political and religious changes that the Enlightenment period brought about. The **Enlightenment** was an intellectual movement predominant in the Western world during the 18th century that advanced secular views based on reason. The ***Haskalah***, or Jewish Enlightenment, began in Galicia (Germany, Poland and Central Europe) and later spread to other parts of Europe. The word *Haskalah* comes from the Hebrew root word, *sekhel*, meaning reason or intellect, and the movement was characterized by a scientific approach to religion. Secular culture and philosophy, once shunned within traditional Jewish circles, became valued. Although it is the norm for us today, at the time of the *Haskalah*, studying secular subjects such as agriculture, science and the arts, and speaking Modern Hebrew were considered radical expressions of Jewish European modernity. However, while some Jews embraced modernization for the promise of prosperity and emancipation, others resisted it by maintaining traditional Jewish views.

While Jews thrived in many European countries for centuries before the Holocaust, Poland was the nexus of Jewish life—it is the birthplace of ***yeshivot*** (houses of learning), of Hasidism (religious renewal movement), and before the Holocaust, it was home to more Jews than anywhere else in the world. By the early 20th century, Poland's population numbered more than 32 million with Jews comprising more than 10 percent. As many as 80 percent of Jews across the world can trace their roots back to Poland. While Poland boasted the greatest number of Jews, German Jews came to represent the elite intellectual vanguard of European Jewry. The ideological trends of the Enlightenment marked the beginning of a new period for the Jews of Eastern and Central Europe, and this was particularly true for German Jews. The Enlightenment gave rise to modern scholarly Jewish study, spawned various religious movements including Reform, Conservative and Modern Orthodox, and enabled German Jews to integrate into modern German society. Poland and Germany serve as illustrative case studies for an exploration of how the *Haskalah* affected Jewish life, as these two countries tend to dominate our collective imagination of European Jewry.

Cultural Responses to the *Haskalah*

Unique Jewish cultures blossomed in pre–World War II Europe in a multitude of forms. Similar to the plethora of offerings available today, Jewish life encompassed political and religious institutions, literary activity, social clubs, theater, music and sports. The range of Jewish educational institutions included both secular and religious primary and secondary schools, colleges and universities, scientific institutes, vocational training, rabbinical seminaries, *yeshivot* and hundreds of Jewish libraries.

As an agricultural country, more than three quarters of the Polish people lived in farming communities. However, because Jews were historically not allowed to own land, most Polish Jews lived in the towns and villages—the centuries old *shtetlach (*plural of *shtetl)*—and earned their living in trade and commerce. Various merchants' associations, artisans' societies and labor unions were established to support and aid the wide range of Jewish business endeavors. In his memoirs, Mordekhai Munesh Kaleko wrote about his mother-in-law's socio-economic success as a shopkeeper:

> My mother-in-law, may she rest in peace, was a young, beautiful woman, real gorgeous, a divorcee. Though she wore a filthy apron, stained with kerosene, pitch tar, and lubricant grease that smelled from a distance, it did not detract from her beauty. She owned a store that appeared small from the outside, but she was well stocked. There were stacks of flour, sugar, raisins, barrels of herring, kerosene, pitch tar, lubricant grease. There was plenty of everything, and she bought all for cash, for she did not suffer from lack of business, but was popular with Jews and Christians alike.[7]

Jewish entrepreneurs, bankers, industrialists and merchants played a major role in the economic industrialization of Poland. As a result, there were some Jews

---

[7]Mordekhai Munesh Kaleko in *There Once Was A World: A 900-Year Chronicle of the Shtetl of Eishyshok* by Yaffa Eliach (Boston: Little, Brown and Company, 1998), 272.

with considerable wealth who were highly integrated into Polish society and thought of themselves as Poles of Jewish faith. Yaffa Eliach describes the affluent summer vacations of some Jewish Poles, "Summer colonies in the pine forests and on the banks of nearby lakes and rivers were popular… [and] favored by the *shtetl's* fashionable set. By the mid-1930s the Vilna crowd had staked out its own preferred resort colonies, disdaining to mix with the *shtetl* vacationers."[8]

Jews figured prominently in German cultural, intellectual, political and social circles as well. Although antisemitism was not uncommon, German Jewry became more prosperous when Imperial Germany collapsed and was replaced by the democratic regime of the **Weimar Republic** in the early 1900s. During this era, burgeoning religious and social Jewish organizations thrived, and certain German Jews had made names for themselves in theater, music, arts, philosophy and science. Remarkably, for example, nine out of 38 Nobel Prize winners in Germany up until 1938 were Jewish. Jews comprised nearly one percent of the total population in Germany with the vast majority living in large cities like Berlin, Frankfurt, Hamburg, and Cologne. The remainder settled in the thousands of small towns and villages that dotted the German countryside. The majority of German Jews were middle class, and most were employed in business. The profusion of German Jewry's scholarly institutions, the establishment of cultural centers, and the wide range of literary and academic periodicals made Germany the center of assimilated Jewish intellectual life in Europe.

The language spoken by Jews also reflected cultural influences and politics. **Yiddish** had been the vernacular of Eastern European and Russian Jews, including Polish and German Jewry. The language uses the same alphabet as Hebrew but is a blend of Hebrew and several European languages, primarily German. Because of rampant persecution over the years in Poland, Jews were increasingly isolated from non-Jewish European society. This isolation gave rise to Yiddish as the common language among Jews enabling them to live in the same areas, trade amongst themselves, and maintain international networks among the numerous Yiddish speaking Jewish communities in Europe. In some ways, it is this fact which formed the basis of the antisemitic myth of a Jewish conspiracy for world domination. Because of years of persecution and a shared common language, Jews in business were at an advantage during the years of intense industrialization at the end of the 19th century.

Beginning in the 19th century, however, Yiddish became more than merely a language of utility to be used in everyday speech and writing. Yiddish promul-

---

[8]Yaffa Eliach, *There Once Was a World: A 900-Year Chronicle of the Shtetl Eishyshok* (Boston: Little, Brown and Company, 1998), 531.

gated the Jewish cultural arena through literature, poetry, drama, music, and religious and cultural scholarship. However, the *Haskalah* also gave rise to the revival of Hebrew as a living language and the adoption of European languages in the host countries where Jews lived. As a result, many Western European Jews, particularly German Jews, grew to disdain Yiddish as a product of the insular, unworldly *shtetl* Jew. German Jews considered Eastern European Jews backwards, primitive, living according to pre-Enlightenment ideals. To the German Jews, they were *OstJuden*, Eastern Jews. In return, Polish Jews considered many assimilated German Jews to be haughty, assimilated, abandoners of tradition, called *Yekkes*. German Jews also increasingly began to enter secular schools and to work in professions where knowledge of German was essential. Wealthy Jews in Germany taught their children German and French to facilitate business and social contacts with non-Jews. By the end of the 1700s, French had become the language of the Jewish elite while German was the spoken language of the middle class. German writers had previously claimed that Jews deceived non-Jews by using Yiddish in business transactions, thus furthering negative attitudes towards Yiddish. Some reformers even called for the removal of Yiddish from Jewish schools and others suggested that Jews refrain from using Yiddish or Hebrew in bookkeeping and business contracts.

Simultaneously, Hebrew was revived with the goals of preparing European Jewry for emancipation. Along with the resurgence of Hebrew came a new form of Hebrew literature. The *Haskalah* writers first tried to capture the attention of readers by writing Hebrew novels modeled after the type of writing that was popular at the time. Set mostly in the Land of Israel, the novels depicted Jews as heroines, romantic lovers and brave warriors. They implied that Jews could change their present situation by taking political action instead of waiting for the *mashiach* or Messiah. *Haskalah* writers also turned to themes like the meaning of Judaism and Jewish identity. They wrote in Hebrew for the intellectuals, though they still used Yiddish for the masses.

For the most part, books published in Yiddish were addressed to women (who were not usually taught Hebrew) and to uneducated men. The Yiddish writers generally wrote fiction while the Hebrew writers composed essays and poetry. Eminent writers like Shalom Aleichem and Isaac Leib Peretz, who today are considered important literary figures by non-Jewish and Jewish critics alike, created classic works in Yiddish during this period. Concurrently, a vibrant, literature scene boasted young Jewish poets who haunted smoky bars decades before the beatnik scene emerged.

Yiddish drama was another important development in this era. More than 20 Jewish theater companies toured throughout Poland, performing in big cities and tiny *shtetl*s to universal accolades. Their repertoire ranged from popular plays that were translated into Yiddish (including such decidedly non-Jewish works as *The Merchant of Venice*), to specifically Jewish pieces written and performed only in Yiddish and showcasing celebrated performers and playwrights. The music scene was equally robust with a Jewish symphony orchestra in Warsaw established by Menachem Kipnis. Like their youthful counterparts in the United States, young Jewish boys and girls in Europe could be found dancing the Charleston during the roaring 1920s.

The Jewish press was perhaps the most widespread manifestation of the cultural changes of this heady time. Countless local and national daily publications and periodicals written in Yiddish, Hebrew and European languages ranged from daily newspapers that carried the latest news, commentary and gossip on people and events to various scholarly journals that dealt with religious, social and political issues.

Equally significant to the existence of a vibrant Jewish culture during this era was the number of Jewish leaders in the political arena. Jews held political positions in the democratic and socialist parties. A prominent Jewish figure served as Germany's minister for economic affairs and later as the foreign minister, and a German Jew named Hugo Preuss was involved in drafting the Weimar Constitution.

After the long process of German emancipation that occurred in 1871, there had been a rise in assimilation, but also in Jewish nationalism, a reflection of the nationalisms that were sweeping all of Europe. Many *maskilim* (members of the *Haskalah*) identified themselves expressly as Germans, not as Jews. German Jews generally were highly assimilated. According to some estimates, by 1927 nearly 54 percent of the approximately 500,000 Jews living in Germany were intermarried. That said, much of the nationalism that Jews expressed was fostered by antisemitism, which, in keeping with the *Haskalah* ideals, led to aspirations for redemption by a human, non-Messianic, means. This was the beginning of the Zionist movement in Germany that developed into a mass movement between 1897 and 1904. However, most German Jews rejected Zionism.

Jews were also politically active in Poland, where Zionist ideas were especially attractive. *Hashomer Hatzair*, a Zionist socialist youth movement was founded in Poland in 1913. Many other youth movements affiliated with the Zionist movements emerged and prepared and encouraged young adults for immigration to Palestine. Young Polish Jews were not just attracted to Palestine; many left for France early in the 20th century. However, the youth movements were so prolific in Poland that 50 percent of the Jewish immigrants to Palestine in the decades between the two world wars were of Polish descent. Esther Katz, who was a member of a Zionist youth group recalls the elaborate celebratory send off that her neighbor Saul Schneider and his family received from the entire *shtetl* when he and is family set off to immigrate:

> The other day I took part in a parade that was organized by all of our *shtetl* institutions and parties, for the purpose of saying farewell to a distinguished family by the name of Schneider, on the night of their departure for *Eretz Yisroel* [the Land of Israel]. …each of the Zionist groups [were] marching as a unit, displaying its own flag, and everybody joining together to sing songs expressing the love of Zion. Alongside the marchers rode young fellows on white horses, carrying burning torches, and behind them were the men, women, and children of the *shtetl,* people of all ages, singing and dancing. ..We all sang *Hatikvah*, the Jewish national anthem. …Our hearts were filled with hope that we too would one day make *aliyah* and join in building the land.[9]

The Zionist youth movement, **He–Halutz** was an association of Jewish youth who resolved to create collective settlements—*halutzim*—in Palestine. *He-Halutz* members were dedicated to cooperatively working the land, with the ultimate goal of establishing a sovereign Jewish nation. The movement spread throughout the Jewish world and came to symbolize Zionist ideology in the 20th century.

The most celebrated exploit of the *He-Halutz* movement during this time is the chronicle of "The 105"—the first *He-Halutz* group to immigrate to the Land of Israel. Despite the British mandate that disallowed immigration to then Palestine, a group of six *halutzim* left Poland in the summer of 1918 and made their way through Odessa and Constantinople, finally reaching Jaffa on December 5, 1918. A second group set out soon after. Their journey made Zionist history as these *halutzim* passed through Czechoslovakia, Austria, Serbia, Croatia, and Italy with neither passports nor visas. However, when they landed in Egypt they were imprisoned by the British military. After six months of hard labor, they reached Palestine in 1919, during Passover—symbolically akin to the Biblical Exodus from Egypt. Upon their arrival, they were greeted by nearly the entire population of Tel Aviv. These *halutzim* inaugurated a new wave of immigration to

---

[9]Esther Katz in Yaffa Eliach, *There Once Was a World: A 900-Year Chronicle of the Shtetl Eishyshok* (Boston: Little, Brown and Company, 1998), 504–505.

the Land of Israel, and reports of their arrival renewed the hope of *He-Halutz* members in Europe. By the 1930s *He-Halutz* inaugurated yet another wave of illegal immigration to the Land of Israel and, during World War II; *He-Halutz* members were among the most active resistance fighters against the Nazis.

Not all of the Jewish political movements in Europe in the early 20th century favored Zionism, though. The largest movement, the secular and socialist **Bund Party** represented the voice of the working class and denounced Zionism as an intransigent utopian dream and even considered the retention of the Yiddish language, as opposed to Hebrew, to be a central part of its platform.

At the other end of the spectrum were political Orthodox movements, like *Agudat* **Israel**, aimed at strengthening religious Jewish life while rejecting secular Zionism as a dangerous modern tendency. As a world Jewish movement and political party, *Agudat* Israel worked to preserve religious life through adherence to *halakhah* (Jewish law) in Eastern and Central Europe. The formation of such a movement was an innovation in its time and can be traced in part to advances made by assimilation as a result of the Enlightenment, by the resurgence of Zionist movements, and by the proliferation of the Bund Party. *Agudat* Israel opposed any attempt to revive Jewish nationhood in the Land of Israel other than one founded through the divine hand of God and based on the law of the Torah. Therefore, they unequivocally opposed the creation of a secular Jewish state and considered the revival of Hebrew as a secular language sacrilegious. Prior to World War II, *Agudat* Israel's strongest and most politically active groups were in Poland, and its members built a number of educational institutions including Talmud Torah schools and *yeshivot*, establishing the pioneering network of *Bet Ya'akov* schools for girls, who had been traditionally excluded from religious education. Though it still maintained a strict religious ideology, after the Nazis' rise to power in Germany, *Agudat* Israel began to coordinate its policies more closely with the Zionist movements.

Jewish religious life in Europe was equally vibrant and increasingly diverse. Hasidic dynasties emerged in the late 18th and early 19th centuries in Europe. **Hasidism** attracted both an enormous following of fervent supporters and a tremendous group of active opponent. Founded in southeast Poland by Rabbi Israel Ben Eliezer—called, the *Baal Shem Tov*, or Keeper of the Good Name—in the second half of the 18th century, Hasidism grew to include a broad base of devout followers in Polish and Lithuanian villages, eventually spreading into northern Lithuania and westward into central Poland. Most Hasidic followers maintained a separation from Zionism, particularly opposing religious Zionism. Moreover,

Hasidism carefully maintained a strict separation from Polish secular society in speaking Yiddish, rather than the local vernacular, and in creating distinct educational institutions, rather than sending their children to Polish ones. Yet, interestingly, the traditional style of Hasidic dress is derived in part on the fashions of medieval Polish nobility.

Hasidism also had its detractors. The most notable among its critics came not from the secular Jewish community, but rather from the Orthodox world. The most prominent opponent of Hasidism was Rabbi Elijah ben Shlomo Zalman, known as the *Gaon of Vilna*, who feared that the veneration of the *Baal Shem Tov* would become idolatrous. He further believed that Hasidic ecstasies, visions and miracles were dangerous delusions, and that the Hasidic focus on prayer negated the Jewish value of Torah study.

The Enlightenment solidified some religious Jews' commitment to their faith and opened the way for others to assimilate into secular culture and society by releasing them from the perceived confines of religious life. Roman Eisner grew up in Lodz, Poland during this era and recalls what he thought of religious Judaism at the time:

> I am a Jewish person. I believe, but without the religion. Why should I dress differently than anybody else? Why should I wear a uniform? It is not that I'm ashamed to be a Jew. I'm proud to be a Jew. But I don't have to advertise it. My home language was Yiddish, my country language was Polish. I had Jewish friends. I had Christian friends too. I obeyed all the traditional holidays in the house; otherwise I was just like anybody else."[10]

Moses Mendelssohn was a significant German Jewish philosopher and writer whose work won him international acclaim in the literary world. Mendelssohn was revolutionary in his time for combining Judaism with modern culture and he is credited as one of the founding fathers of the Jewish Enlightenment. Likened to Plato, Socrates and the Biblical Moses, in 1783 Mendelssohn translated the Bible into German. The translation was hailed by rabbis in Germany, Holland, France and England who supported the Enlightenment. However, it was also banned by more conservative rabbinic leaders. Mendelssohn's translation of the Bible had an important effect on Jewish life in Europe, inaugurating a new era of religious culture and education.

One of the most historically significant religious changes that emerged during this time came from a group of German Jews who began what came to

---

[10] Roman Eisner from an interview in *Image Before My Eyes*, produced by Josh Waletsky and Susan Lazarus, 1980

be known as the **Reform Movement**. They wanted to remain Jewish while taking advantage of the new liberties and opportunities brought on by the Enlightenment. The Reformers viewed traditional Jewish customs and lifestyles as barriers to acculturating into mainstream German society. They also tried to stem the tide of conversions to Christianity by Jews who were estranged from traditional Jewish observance.

The first Reform synagogue opened in Hamburg, Germany in 1818 and included many new rituals—borrowed from Christianity and European customs—including sermons, and an organ (although a non-Jew was hired to play it on the Sabbath). The service was conducted in German in an attempt to emphasize nationalistic loyalty and identity and a prayer book was published in 1819 that included prayers in German and eliminated prayers mentioning a desire to return to Zion. However, even before the synagogue was established in Hamburg, Israel Jacobson, a philanthropist and Reform leader, held services in his home as early as 1815 with abbreviated liturgy.

Furthermore, as we mentioned earlier, the Jews of Germany wanted to show their allegiance to their country of residence, which in turn meant disavowing Yiddish as a mother tongue. The Reform Movement instituted other modern customs including mixed gender seating in the congregation. They also shifted adherence of Jewish law from ritual observance to honoring ethical commandments. All of these were radical introductions at the time and were subsequently offensive to many other European Jews. Despite and because of the controversy it aroused, the Reform Movement is credited with taking the lead in trying to reshape and retain Jewish religious expression within the culture of the Enlightenment.

However, the Reform Movement—like any other burgeoning coalition—was not an entirely unified movement. The changes it introduced were not accepted by all the leaders in the movement, nor adopted in all Reform synagogues. The Movement had its liberal, center and conservative branches. These various branches shared an easy coexistence for the first few decades of the century, but as the Movement grew, the need for greater clarity could not be ignored. The result was a series of conferences, convened by the rabbis of the Reform Movement, designed to provide a forum for achieving consensus on the substance and pace of reform. The second of these conferences, held in Frankfurt in May 1845, proved to be pivotal in the history of modern Judaism.

Rabbi Zechariah Frankel the chief rabbi of Dresden, Germany attended the conference. A major topic of the conference was whether Hebrew should be the only permitted language of prayer in synagogue. The discussion was heated because Hebrew represented the bond that had united Jews in prayer for over 2,000 years. The vote on the issue was far from definitive: 15 conference members voted that Hebrew should not be the exclusive language of Jewish prayer, 13 voted that it should be, and three abstained. Frankel spoke passionately against the majority position and, upon hearing the result, walked out. Two months later, he defended his action in a letter to his colleagues. Frankel was fully aware that *halakhah* did not mandate that Hebrew was essential to prayer; therefore, his appeal was not to Jewish law, but to history. He argued that Hebrew had been the language of Scripture throughout Jewish history and serves as the tie that binds together Jews throughout the world.

While Frankel rejected the approach of German Reform, which he saw as radical and hasty, he simultaneously maintained the position that changes in the central beliefs and practices of Judaism were possible—that the Jewish religion was not immune to cultural and historical influences. In 1854, nine years after walking out of the Reform Movement conference in Frankfurt, Frankel became the new head of a rabbinical school, the Jewish Theological Seminary of Breslau. Thus, the **Conservative Movement**—grounded in both *halakhah* and history—was born.

The **Modern Orthodox Movement** also emerged as another example of how European Jews struggled to reconcile traditional, observant Judaism and the modern world. **Rabbi Samson Raphael Hirsch**, recognized as the founding father of modern Orthodoxy, set the terms for the Orthodox response to modernity. He argued that to the German Reformers, progress is the absolute and religion is to be governed by progress, whereas to the Orthodox, religion is the absolute, and progress must be governed by religion. In short, if Judaism and modernity conflict, modernity must yield.

Although Hirsch opposed the liberal leanings of both the German Reformers and of Frankel, he was, nevertheless, also influenced by modernity. Hirsch was educated in secular German schools and received his Jewish education from rabbinic tutors. As a result, he supported the integration of secular studies, specifically literature and culture, into Orthodox education. He also emphasized study of the Biblical text, a somewhat new introduction at the time. However, he insisted on preserving rabbinic law as the best method for safeguarding Judaism. He further introduced the idea that the commandments contained symbolic teachings and the belief in Jewish peoplehood and community as integral expressions of Judaism.

These new forms of Jewish expression that were introduced, to a greater or lesser extent, by the early reformers and by the Conservative and Modern Orthodox movements may not seem like radical innovations today. In their time, though, these changes shook European Jewry to its core. Moreover, these changes have defined and shaped the way Jews live and experience Judaism to this day.

Teaching Ideas

1. **Archeological Time Capsule:** Ask students to become archeologists by imagining that they have discovered a time capsule from pre-Holocaust Europe. What might the time capsule include and what would the objects teach them about Jewish life in Poland and Germany during that era? Then, have students create their own time capsule. Ask them to identify objects that exemplify Jewish life today. What would they include and exclude and why? How do the artifacts they selected to represent Jewish life in pre-War Europe compare and contrast to the artifacts that they would place in the time capsule representing Jewish life today? This can be an imagined activity or a real one. If you can, bury a real time capsule.

2. **The Punch Line is Always in Yiddish:** Many of us remember the anticipatory joy we felt when our parents let us stay up past our bedtimes to eavesdrop on their late night dinner conversations. Unfortunately, the let down came fast when Uncle Leo told a long winded joke leading up to a racy punch line. Of course, while the joke was told in English, the punch line was always delivered in Yiddish, followed by waves of laughter from the adults and blank stares from the kids.

   Teach your students Yiddish jokes. They're usually not that racy and sometimes they're even funny. Start by making a list of all the Yiddish words your students already know. They might be surprised to find out how much Yiddish has crept into the English vernacular.

   Two wonderful resources are **Naftali the Storyteller and His Horse, Sus**, a delightful collection of stories for children translated from Yiddish, and the **Yiddish Radio Project** which features classic Yiddish radio recordings with simultaneous English text translations that can be accessed via National Public Radio's website.

3. **Yiddish Theater:** If your local community theater boasts a revival of Yiddish theater, attend a performance with your students. If not, stage your own production. An Israeli drama educator, whom Debbie observed, created *Playing Our Roots* at a Jewish Community Center in Northern California.

Teens interviewed seniors about their lives then turned their stories into a play, which they performed for the entire community. Create your own *Playing Our Roots* based on stories of Jewish life before the Holocaust. You can start by viewing **Yidl Mitn Fidl** (Yiddle with his Fiddle), an original Yiddish musical produced in Poland in 1936.

4. **Music:** Eastern European Jewry contributed immensely to the body of Jewish and secular music including Yiddish folksongs, Klezmer and synagogue music. Teach the students some songs from this era to illuminate the various genres of music as a window into European Jewish life. Thanks to Steven Spielberg's Virtual Cinema Project you can access music compilations from the Israel Music Heritage Project including **Ashkenazi Music of the Jews of Eastern Europe** and **European Jewish Music of the Nineteenth Century.**

5. **Role Play/Debate:** Have students research then role play or debate a conversation between Rabbi Zechariah Frankel, the founder of the Conservative Movement's Jewish Theological Seminary, Rabbi Samson Raphael Hirsch, the father of Modern Orthodoxy, and Moses Mendelssohn, one of the early Reformers in Germany. The various movements' websites provide succinct historical summaries (**United Synagogue of Conservative Judaism,** the **Orthodox Union,** and the **Union for Reform Judaism.**)

6. **Films: The Steven Spielberg Jewish Film Archive, Virtual Cinema Project** contains over 100 films and will eventually archive over 500 Jewish documentary films viewable over the Internet. Our favorites are the ones that depict Jewish life in pre-war Europe including: *Ashkenazi Music of the Jews of Eastern Europe* (28 minutes) which opens a window into the world of Yiddish folksongs, Klezmer music and Eastern European synagogue music. *European Jewish Music of the Nineteenth Century* (30 minutes) which presents European Jewish music in the 19th century, and *Jewish Life in Five Polish Cities on the Eve of World War II* (10 minutes each) which encompasses five delightful films of original footage of Jewish life in Bialystock, Cracow, Lvov, Vilna and Warsaw in 1939 which were made to attract tourists. Some other good films depicting Jewish life in pre-War Europe include: **Camera of My Family,** which portrays four generations of a German Jewish family from 1845-1945; **Echoes That Remain** presents Eastern European Jewish *shtetl* life; **Image Before My Eyes** is one of the best video compilations of rare film, photographs, memorabilia, music and interviews with survivors; and another great video is **The *Shtetl*,** which uses original photographs to

trace American Jewish life to the *shtetl*. **Centropa** is a good website that includes photos and family histories of pre-War European Jewry.

Resources for Teaching

Auschwitz Jewish Center Foundation. Web site: www.ajcf.org. *Preserves pre-war Jewish history in Oswiecim, Poland.*

Camera of My Family: Four Generations in Germany, 1845–1945. Produced by the Anti-Defamation League of B'nai B'rith, 1978, 18 minutes. *Linking the past to the present, four generations of a German Jewish family are brought to life.*

Centropa. Website: www.centropa.org/mainpage/archive.asp, a project of the Central Europe Center for Research and Documentation. *The site includes photos of pre-war European Jewry and family histories.*

Echoes That Remain. Produced by the Simon Wiesenthal Center, 1991, 60 minutes. *Depicts of Jewish* shtetl *life before the Holocaust by combining rare archival photos and footage with live sequences shot on location at the sites of former Eastern European Jewish communities.*

Image Before My Eyes. Produced by Josh Waletsky and Susan Lazarus, 1980, 90 minutes. *Through rare film, photographs, memorabilia, music and interviews with survivors this film vividly recreates Jewish life in Poland from the late 19th century through the 1930's.*

Naftali the Storyteller and His Horse, Sus. Written by Isaac Bashevis Singer and published by Farrar, Straus, Giroux, New York, 1976. *A delightful collection of stories for children translated from Yiddish.*

The *Shtetl*. Distributed by Behrman House, 1994, 16 minutes. *Using original photographs this short film traces American Jewish life to the* shtetl.

The Steven Spielberg Jewish Film Archive, Virtual Cinema Project. Website: www.spielbergfilmarchive.org.il/. *Jewish documentary films viewable over the Internet including:* Ashkenazi Music of the Jews of Eastern Europe *(28 minutes) which opens a window into the world of Yiddish folksongs, Klezmer music and Eastern European synagogue music.* European Jewish Music of the Nineteenth Century *(30 minutes) which presents European Jewish music in the 19th century, and* Jewish Life in Five Polish Cities on the Eve of World War II *(10 minutes each) which encompasses 5 delightful films of original footage of Jewish life in Bialystock, Cracow, Lvov, Vilna and Warsaw in 1939 which were made to attract tourists.*

Orthodox Union. Website: www.ou.org/. *The Orthodox Union is the central coordinating agency for American and Canadian Orthodox Jewish congregations.*

Union for Reform Judaism. Website: www.urj.org. *The Union for Reform Judaism is the central body of the Reform Movement in North America.*

United Synagogue of Conservative Judaism. Website: www.uscj.org/. *The United Synagogue of Conservative Judaism is the association of Conservative congregations in North America.*

Who Was the Woman Who Wore the Hat? Written and illustrated by Nancy Patz and published by Dutton Books, New York, 2003. *Appropriate for younger children, this book is a poetic meditation on a woman's hat with simple wonderment at who she might have been like.*

Yiddish Radio Project. Website: www.npr.org/programs/atc/features/2002/ yiddish. *A 10-part series from National Public Radio and the Yiddish Radio Project that features classic Yiddish radio recordings with simultaneous English text translations.*

Yidl Mitn Fidl. Produced by the National Center for Jewish Film at Brandeis University, 1936, 92 minutes. *An original Yiddish musical produced in Poland in 1936*

Resources for Further Learning

Ashkenaz: The German Jewish Heritage. Edited by Gertrude Hirschler and published by Yeshiva University Press, New York, 1988. *Six scholars document the fabric of Jewish life in Germany from the Middle Ages to the Holocaust.*

Image Before My Eyes: A Photographic History of Jewish Life in Poland, 1864–1939. Written by Lucjan Dobroszyck and Barbara Kirschenblatt-Gimblett and published by Schocken Books, New York, 1977. *This compilation can act as a companion guide to the video or it can stand on its own. It includes hundreds of still photographs spanning a 75-year period that vibrantly portray Jewish life in Eastern Europe.*

The Jews of Germany: A Historical Portrait. Written by Ruth Gay and published by Yale University Press, New Haven, 1992. *Through texts, pictures and contemporary accounts, this book provides a panoramic overview of the 1500-year history of German Jewry.*

There Once Was a World: A 900 –Year Chronicle of the *Shtetl* Eishyshok. Written by Eliach Yaffa and published by Little, Brown and Company, Boston, 1998. *Through the particular lens of the Eishyshok shtetl, Eliach presents an illuminating and comprehensive picture of shtetl life.*

PAVING THE WAY

German spectators at the 1937 Reich Party Day celebrations in Nuremberg, Germany.
USHMM, courtesy of Julien Bryan.

When Simone asks college students taking her course on the Holocaust to think for a moment and then list as many reasons as they can for the Holocaust to have occurred, their lists are revealing. Usually coming out of American public high schools, the students include typical textbook answers in their lists, factors like: Germany's loss in World War I, the harsh conditions of the Versailles Treaty, Germany's economic devastation as a result, the weakness of the Weimar government, Germany's seeking world domination, Adolf Hitler's personal insecurities and/or mental illness, societal needs for scapegoats in hard times, etc. Conspicuously absent are usually the factors we think of as being most important, the necessary if not sufficient conditions for the Holocaust to have occurred: the histories of antisemitism, racism and prejudice in general. Because these histories are typically absent in history textbooks or glossed over in public school classrooms, it's especially important to cover them. We'd argue that one can't understand the Holocaust without understanding these histories.

One of the main teaching pitfalls that can come into play when teaching these histories is what Simone calls **double victimization**. In teaching about the history of antisemitism, for example, it's easy to inadvertently dehumanize Jews in your teaching and in that way to mimic the very history that's being taught, thereby doubly victimizing them. First victimized in the Holocaust, they are doubly victimized by being dehumanized in its teaching. A specific example may help in understanding this pitfall. One of the teaching tools Simone especially likes is a slide show of historically antisemitic images of Jews. Tracing five different anti-Jewish myths, Simone likes to show these slides as a way to explain the stereotypes. However, for the duration of that slide show, the only image of Jews that exists in her darkened classroom is one where they are grotesque, demonized and offensive. Of course these images of Jews are fabricated fantasies that do not reflect on actual Jews; nonetheless, these kinds of images can be powerful and haunting for your students. And therein lie the real dilemmas of teaching this material. On the one hand, you can't skip teaching about it or showing its images as they are central to understanding the Holocaust. On the other hand, in teaching these histories, you risk reifying negative stereotypes. In some classes, your students may not even be familiar with the stereotypes in the first place. Are you then perpetuating hatred or paving its way by introducing its symbols to your students?

Our suggestions do not resolve this teaching dilemma, but rather offer one perspective on how to handle it. Our feeling is that as long as antisemitism, racism and other forms of prejudice are still flourishing, it's important to teach students how to recognize their appearances in our culture. That means that you do expose students to these ideas and images, as ugly as they are and as unpleasant as it is to serve in that capacity as a teacher. You can mitigate the impact of propagandistic images like the ones in Simone's slide show by making sure to intersperse real images of Jews, diverse Jews, not only the ubiquitous image sometimes thought of as the quintessential 'real Jew': a bearded, black-hat wearing Hasidic Jewish man. In addition, it's vitally important to discuss how stereotypic images work, analyzing the propaganda as propaganda and thereby debunking its power. Reminding your students that stereotypes inform us more about those who stereotype than about those who are stereotyped is useful as well. Finally, too, it's important to realize that the histories of particular prejudices are interlinked, and that each has a place within the vast array of factors that paved the way for the Holocaust.

Though the combination of factors didn't make the Holocaust inevitable, each contributed significantly to its eventuality. And therein lies a final tension in the teaching of this chapter's content. It's very hard to present a history of antisemitism without conveying the sense that the Holocaust was its culmination. As Saul Friedlander puts it, "no historian can forget the end of the road."[11] While the Holocaust couldn't have happened without the histories of antisemitism, racism and other prejudices, these histories didn't lead inevitably to the Holocaust either. As teachers, therefore, we need to balance knowing the outcome with presenting other possibilities for Holocaust history.

A number of **metaphors** have been used to help people consider both the different kinds of factors that enabled the Holocaust and the different ways they coalesced. In the tree metaphor, the Holocaust can be viewed as having deep roots that anchor the tree and other, proximal roots that are shallower. In this version, the history of antisemitism forms a deep root with extensive off-shoots, whereas, for example, Germany's defeat in World War I or the weakness of the Weimar government form shallower roots, ones closer to the surface. Doris Bergen, a historian who has written extensively about antisemitism, uses the metaphor of a conflagration, which seems more appropriate as a symbol of mass-murder than does the growth metaphor of the tree. (The tree, after all, is a positive Jewish symbol, the *etz chayim*, or tree of life, which is often associated with the Torah and the growth of Jewish life and learning.) "In order for a house to burn down," Bergen explains, "three things are required. The timber must be dry and combustible, there needs to be a spark that ignites it, and external conditions have to be favorable—not too damp, perhaps some wind."[12] Bergen likens Hitler's regime to the spark, and World War II to the favorable conditions. But, she notes, the "dry timber" was already there: the attitudes that Germans and other Europeans already held toward particular "others" fueled the mass murder. In the hopes that your students will be better informed than the students who begin Simone's college classes sometimes are, in this chapter we highlight some of the most important preconditions that paved the way for the Holocaust to occur.

The big ideas of this chapter are that:

- There were very different kinds of preconditions that enabled the Holocaust to occur, and students need to be aware of their differences.

- Of those, the histories of antisemitism, racism and prejudice are often overlooked and vitally important to teach about.

---

[11]Saul Friedlander, *Nazi Germany and the Jews* (New York: HarperCollins, 1997), 4.

[12]Doris Bergen, *War and Genocide: A Concise History of the Holocaust* (Lanham, MD: Rowman & Littlefield, 2003), 1.

- The pat accounts of Germany's interwar years portrayed in history text-books are often perfunctory. Teaching students carefully about these years should allow them to serve as guides to learn beyond the traditional text-book versions.

Key terms of this chapter include: double victimization, metaphors, religious antisemitism, pogroms, anti-Roma stereotypes, eugenics, *volkesgemeinschaft, volk*, racial antisemitism, political antisemitism, 'anti-Semitism', *Judenhass*, Weimar government, Treaty of Versailles, the Great War, Nazi Party —National Socialist German Workers' Party, and 'stabbed in the back.'

Histories of Hatred

Holocaust historian, Raul Hilberg, famously summarized the history of anti-semitism in a single sequence of interlinked sentences: "You cannot live among us as Jews; You cannot live among us; You cannot live." (A teacher Simone once observed wrote the first sentence on the board, crossing out each phrase as she explained the history of antisemitism.) Where the Crusades typify the first line, and the ghettoization of Jews illustrates the second, the Holocaust is summed up by the third. The three sentences, in other words, describe the history of antisemitism as culminating in the Holocaust's mass murder of Jews. As a crystallization of antisemitism, then, the sentence string works to capture its essence; the actual history of antisemitism, however, is much more complex, as it has both different types and interlinked histories. As some indication of that complexity, Bauer characterizes antisemitism as having three variants: religious, racial and political.

Religious antisemitism is mainly considered to have followed the birth of Christianity. Though Jesus of Nazareth was himself an observant Jew put to death by the Romans (crucifixion was in fact a common form of punishment in the Holy Roman Empire), his death would be repeatedly imagined and explained as "the Jews" having killed him, a myth that would become foundational for antisemitism to thrive. More historically accurate would be a portrait of two groups of Jews fighting intensely about how to accommodate Roman rule at that time: whether to defend Jewish rituals and observances through armed uprising (the position of the Pharisees) or whether to compromise with Roman dictates which the upper classes and priestly caste favored (the position of the Sadducees). Jesus was in all likelihood a Pharisee rabbi, whom a small group of followers upheld as a new messiah after his death. Those who believed this and who sub-sequently studied his teachings and proclaimed him the Son of God (Christ) became known eventually as Christians; those who considered Jesus to have been a Jewish teacher, a remarkable leader but human throughout, remained Jews. It's worth remembering that for the first hundred years after Jesus' death, these groups worshipped together, and that Jesus' apostles were also Jews. In the centuries after Jesus' death, however, the new Christians de-emphasized Christianity's commonalities with Judaism, largely as a way to accommodate living under the Holy Roman Empire.

By the Middle Ages, Jesus' Judaism was effectively lost, denied and rendered invisible, and a number of profoundly anti-Jewish myths circulated wildly. Some scholars understand this development in Freudian terms—as the desire of a new religion to kill off the father's religion, or, more generally, as the need of an adolescent religion to rebel against its parent. Either way, the anti-Jewish myths were powerful in both the imaginations of Europe's peasants and upper classes, laying the groundwork for tremendous mistreatment of Jews and **pogroms**, organized attacks against individual Jews, Jewish communities, and sometimes entire regions. Among these myths were included the notions that Jews were aligned with the devil, (an inversion of the idea that Jews were God's chosen people,) that Jews sought control of the world (in line with the devil's desires), that Jews murdered Christian children and used their blood in Jewish rituals (an inversion of the reality that Jews practiced *kashrut*, draining the blood of animals they slaughtered to be eaten), that Jews poisoned wells and caused diseases (like the Black Plague) and that Jews wandered the earth, seeking money and perpetrating evil. As these myths attest, many had grains of truth whipped up into paranoid delusions. This last myth, for example, the myth of the wandering Jew, resulted from the mass expulsions and persecutions of Jews throughout Europe, causing them to wander in attempt to find places where they would not be harassed, exploited, attacked and murdered. Confined to particular occupations (like usury) and banned from many others (like land ownership), Jews were sometimes forced to live in particular locales or to wear distinctively marked clothing, all practices that the Nazis would later adopt.

The **anti-Roma stereotypes** of the Middle Ages mimicked anti-Jewish ones. The Roma, (formerly known as 'Gypsies' because they were wrongly thought to have originated in Egypt) were accused of wandering, stealing, poisoning wells, kidnapping Christian children for ritual purposes, and generally being aligned with the devil, perpetrating crimes and spreading bad luck. While the Jews were accused of having murdered Jesus, the Roma were accused of having crafted the nails with which he was crucified—this despite the fact that some Roma were themselves Christian. (The Roma, because they were confined to particular professions like metalwork, were sometimes expert craftsmen.) Like the Jews, then, the Sinti and Roma became accustomed during this period to being persecuted, chased from towns, falsely blamed for theft or outbreaks of disease and more generally used as societal scapegoats. More importantly, however, white, Christian Europeans became used to the habits of thought that enabled victimization. Unlike the racism that Nazism would embrace, for most of these centuries, religions and ethnicities were not considered utterly inescapable; baptism and conversion allowed Jews other futures, for example, if not Jewish ones.

In the 19th century, however, racial discourses began to flourish, ideas that biologized Christian antisemitism, institutionalized racisms and prejudices of all sorts: against Blacks, against Roma, against gays, the disabled, and others. What the Church had served to do for Christian antisemitism, science did for racial hierarchies. Social Darwinists had applied the scientific discoveries of Charles Darwin to human arenas (despite the fact that Darwin never intended for them to be), claiming that certain classes of people (Nordic, Germanic, so-called 'Aryans') deserved dominance over others based on heredity. At its heart, racializing discourses claimed that what mattered most about people was their genetic make-up, which scientists at the time thought of as entirely inescapable and utterly unchangeable. The idea of managing populations' genetics, known as **eugenics**, gained credence, and by the beginning of the 20th century, groups across Europe proposed methods for population management: forced or voluntary sterilization and other birth control policies for so-called 'defectives,' breeding policies for those considered racial superiors.

Eugenic ideas became popular not only in Europe but in the United States as well. In 1907, for example, Indiana passed a law requiring sterilization of people deemed inferior. These ideas were especially popular in Germany. Since the 19th century, German intellectuals had embraced a notion of the ***volkesgemeinschaft***, the German people as a national community or ***volk***, united in purpose, goals and vision. Such a community demanded the submission of individuals for its greater good, an idea that Nazi fascism would exploit. Houston Stewart Chamberlain's *The Foundations of the Nineteenth Century* became a best-selling book in Germany by wedding eugenic, *volkische*, racist and antisemitic ideas. An eloquent writer admired by Theodore Roosevelt among others, Chamberlain argued that Germans were intellectual superiors to other nations that they were responsible for the march of history, and that Jews, by contrast, had served as its obstacles. (Chamberlain also argued that Jesus had been an 'Aryan' rather than a Jew.) In his works, Jews were not only a blight on the German national body, but they were linked with other movements considered detrimental by the right wing: liberalism, communism, socialism, modernization, secularization, industrialization.

Just as **racial antisemitism** contained the themes of Christian antisemitism, so too **political antisemitism** built on its two predecessors, using their ideas as the platform of a political group or party. In some ways, Wilhelm Marr was the founder of political antisemitism. Marr coined the term **'anti-Semitism'** in 1879, in the hopes of replacing *Judenhass*, or Jew hatred, with a more scientific-sounding phrase. He wanted his hatred of Jews to seem rational rather than religious. Thus he invented the category of the 'Semite,' which as part of antisemitism, was associated specifically and only with Jews. (As a result, we choose to spell the word as "antisemitism"—that is, without a hyphen and without capitalizing the "s".) Like social Darwinists, Marr believed that Jews and Germans were locked in a struggle for dominance, and that, as of the end of the 19th century, Jews were winning. Marr believed that the power of Jews would result in the disappearance of Germans. Marr therefore founded the League of Anti-Semites in 1879 in order to combat such an imagined (and imaginary) victory. Marr's was not the only antisemitic group. In 1887, Otto Boechel became the first political antisemite to be elected to the Reichstag in Germany. Another political antisemite, Karl Lueger, served as mayor of Vienna during Adolf Hitler's youth there.

Nazism thus drew from three types of antisemitism, from racializing discourses, from common prejudices, from long-standing traditions of scapegoating, and from the brutality associated with imperialistic colonialism more generally. Throughout the 19th century, European nations had carved up Africa and the Asian continents, brutally massacring local populations for material gain and political power. The condescension towards and exploitation of native peoples, their families, cultures, homelands and goods, also habituated Europeans to behaviors that paved the way for the Holocaust to occur. As Doris Bergen's excellent summary suggests, Nazism's versions of these hatreds were thus "extreme, but not unique."[13] The groundwork for Nazi patterns of atrocity had already been laid in the previous centuries.

Germany Between the Wars

Most textbook accounts of World War I summarize the Versailles Treaty, which ended the war, as unfairly imposed by the victors on the vanquished, as

---

[13]Ibid, p. 11.

extracting exorbitant payments from the German people which then catalyzed the hyperinflation of the 20s, crashing Germany's already weakened economy. The Versailles Treaty is usually described as rankling Germans because of the War Guilt clause and as being overly punitive in general. As a result of the treaty's terms, Germany had to demilitarize substantially, eviscerating its armed forces. Germany was forced to give up Alsace/Lorraine and large swaths of land and people around the Rhine River. And, in essence, a democratic government was imposed, the utterly weak **Weimar** government, under which the arts and culture would flourish wildly, but which, attacked from both the right and the left, would collapse within a few short years.

While much of this typical account is accurate, Doris Bergen argues that "the treaty was not exceptionally harsh."[14] She claims, in fact, that by comparing the **Treaty of Versailles** and the Treaty of Brest Litovsk, "which the Germans had imposed on the defeated Russians just a year earlier, you might almost call it [the Treaty of Versailles,] generous."[15] She explains:

> In March 1918 the Germans had demanded that the Russians cede about 30 percent of their territory, including much of their agricultural, industrial and mineral wealth. Under the terms of the Treaty of Versailles the Germans lost about 10 percent of their territory, much of it fairly recently acquired; Alsace and Lorraine, for example, taken in 1870 from France. Contrary to what is often said, the Treaty of Versailles did not blame the Germans for the war itself. Article 231, often referred to as the 'war guilt clause,' was in fact not a moral judgment but a general, legal statement stipulating that Germany was responsible for paying for damages in the places outside Germany where most of the fighting had occurred. A similar clause appeared in the treaties with Germany's former allies, Austria, Hungary, and Turkey. [And,] as for reparations, the Germans paid only a very small amount of the bill originally presented to them, which was repeatedly adjusted downward. The victorious nations, above all the British and the French, had neither the ability to make Germany pay nor the will to risk another war after all the suffering and loss they had experienced.[16]

Thus, while Germans of the time experienced their defeat as a tremendous blow—they had, after all, been told for years that they were winning and winning

---

[14] Ibid, p. 26.
[15] Ibid.
[16] Ibid, p. 27.

well—they nonetheless experienced the similar (even less extreme) economic hardships that most European nations experienced post-war. **The Great War** (as the First World War came to be known) had laid the groundwork for the Holocaust in much subtler ways.

The massive carnage of the First World War had accustomed people to slaughter. While on the one hand that cheapening of life led to social upheaval, the Russian revolution and the threat of revolution elsewhere, on the other hand, it also made many fearful of conflict, favoring insularity or isolationism rather than the possibility of renewed warfare. The war had wiped out almost an entire generation of young men, who fought along the Western Front for years as it moved within only a few miles, consuming the living as though the trenches were the gaping mouths of giants. Life in the trenches was so vile—filthy, cramped, bloodied, dismembered, infested, infected, etc.—that many men committed suicide, or shot off their own limbs in order to be released from continued warfare. Both sides in the war experimented with the use of gas—mustard gas being the worst type—to make death especially excruciating.

Rudolf Binding was 46-years-old when he joined the Hussars, and he spent most of World War I serving on the Western Front. After the war, he published a collection of his writings, entitled, *A Fatalist at War*. In a letter home, dated April 19, 1915, Binding had written a description that aptly summarizes many experiences of war and atrocity, specifically, the inability to communicate about them:

> I have not written to you for a long time, but I have thought of you all the more as a silent creditor. But when one owes letters one suffers from them, so to speak, at the same time. It is, indeed, not so simple a matter to write from the war, really from the war; and what you read as Field Post letters in the papers usually have their origin in the lack of understanding that does not allow a man to get hold of the war, to breathe it in although he is living in the midst of it.

> The further I penetrate its true inwardness the more I see the hopelessness of making it comprehensive for those who only understand life in the terms of peacetime, and apply these same ideas to war in spite of themselves. They only think that they understand it. It is as if fishes living in water would have a clear conception of what living in the air is like. When one is hauled out on to dry land and dies in the air, then he will know something about it.

So it is with the war. Feeling deeply about it, one becomes less able to talk about it every day. Not because one understands it less each day, but because one grasps it better. But it is a silent teacher, and he who learns becomes silent too.

When those who survived did return home, shell-shocked, war-torn and emotionally devastated, some sought refuge in the paramilitary groups which sprang up. Such groups supplied them with opportunities for continued violence, for the camaraderie of male friendship and with avenues to perpetuate the wartime lifestyle they had come to know best. Some groups also fanned the flames of resentment, especially within Germany. Adolf Hitler, who had earned an Iron Cross, First class, as a runner in the trenches, who had been blinded temporarily by a gas attack, and who was one of the 'lost generation' to return to Germany post-war, joined a military intelligence unit after the war. Working as a police spy, he infiltrated one such group, a right-wing, *volkische* paramilitary organization which eventually, under his direction, became the **Nazi Party, the National Socialist German Workers' Party**. Convinced that Germany had not surrendered of her own volition at the end of the First World War but instead had been **'stabbed in the back'** by internal 'elements'—Jews, Communists, and Socialists—Hitler's group gained momentum.

Teaching Ideas

1. **Discussion prompts:** Have your students discuss the following prompts in some depth, making sure that they've covered a whole host of possibilities before allowing them to change the topic.

   - What's wrong with the sentence: "The Jews killed Christ"? What would you say to someone who uttered this sentiment?

   - The eminent historian Saul Friedlander calls the kind of antisemitism that Hitler developed 'redemptive antisemitism.' For Friedlander, what distinguished Hitler's brand of antisemitism was its "synthesis of a murderous rage and an 'idealistic' goal [of total annihilation]."[17] This kind of antisemitism was "different, albeit derived from other strands of anti-Jewish hatred."[18] As an exercise to understand the various forms of antisemitism, ask your students how 'redemptive antisemitism' seems similar to and different from its previous variants.

---

17 Friedlander, p. 3.
18 Ibid.

- **Supercession** is the idea that Christians displaced Jews as God's chosen people. In other words, when Jews rejected Jesus as their messiah, God decided that Christians had superceded Jews and that Christians were God's new favorite people. (This is why the New Testament is called the New Testament; it makes the Hebrew Bible into the 'Old Testament.') Ask your students to compare Jewish chosenness and Christian supercession. How are they similar and how are they different? What are the implications of both worldviews for people who are neither Christian nor Jewish?

2. **Nazi Party Platform Simulation:** As an entry point for thinking about the political platform of the early Nazi Party, Simone sometimes distributes a doctored version of their statement of principles from 1920, one which is abridged and where all references to Germany/Germans, etc. are replaced with references to America/Americans, etc. Before revealing what the original document claims, see if your students would sign such a petition and why. This exercise is helpful for illuminating the slipperiness of policy language.

> We demand the union of all Americans in a Great America on the basis of the principle of self-determination of all peoples.
>
> We demand that Americans have rights equal to those of all other nations and that the economic treaties that bind us [originally worded as the Peace Treaties of Versailles and St. Germain] shall be abrogated.
>
> We demand land and territory for the maintenance of our people and the settlement of our surplus population.
>
> Only those who are our fellow countrymen can become citizens. …Those who are not citizens must live in America as foreigners and must be subject to the law of aliens.
>
> We demand that the State shall above all undertake to ensure that every citizen shall have the possibility of living decently and earning a livelihood. If it should not be possible to feed the whole population, then aliens (non-citizens) must be expelled….
>
> Any further immigration of non-citizens must be prevented.
>
> All citizens must possess equal rights and duties.

The first duty of every citizen must be to work mentally or phys-ically. No individual shall do any work that offends against the interest of the community to the benefit of all.

We demand that ruthless war be waged against those who work to the injury of the common welfare. Traitors, usurers, profiteers, etc., are to be punished with death, regardless of creed or race.

3. **Textbook Detectives:** Have your students obtain the American or world history textbooks that their local public school district approves for the teaching of World War I and the Treaty of Versailles. (As a side note, edu-cational research suggests that 90 percent of public school teachers still use a single textbook as their source of educational material for the teaching of history.) Have your students compare the textbook versions with Doris Bergen's version (summarized above). Why, in their opinion, can history have more than one version? How can they determine which one is right, or, in what ways each is right (or not)? After having students compare ver-sions, supply them with primary source material and ask them to write letters to their public school teachers, sharing their findings and opinions about the textbook coverage. Alternatively, have them write a better text-book entry.

4. **Metaphors:** After discussing and documenting the various events and his-tories that paved the way for the Holocaust, have your students, in small groups, generate metaphors for the factors. (You can give them the examples of the tree metaphor, the fire metaphor, and the roadway metaphor—the title of this chapter, as examples of metaphors.) Distribute a large piece of poster paper and a set of markers to each group for them to draw their met-aphor and label its parts. Then each group can share out their metaphors. Don't stop there, though; make sure to compare the metaphors, asking which works best as an explanatory framework, in what ways, and for which aspects of explaining the Holocaust. Which metaphor seems most appropriate morally? How do metaphors shape our thinking, and why are they important?

5. **Investigating antisemitism**: Have your students, in small groups, do research projects that will broaden their understandings of antisemitism and then present their findings to the class. They might choose to examine historical antisemitism or antisemitism today. Be warned, though, that if you assign your students to use the Internet for research, they are very likely to encounter websites that are supported by antisemitic groups that deny

the Holocaust. That in itself is worth discussing with your students. Below are recommended topics, and a few reliable websites your students can use to begin their research.

Historical antisemitism: *The Protocols of the Elders of Zion* was an infamous forgery that imagined Jews to be plotting to take over the world. Published in the wake of the First Zionist Congress in Basel, the book was translated into many languages. Have your students read excerpts of the book, discuss why some could believe this as an authentic document, and compare the horrendous images that grace the covers of different translations. Another complex topic to research is Martin Luther. Have your students read excerpts of his book, *On the Jews and their Lies,* as it is well documented that Hitler appropriated many of Luther's ideas. For a fascinating portrait of a famous German Jewish industrialist murdered by antisemites, have some students investigate Walter Rathenau, who participated in the Versailles negotiations and was later assassinated. His biography can help students understand that antisemitism still existed in the interwar period. And of course, Hitler's antisemitism is an interesting topic.

Antisemitism today: Sadly, antisemitism is not gone and forgotten. A number of reliable websites track antisemitic behavior worldwide. **The Anti-Defamation League's** website is informative and reliable, and **The Southern Poverty Law Center's** website is entitled "Hatewatch" and tracks not only antisemitic activity, but racist and prejudicial activity in general. **Holocaust denial** is one potent form of antisemitic activity today. For more information about denial, you may want to share excerpts from Deborah Lipstadt's phenomenal book, **Denying the Holocaust**. (Her appendixes alone have concise, one to two page readings on some of the most widely circulated denial myths—that, for example, Anne Frank's diary was forged and that Zyklon B was never used to murder people.) Another fascinating topic to research would be the David Irving v. Penguin Books and Deborah Lipstadt trial, in which a Holocaust denier, David Irving, brought a libel suit against Lipstadt and her publisher, Penguin Books, in England. For more on that trial, **Holocaust Denial on Trial** has an excellent website to start students off.

6. **Media**: The history of antisemitism is sadly rich in images that make for an informative slide show. Though somewhat technologically arcane, we like the format of a slide show because it enables you to pace the images in accordance with your students' understandings. (You'll need to talk them through

what each image projects as, in all likelihood; they won't even be able to understand what they're seeing without detailed explanation.) We like to follow this set of images with Nazi propagandistic images of Jews, since by that point, your students will be able to make the linkages themselves as to which stereotypes were being called up. A great website containing useful images and explanations of historical antisemitism is maintained by the **Florida Holocaust Museum**. The website organizes their timeline of antisemitism into phases: pre-Roman, Roman Empire, Crusades, Spanish Inquisition, Reformation, Enlightenment, Emancipation, 19th century, and post-World War I. As a side note, if you are planning a slide show presentation on all the factors, see the website, **Photographs of the Great War**. For a very informative film on the history of antisemitism, which is useful to excerpt in the classroom, see **The Longest Hatred**. Simone also likes to use the famous segment from Claude Lanzmann's film, **Shoah**, where a sole survivor of Chelmno (Simon Srebnik) has returned there decades later. A group of elderly, rural Poles are just exiting a church service and Lanzmann gets them to discuss what happened to the local Jews and the reasons they were gassed nearby. The excerpt is no more than five minutes, but Srebnik's standing among them and listening to their explanations, concisely and painfully exhibits the tenaciousness of anti-Jewish stereotypes to this day.

Resources for Teaching

Anti-Defamation League. Website: http://www.adl.org/adl.asp. *Tracking antisemitic and genocidal activity worldwide, the website has many useful links.*

Denying the Holocaust: The Growing Assault on Truth and Memory. Written by Deborah Lipstadt and published by Plume Books, New York, 1994. *An excellent and careful dissection of the Holocaust denial industry: who says what, why, and with what language.*

Florida Holocaust Museum. Website: http://www.flholocaustmuseum.org/ history_wing/antisemitism/. *Well organized and concise, this website houses many images that document the strands of antisemitism in various periods of European history.*

Holocaust Denial on Trial. Website: http://www.holocaustdenialontrial.org/ nsindex.html. *This website is housed at Emory University's Witness to the Holocaust program (where Deborah Lipstadt has her faculty appointment). It is thus one of the most comprehensive and careful websites for documenting the David Irving libel case. Included are transcripts from the trial and other official documents of all sorts.*

The Longest Hatred. Directed by Rex Bloomstein and produced by WGBH Boston Video, Boston, 1997, 90 minutes. *This three-part documentary film orga-*

nizes the history of antisemitism coherently into its usefulness during early Christianity, its culmination during the Holocaust, and its entanglement in the conflict between Jews and Arabs. The footage is great, if often disturbing, and the narration is comprehensible for high school students. A fabulous resource for background knowledge and for classroom use (in excerpted form).

Photos of the Great War. Website: http://www.gwpda.org/photos/greatwar. htm. *This archive has lots and lots of useful images despite the ugliness of the portal. For a stunning visual summary of the ruinous remains of World War I, click on the category, "Death and Destruction," and see the "Before and After" photographs.*

Shoah. Directed by Claude Lanzmann and distributed by New Yorker Films, New York, 1985, 566 minutes. *Technically 566 minutes long, this documentary is difficult for kids to watch. The layers of translations and the slowness of the pacing put students off. That said, there are numerous sections of the film, which, if discussed with students before watching, can be exceedingly powerful.*

Southern Poverty Law Center. Website: http://www.splcenter.org/intel/hate-watch/. *Especially dedicated to fighting racism nationally, the Southern Poverty Law Center's website is informative and interesting, visually stimulating and provocative. They also publish a teaching journal called "Teaching Tolerance."*

Resources for Further Learning

Fallen Soldiers: Reshaping the Memory of the World Wars. Written by George Mosse and published by Oxford University Press, Oxford, 1990. *A riveting history of the memory of wars.*

The First World War: A Complete History. Written by Martin Gilbert and published by Henry Holt, New York, 1996. *Martin Gilbert is a brilliant historian who can explain large events in clean prose. This book is a great history for those unfamiliar with World War I.*

A History of the Holocaust. Written by Yehuda Bauer and published by Scholastic Books, New York, 2001. *A fabulous and thorough textbook. Useful as a reference text.*

Nazi Germany and the Jews. Written by Saul Friedlander and published by HarperCollins, New York, 1997. *A detailed, but readable history which foregrounds Hitler and antisemitism.*

War and Genocide: A Concise History of the Holocaust. Written by Doris L Bergen and published by Roman & Littlefield Publishers, Inc., Baltimore, 2003. *A provocative history, which intertwines the history of Jews in the Holocaust with other groups' experiences.*

GERMANY 1933–1939

Businesses and properties owned by Jews were the target of vicious Nazi mobs during Kristallnacht.
© Bettmann/CORBIS.

It was a terrific time to be young in Germany. If you were a healthy teenager, if you were a patriotic German, if you came from an Aryan (non-Jewish) family, a glorious future was yours. The Nazis promised it. You were one of Adolf Hitler's chosen people. You were part of his Master Race whom he considered the highest class of human beings on earth.

Unlike our elders, we children of the 1930s had never known a Germany without Nazis. From our very first year in the *Volksschule* or elementary school, we received daily doses of Nazism. These we swallowed as naturally as our morning milk. Never did we question what our teachers said. We simply believed whatever was crammed into us. And never for a moment did we doubt how fortunate we were to live in a country with such a promising future.

[My teacher] Herr Becker, like many other people in Wittlich, was both a good Catholic and a good Nazi. He never tried to hide his belief that Jews were different. Once a week we had 'racial science' class where we learned how and why they were different. 'Just look at the shapes of their noses,' he would say. 'If they are formed like an upside-down 6 that shows their Jewishness. ...No German boy can ever be friends with a Jewish boy. No matter how nice he seems, he'll grow up to be your enemy.' I didn't see how this could be true, but I figured it must be, since Herr Becker knew everything.[19]

Alfons Heck was a young German when Hitler came to power in 1933. His faithfulness and obedience to the Nazi Party led him to join Hitler's youth movement when he was just 10-years-old and to rise to high rank over the next 12 years. The *Hitlerjugend* **(Hitler Youth)** organization mobilized boys into the National Socialist community and prepared them for combat in war by indoctrinating them in all aspects of Nazi ideology, particularly in racial science. By 1935, 60 percent of German children had joined the Hitler Youth.

The Hitler Youth movement's philosophy and organizational structure were outgrowths of Hitler's own ideology in which the younger generation would ensure his vision of a '**Thousand Year Reich**.' Boys were eligible to join the Hitler Youth at the age of 10 and, as part of their militaristic training for the future, were divided into platoons and given uniforms and bayonets. When the boys turned 19, they were drafted into the *Reich* Labor Service and then enlisted in the Third *Reich's* armed forces. Children did not need their parents' consent to join the Hitler Youth. In fact, parents who tried to keep their children from joining could be sent to prison. This process enabled the Nazi Party to supervise and control German youth from an early age. As Heck describes it,

Of all the branches in the Nazi Party, the Hitler Youth was by far the largest and by far the most fanatic. Its power increased each year. Soon, even our parents became afraid of us. Never in the history of the world has such power been wielded by teenagers. Far from being forced to enter, I couldn't wait to join. It promised to be an exciting life, filled with 'duties' that were more like pleasures. In a way, it was like the Boy Scouts—hiking, camping, sports, competition—with more emphasis on discipline than politics.[20]

---

[19]Eleanor Ayer with Helen Waterford and Alfons Heck, *Parallel Journeys* (New York: Atheneum Books for Young Readers, 1995), 1, 7-8.

[20]Ibid, p 8.

Throughout the 1930s, Nazi doctrines and practices exerted an increasing influence on every aspect of German life, not only on male youth. This chapter provides a historical synopsis of the changes that occurred in Germany from the time that Hitler came to power in 1933 until the outbreak of World War II in 1939.

The big ideas of this chapter are that:

- Under the Nazi regime, every aspect of German life was impacted: culture, economy, education, law, military, domestic and foreign public policies, domestic life and religion, among others.

- During this time period, the Nazi regime began enacting increasingly draconian legislation that deprived Jews of the most basic human rights.

- The Holocaust could not have occurred without the passive assistance of the German populace and the rest of the world. Their noninterference and even complete indifference to the plight of European Jewry contributed to the Nazis' plan. As Michael Berenbaum has written, "…neutrality helped the killer, never his victim."[21]

Key terms of this chapter include: *Hitlerjugend* (Hitler Youth), 'Thousand Year Reich,' National Socialist German Workers' Party—Nazi Party, *Führer,* totalitarian state, political prisoners, propaganda, book burnings, 'Aryan,' anti-Jewish legislation, *Kristallnacht*—The Night of Broken Glass, Nuremberg Laws, The Law for the Protection of German Blood and Honor, *lebensraum,* and Nazi-Soviet Pact.

The world-wide economic depression of the 1930s left millions of Germans out of work. The German people lacked confidence in their weak government, and many were desperate for a way out of the grim political and economic situation. These conditions provided the groundwork for Hitler and his **National Socialist German Workers' Party,** known as the **Nazi Party,** to rise to power and create a loyal following in Germany. Hitler was a charismatic, powerful speaker who promised a better life for Germans. On January 30, 1933, Hitler was appointed German chancellor by German President Paul von Hindenburg. When Hindenburg died on August 2, 1934, Hitler combined the offices of chancellor and president, declaring himself *Führer*—the leader of the German state and commander-in-chief of Germany's Armed Forces. The Nazi Party referred to their government as the **Third *Reich*** or third German empire. (The First *Reich* began with the Holy Roman Empire and lasted until its dissolution in 1806. The Second *Reich* was the German empire that ended when Germany lost

---

[21]Michael Berenbaum, ed., *Witness to the Holocaust* (New York: Harper Collins, 1997), 113.

World War I.) From 1933 to 1945, the Third *Reich* controlled Germany and took most of Europe by storm.

Within months of his appointment as chancellor, Hitler instituted a consolidated one-party dictatorship whereby all individuals and institutions were aligned to Nazi Party goals. During the next six years, Hitler transformed Germany into a police state. Nazi domestic policies came to govern and guide every facet of German life. German culture, economy, education, law, military, public policy, the majority of Catholic and Protestant churches, and even personal social practices all came under Nazi control, forming what has come to be called a **totalitarian state**. Storm Troopers set out to identify and arrest political opponents of the Nazi regime. Socialists, Communists, trade union leaders, and anyone who differed with the Nazi Party could be arrested and even killed.

On February 28, 1933, Hitler's cabinet declared a state of emergency and ended many individual freedoms including freedom of press, speech and assembly. Individuals lost rights to privacy—that is; Nazi government officials could read people's mail, listen in on telephone conversations and search private homes. By the middle of 1933, the Nazi Party was the only political party left in Germany, and nearly all overt opposition to the Nazi regime had been eliminated. The Nazi Party also began erecting concentration camps to imprison so-called **political prisoners**, anyone who opposed the Nazi government. In 1933, camps for political prisoners were built in Oranienburg, Esterwegen, Sachsenburg and Dachau, which was first established on March 22, 1933.

Hitler professed the belief that Germans were a racially superior people who were biologically destined to rule all of Europe, the Soviet Union, and eventually the world. Within this framework, so-called inferior people such as Jews, Sinti and Roma (formerly known as 'Gypsies'), homosexuals, and those who were physically challenged, deaf or blind, would be eliminated. Of these groups, the Jews were Hitler's primary target.

To spread Nazi racist philosophies throughout Germany and to win the loyalty and cooperation of the German people, massive **propaganda** campaigns were initiated. The Nazi Propaganda Ministry took control of all forms of communication: newspapers, magazines, books, public meetings, rallies, art, music, movies, and radio. Publicly displayed posters, radio broadcasts, films, and newspapers constantly reiterated Nazi ideology and antisemitic rhetoric. The Nazi Propaganda Ministry published and displayed 'weekly quotation posters' to encourage German citizen's active participation in creating a German revolution. A March 1933 poster included the caption: "The *Reich* will never be destroyed if you are united and loyal."[22] Any viewpoints seen as even remotely threatening to Nazi beliefs were censored or eliminated entirely.

On the night of May 10, 1933, *Deutsche Studentenschaft*—the German student organization—raided libraries, schools and bookstores throughout Germany, publicly burning more than 25,000 books that were considered a threat to the German 'Aryan' community. Book burnings took place in university towns throughout Germany. While some of the confiscated books were by Jewish writers, including Albert Einstein and Sigmund Freud, most were by non-Jewish writers, including such famous Americans as Jack London, Ernest Hemingway, Helen Keller and Sinclair Lewis. The world press expressed shock and dismay at the Nazi **book burnings**. In an eerily prophetic foreshadowing of things to come, several journalists recalled the poet Heinrich Heine who, in 1822 wrote, "Where one burns books, one will soon burn people."[23]

German teachers spread Nazi propaganda in their classrooms. Newly written textbooks taught students obedience to the Nazi Party, encouraged unconditional loyalty to Hitler, and promulgated antisemitic beliefs. A children's board game that students with free time might play in elementary school was called, "Jews Get Out!" Extra-curricular activities like those of the Hitler Youth trained school children from a young age to be faithful to Hitler and the Nazi Party over and above their parents. A 'German National Catechism' booklet included several antisemitic references such as, "The German people [are] the most racially pure of the European peoples. Which race must the National Socialist race fight against? The Jewish race. Why? The goal of the Jew is to make himself the ruler of humanity. Wherever he comes, he destroys works of culture. He is not a creative spirit, rather a destructive spirit."[24]

The Nazis also put their ideology into practice by encouraging and supporting German scientists whose work supposedly 'proved' that the human race should rid the world of those considered inferior. Known as the Law for the Prevention of Offspring with Hereditary Diseases, and passed on July 14, 1933, German physicians began performing state sanctioned, forced sterilizations of Sinti and Roma, physically handicapped individuals, the mentally ill, and those with certain diseases to prevent them from producing children.

[22]Randall Bytwerk, *In German Propaganda Archive,* (Calvin College: Grand Rapids, Michigan, 2003).

[23]As quoted in Guy Stern, *The Burning of the Books in Nazi Germany, 1933: The American Response,* (Los Angeles: Simon Wiesenthal Center Annual 2, 1985), 95.

[24]Werner May, *Deutscher National-Katechismus* 2nd edition (Breslau, Germany: Verlag von Heinrich Handel, 1934), 22-26, in German Propaganda Archive, Randall Bytwerk, Calvin College, Grand Rapids Michigan, 2003.

Women also played an important role in the plan to make the German national body 'pure of infection' and strong in numbers. The central role of 'Aryan' women was to be mothers and to educate the next generation of pure German youth. Hitler's propaganda minister, Paul Joseph Goebbels said, "The mission of woman is to be beautiful and to bring children into the world. This is not at all as rude and unmodern as it sounds. The female bird pretties herself for mate and hatches the eggs for him. In exchange, the mate takes care of gathering the food and stands guard and wards off the enemy."[25] The Third *Reich's* population policy even encouraged 'racially pure **Aryan**' German women to bear as many children as possible. Though never wholly enforced, the policy went so far as to prescribe that every member of the SS father four children, whether he was married or not. Furthermore, the Nazi regime bestowed the Cross of Honor medal on women who gave birth to four or more children, and 'pure Aryan' women who had abortion could be imprisoned for up to two years. Nazi racial laws also prohibited marriage between 'Aryans' and anyone considered undesirable or inferior, including Jews, those with handicaps or certain diseases. The Nazi League of German Girls, a branch of the Hitler Youth, trained young girls to become the future mothers and homemakers of an anticipated 'racially pure' Germany. In a 1937 speech, Hitler thanked Germany's women for sacrificing their children to his cause:

> …And all of us, gentlemen and members of the *Reichstag*, hereby join together in tendering our thanks to the women of Germany, to the millions of those German mothers who have given their children to the Third *Reich*. During these four years every mother who has presented a child to the nation has contributed by her pain and her joy to the happiness of the whole people. When I think of that healthy youth which belongs to our nation, then my faith in the future becomes a joyful certainty.[26]

While the totalitarian state of Nazi Germany coerced people's cooperation, many writers emphasize that Germans actually embraced Nazism. As Raphael Lemkin wrote in 1944, "The present destruction of Europe would not be complete and thorough had the German people not accepted freely [the Nazi] plan, participated voluntarily in its execution, and up to this point profited greatly therefrom."[27]

---

[25]As quoted in George L. Mosse, *Nazi Culture*, (Grosset & Dunlap, New York, 1966), 47.

[26]"On National Socialism and World Relations," speech delivered by Adolf Hitler in the German Reichstag on January 30, 1937, in German Propaganda Archive, Randall Bytwerk, Calvin College, Grand Rapids Michigan, 2003, translated by H. Müller, Berlin.

[27]Samantha Power, *A Problem From Hell: America and the Age of Genocide* (New York: HarperCollins, 2002), 40.

Anti-Jewish Legislation

Hitler began implementing his plan to rid Germany of its Jewish population by enacting legislation that deprived Jews of the most basic human rights. Holocaust-era **anti-Jewish legislation** can be divided into three distinct waves. The onset of the first wave occurred just after Hitler's appointment as chancellor and signaled the beginning of legal measures aimed at limiting, and eventually eliminating, Jewish life in Germany. The second major wave of anti-Jewish legislation came on September 15, 1935 when the German government passed the Nuremberg Laws, a series of legal edicts that severely restricted the civil rights of Jews. Other laws passed in 1935 include the *Reich* Flag Law that established the swastika flag as the official flag; and the Law for the Protection of the Hereditary Health of the German People and the National Law of Citizenship established the official definition of 'Jew.' Beginning in 1936, the third wave of anti-Jewish legislation stripped Jews of engaging in economic activity. It reached a crescendo in 1938 with a violent pogrom that has come to be known as ***Kristallnacht*—The Night of Broken Glass**—for the shattered glass from burned synagogues and store windows that littered the streets in its aftermath.

In the countries allied with Germany, or conquered and occupied by it, the extent and severity, swiftness and efficiency of anti-Jewish legislation varied. For example, in Austria racial legislation was applied swiftly and brutally. However, the Danes were able to maintain some political autonomy and to protect Danish Jews from the most severe forms of anti-Jewish legislation.

The First Wave: Enacted in April 1933, the Law for the Restoration of the Professional Civil Service, aimed at curtailing the rights of Jewish citizens, was the first anti-Jewish law in Germany. It prohibited Jews and those considered to be politically undesirable from working as civil servants. The law dictated that Jewish civil servants be dismissed from office even when there were no grounds for such action under prevailing law. The Law Against the Overcrowding of German Schools similarly restricted the number of Jewish students in schools and universities to five percent. These early laws were significant because they become the model for future measures that increasingly marginalized Jews from German society, and marked the beginning of the legal precedence of Nazi rule eclipsing any previous or existing German laws.

During this time, the Nazi government took over the auxiliary police force, further increasing its power in German society. The Nazis offered the police great latitude in making arrests and in the treatment of prisoners. Referred to as 'protective custody', this meant that anyone suspected of being an opponent of the regime could be arrested and kept in custody without benefit of a trial.

The Second Wave: By 1935, at an annual Nazi rally held in Nuremberg, new laws were announced that further deprived Jews of the most basic civil and political rights, including citizenship and the right to marry or engage in sexual relations with a person of so-called 'German blood.' These laws, which became known as the **Nuremberg Laws**, triggered a complicated classification system defining various degrees of Jewishness.

The Nuremberg Laws defined a Jew as anyone who had at least three Jewish grandparents, whether or not that person considered him or herself to be Jewish. Even individuals who had long ago converted from Judaism to another religion were defined as Jewish. A supplementary regulation, **The Law for the Protection of German Blood and Honor** further defined Jews as a separate race. Judaism was thus determined solely by ancestry, rather than by religious beliefs or practices. As a result, thousands of Germans who had not previously considered themselves to be Jewish found themselves defined as such by the German government.

More than 120 laws, decrees, and ordinances were enacted between September 1935 and September 1939—before the outbreak of World War II. These laws prohibited Jews from employing German women as domestics; from displaying the *Reich* and national flags or the national colors; from immigrating into Germany; from voting or holding any public office; even from walking on the sidewalk if an 'Aryan' was passing by. Jewish students were barred from public schools and universities; curfews were instituted; and Jews were banned from public parks, swimming pools, resorts, and forests.

The Third Wave: Nazi Germany hosted the 1936 Olympic Games in Berlin. Hitler viewed it as a public relations opportunity to introduce the glories of Nazism to the rest of the world. State-of-the-art stadiums and facilities were constructed as Nazi showpieces, and a propaganda film was commissioned to promote 'Aryan superiority.' However, international political unrest preceded the games. Several countries questioned whether the Nazi regime would accept the terms of the Olympic charter that guaranteed unrestricted participation regardless of class, creed and race.

A number of U.S. politicians, religious leaders and athletes called for a boycott of the Games unless the Nazis could assure the world that they would allow German Jewish athletes to compete. Judge Jeremiah Mahoney, president of the Amateur Athletic Union, argued that if the U.S.A. participated in the

Games, it would be seen as an endorsement of Hitler's *Reich*. The governors of New York and Massachusetts also opposed sending a U.S. team to Berlin. The American Jewish Congress, the Jewish Labor Committee, and the non-sectarian Anti-Nazi League, staged mass rallies in protest of the upcoming Games. Two Jewish athletes, Milton Green, captain of Harvard University's track team, and his teammate, Norman Cahners, boycotted the national Olympic trials.

In the end, however, a widespread U.S. boycott never took place and, while German officials allowed one athlete with scant Jewish ancestry to compete, one of the world's top high jumpers, a German Jewish athlete named Gretel Bergmann, was barred from competing. One important, albeit symbolic, blow was delivered to Nazi Germany at the Games nonetheless. While Hitler had hoped to use the Games to prove to the world his theories of 'Aryan racial superiority', ironically, an African-American sprinter and long jumper named Jesse Owens was the undisputed hero of the Games, winning four gold medals.

Hitler emerged seemingly unscathed by the public relations set back. In the same year as the Olympic Games, he enacted sweeping measures to seize Jewish assets and property and to cripple most Jews' abilities to earn a living. By 1937, the Third *Reich* further increased economic restrictions against the Jews, taking over all Jewish owned businesses and prohibiting Jewish doctors and lawyers from practicing their professions. Within a year, Nazi leaders enforced further measures that segregated Jews from so-called 'pure Germans'. Jews were barred from all theaters, sports facilities and from any areas designated as 'pure Aryan zones.' To enable the police to identify Jews more easily, new middle names were given to those Jews who did not have recognizable 'Jewish' first names. For males, the name Israel was added, for females, the name, Sarah.

Antisemitism reached an apex in pre-war Germany on November 9-10, 1938 with *Kristallnacht*—the first major physical attack on the Jewish population of Nazi Germany. Just a couple of weeks earlier, on the night of October 27th, 18,000 Polish Jews were deported from Germany, but were refused entry into Poland by the Polish authorities. Not able to return to Germany, and with nowhere else to go, the Jews were forced to set up makeshift shelters. When 17-year-old Herschel Grynszpan, a student in Paris, learned that his family was among the 18,000 Jews caught in this Nazi trap, he shot the third secretary of the German Embassy, Ernst Yom Rath. The Germans used this assassination as a welcome excuse to 'retaliate' against the Jewish community. Paul Joseph Goebbels, Hitler's Propaganda Minister initiated the riot; SS Security Service chief Reinhard Heydrich ordered security agencies to destroy synagogues; a Gestapo chief sent a telegram to all police units that read, "In shortest order, actions against Jews will take place in all Germany. These are not to be interfered with." The young Hitler Youth, Alfons Heck witnessed the mayhem of *Kristallnacht:*

> We were on our way home from school when we ran into small troops of SA and SS men…. We watched open-mouthed as the men jumped off trucks in the marketplace, fanned out in several directions, and began to smash the windows of every Jewish business…. Paul Wolff, a local carpenter who belonged to the SS, led the biggest troop, and he pointed out the locations. One of their major targets was Anton Blum's shoe store next to the city hall. Shouting SA men threw hundreds of pairs of shoes into the street. In minutes, they were snatched up and carried home by some of the town's nicest families—folks you never dreamed would steal anything.
>
> Four or five of us boys followed Wolff's men when they headed up the Himmeroder Stasse toward the Wittlich synagogue. Seconds later the beautiful lead crystal window above the door crashed into the street, and pieces of furniture came flying through doors and windows. A shouting SA man climbed to the roof and waved the rolls of the Torah, the sacred Jewish religious scrolls. 'Use it for toilet paper, Jews,' he screamed. At that, some people turned shamefacedly away. Most of us stayed, as if riveted to the ground, some grinning evilly.
>
> It was horribly brutal, but at the same time very exciting to us kids. 'Let's go in and smash some stuff,' urged my buddy Helmut. With shining eyes, he bent down, picked up a rock and fired it toward one of the windows.[28]

Riots like the one Heck witnessed took place throughout Germany and Austria that night. Nearly 1,000 synagogues were set afire, 7,000 Jewish businesses and homes were looted, and more than 100 Jews were killed as police and fire fighters stood by, making sure that the fires didn't spread to neighboring buildings that served non-Jews. The morning after *Kristallnacht,* as many as 30,000 Jews were arrested for the 'crime' of being Jewish and sent to concentration camps.

Yitzhak S. Herz, a German Jew who was the director of the Dinslaken Orphanage for Jewish children remembers the violent events of *Kristallnacht:*

> At 7 A.M., the morning service in the synagogue of the institution was scheduled to commence. Some people from the town usually participated, but this time nobody turned up. …At 9:30 A.M. the

---

[28]Eleanor Ayer with Helen Waterford and Alfons Heck, *Parallel Journeys,* Atheneum Books for Young Readers, 1995, pp. 27 and 29.

bell at the main gate rang persistently. I opened the door: about 50 men stormed into the house, many of them with their coat or jacket collars turned up. At first they rushed into the dining room, which fortunately was empty, and there they began their work of destruction, which was carried out with the utmost precision. The frightened and fearful cries of the children resounded through the building. In a stentorian voice I shouted: 'Children go out into the street immediately!' This advice was certainly contrary to the order of the Gestapo. I thought, however, that in the street, in a public place, we might be in less danger than inside the house. The children immediately ran down a small staircase at the back, most of them without hat or coat—despite the cold and wet weather. We tried to reach the next street crossing, which was close to Dinslaken's Town Hall, where I intended to ask for police protection. ...This was not very long in coming; the senior police officer, Freihahn, shouted at us: 'Jews do not get protection from us!'

...Facing the back of the building, we were able to watch how everything in the house was being systematically destroyed under the supervision of the men of law and order—the police. At short intervals we could hear the crunching of glass or the hammering against wood as windows and doors were broken. Books, chairs, beds, tables, linen, chests, parts of a piano, a radiogram, and maps were thrown through apertures in the wall, which, a short while ago, had been windows or doors.

In the meantime, the mob standing around the building had grown to several hundred. Among these people I recognized some familiar faces, suppliers of the orphanage or trades people, who, only a day or a week earlier had been happy to deal with us as customers. This time they were passive, watching the destruction without much emotion.[29]

For many Jews, the hardest thing to understand was that their own neighbors and friends had participated in *Kristallnacht*. Moreover, Jewish business owners and synagogue members were forced to pay for and participate in the clean-up activities of that night.

---

[29]As quoted in *Kristallnact at the Dinslaken Orphange, Reminiscenes* (Los Angeles: Museum of Tolerance Online Multimedia Learning Center Beit Hashoah, 1999), Introduction, #3.

The Nazis tried to rid Germany of its Jews by making life so difficult for them that they would be forced to leave the country. While *Kristallnacht* was not the first example of this tactic, at the time, it was the most violent. While many German Jews would have readily left the country at that point, they were unable to; most Jews were unable to find countries willing to take them. Though *Kristallnacht* was widely reported in the U.S. media, in the midst of the Great Depression, many Americans were reluctant to welcome European Jews out of fear that the refugees would compete with them for scarce jobs and deplete their limited social service benefits. Even the Land of Israel, then-Palestine, closed its doors to Jewish refugees. Britain, which controlled Palestine at the time, severely limited the number of Jewish refugees who could immigrate.

Instigating World War II

Hitler began an aggressive campaign for what he called *lebensraum* (more living space). The Third *Reich* attempted to dominate all of Europe through militaristic acquisition. Without engaging in war and with the overwhelming support of the Austrian people, Germany annexed neighboring Austria. Within a few months, Hitler's troops marched into the Czech Sudetenland which was largely populated by Germans who enthusiastically welcomed the invaders as fellow countrymen. In March, 1939, German troops entered Bohemia and Moravia. Hitler informed the world that "Czechoslovakia has ceased to exist."

After securing the Soviet Union's neutrality with the **Nazi-Soviet Pact**, German troops attacked Poland on September 1, 1939. Two days later, Britain and France, Poland's allies, declared war on Germany. Within a month, Poland was defeated and divided as conquered territory by the German and Soviet forces. World War II had begun.

Teaching Ideas

1. **Jewish Responses:** Jewish responses to anti-Jewish legislation in Germany were as varied as Jews themselves. Some vehemently argued that the growing antisemitism in Germany was a curious phase that would pass quickly and quietly. As a result, they felt the best response was no response at all. (For a brilliant illustration of this response, there is an Italian film, **The Garden of the Finzi Continis**, which is too long and mostly too dull to show to students, but in it, there is a short scene in which a wealthy Jewish Italian family discusses, over dinner, what they think about Italian Fascism. Also, the excerpt from **The Pianist** where the members of the family have

utterly different opinions portrays this nicely.) Others steadfastly believed that the brewing storm would only intensify throughout Europe and the only option for the Jews was immigration to Palestine. Others believed the right course of action was to proudly proclaim one's allegiance to Germany. Still others thought it best to stand proudly merely as Jews. We've excerpted two articles written by German Jews in response to the growing body of anti-Jewish legislation in the 1930s. Have your students read these (and others). Afterwards ask your students to write "letters to the editor" supporting or opposing each position.

...April 1, 1933, can become the day of Jewish awakening and Jewish rebirth. If the Jews will it. If the Jews are mature and have greatness in them. If the Jews are not as they are represented to be by their opponents. ...Even if we stand shattered by the events of these days we must not lose heart and must examine the situation without any attempt to deceive ourselves. One would like to recommend in these days that the document that stood at the cradle of Zionism, Theodor Herzl's 'Jewish state' be distributed in hundreds of thousands of copies among Jews and non-Jews.... Many Jews suffered a crushing experience on Saturday. Suddenly they were revealed as Jews, not as a matter of inner avowal, not in loyalty to their own community, not in pride in a great past with great achievements, but by the impress of a red placard with a yellow patch. The patrols moved from house to house, stuck their placards on shops and signboards. ...In addition to other signs and inscriptions one often saw windows bearing a large Magen David, the Shield of David the King. It was intended as dishonor. Jews, take it up, the Shield of David and wear it with pride!

—Excerpted from "Wear It With Pride, The Yellow Badge" by Robert Weltsch, published by Judische Rundschau, No 27, April 4, 1933.

...the great majority of German Jews remains firmly rooted in the soil of its German homeland, despite everything. There may be some who have been shaken in their feeling for the German Fatherland by the weight of recent events. They will overcome the shock, and if they do not overcome it then the roots which bound them to the German mother earth were never sufficiently strong. But according to the ruling of the laws and regulations directed against us only the 'Aryans' now belong to the German people. What are we, then? Before the Law we are non-Germans without equal rights; to ourselves we are Germans with full rights. We reject it, to be a folk or national minority, perhaps like the Germans in Poland or the Poles in Germany, because we cannot deceive our innermost feelings. We wish to be subject as Germans with equal rights to the new Government.... Thus we are suspended between heaven and earth. We will have to fight with courage and strength in order to get back to earth, in the eyes of State and Law, too....

—Excerpted from Alfred Wiender, of the leadership of the CentralVerein "Between Heaven and Earth," CV-Zeitung, No, 22, June 1, 1933.

2. **Just and Unjust Laws:** Ask your students to contemplate the role of the rule of law in society. The Nazi regime enacted unjust laws against its Jewish citizenry. What makes laws just or unjust? Are there unjust laws today? If so, which ones are considered unjust and why? In what ways are unjust laws today similar to or different from those enacted in Nazi Germany? What can citizens do today to fight unjust laws? Have them compare laws that were enacted by the Nazi regime (Nuremberg Laws; The Law for the Protection of German Blood and Honor) with those enacted by the U.S. government during the same period (immigration restrictions, the Supreme Court decision in Korematsu v. United States—the 1944 law that sequestered Japanese Americans).

3. **Civil Rights:** Similarly, ask your students to consider the issue of civil rights. Using primary sources, ask your students to read the 1933 Law for the Restoration of the Professional Civil Service—the first Nazi legislation aimed at curtailing the rights of Jewish citizens in Germany—and the 1935 Nuremberg Laws. (They are surprisingly brief and succinct and readily available on the Internet.) Then, over a one or two-week period, ask your students to scan current print or on-line newspapers and clip articles that address issues of civil rights today (e.g. African-Americans, gays and lesbians, obese or physically handicapped people). As a class, compare today's prejudices and issues of civil rights with those 'legalized' against the Jews by Nazi legislation. How are the two worlds the same? How are they different? Why do prejudice and inequality remain with us?

4. **Propaganda:** One of the odd 'contributions' that Nazi Germany made in world history was its utterly sophisticated use of propaganda. Hitler used an airplane to campaign for election, allowing him to seem 'ever-present' in Germany. Moreover, the many organizations that controlled the media in

Nazi Germany saturated the cultural environment, creating what is sometimes called a 'total environment.'

Ask students to consider and discuss various definitions of the purposes of propaganda. Some examples include:

- "Propaganda is the art of very nearly deceiving one's friends without quite deceiving one's enemies."[30] –F. M. Cornford

- "Propaganda is a set of methods employed by an organized group that wants to bring about the active or passive participation in its actions of a mass of individuals, psychologically unified through psychological manipulation and incorporated in an organization."[31] –Jacques Ellul

- "Every day we are bombarded with one persuasive communication after another. These appeals persuade not through the give-and-take of argument and debate, but through the manipulation of symbols and of our most basic human emotions. For better or worse, ours is an age of propaganda."[32] –Anthony Pratkanis and Elliot Aronson

Then, using primary source materials, ask your students to interpret Nazi propaganda posters, cartoons, films, and pamphlets. **Art of the Third Reich** by Adam Peter includes hundreds of examples of officially sanctioned artwork that demonstrate how the Nazi regime used fine arts including film, painting and architecture as manipulative propaganda tools. You can also access and down-load examples of Nazi Germany propaganda from **A Teacher's Guide to the Holocaust** and from the **U.S. Holocaust Memorial Museum.** We've also included, below, a few examples of common Nazi slogans:

- Germany Awake! Judah Perish!

- Whoever knows the Jews, knows the Devil!

- The Jews are our Misfortune!

- Germany is Hitler! Hitler is Germany!

Some questions for your students to consider when reviewing Nazi propaganda art and slogans include:

---

[30]F. M. Cornford, *Before and after Socrates* (Cambridge: Cambridge University Press, 1932), 18.

[31]Jacques Ellul, *Propaganda: The Formation of Men's Attitudes* (New York: Vintage Books, 1973), 61.

[32]Anthony Pratkanis and Elliot Aronson, *Age of Propaganda : The Everyday Use and Abuse of Persuasion* (New York: Owl Books, 2001), 48.

- Who do you think is the intended audience of the propaganda material (men, mothers, young people, the unemployed, etc.)? What symbols (if any) are depicted?

- Are the messages used primarily visual, verbal or both? What is the difference in the messages' impact?

- What Nazi purposes are served by the material?

- The most effective propaganda materials use symbols that are unusual, simple, and direct. Why do you think that is the case?

5. **Dramatic Movement:** Have your students interpret the changes and uncertainty of Germany in the 1930s through movement. As with any movement activity, much depends on your comfort level and that of your students. It's important to set up and maintain a safe environment for your students to express themselves creatively. Move desks and chairs out of the way so your students have room to move freely, or if possible, go outside. You may also incorporate musical instruments like tambourines, drums, bells, or shakers. Start by asking your students to imagine that they are at a celebratory Jewish wedding or a Passover *seder* in Germany in the late 1920s. Ask them to move their body to express how they feel in the moment. What does it feel like physically? What does it sound like? Then read to them excerpts from anti-Jewish legislation like the "Law for the Restoration of the Professional Civil Service," which was the first legislation aimed at curtailing the rights of Jewish citizens in Germany, or the Law Against the Overcrowding of German Schools that restricted the number of Jewish students in schools and universities. Ask your students to dramatize what it might feel like to be banned from public parks and swimming pools. How might they walk if forced to step off the sidewalk and into the street since a 'proper Aryan' was passing? How might they physically express *Kristallnacht*?

Afterwards, debrief the activity with your students. Ask them to reflect on their movements and music for each interpretation. At what moment was their dramatic movement or sound staccato (short, quick, sharp movement), sustained (continuous, slow movement), percussive (strong, forceful movement), swinging (back and forth to an even rhythm), open (flowing movement), bound (closed, tense)? What did each convey and why? Ask them to reflect on the speed of their movement and sound. What did the different tempos convey and why? Ask them to reflect on the amount of space they used in their dramatic interpretation (e.g. did they stand in one place or move around a lot)? Ask about the direction of their movement. Did they move forward, backward, sideways, diagonal, or in a pattern such as a circle, straight line or zigzag? Were they close to the ground (sitting or crawling) or reaching up on tip toes? Again, ask them to interpret what each movement meant to them and why. It is useful to do this exercise several times as students often need time to feel comfortable with the activity, thus enabling new images and meanings to emerge.

6. **Olympic Games:** The official charter of the International Olympic Committee states that the goal of the Games is to achieve the harmonious development of human kind through sport with a view to encouraging the establishment of a peaceful society. Nearly every nation in the world sends athletes to compete in the Games with the purpose of fostering the ideals of friendship among nations. However, the Olympics have had their share of human rights controversies. For example, during the 1908 Games in England, Irish athletes who wanted to represent their country were ordered to compete on behalf of Great Britain, and many of them withdrew from the Games as a result. At the 1972 Olympic Games in Munich, 11 Israeli athletes were murdered by Palestinian terrorists. And, as described earlier in this chapter, Nazi Germany hosted the 1936 Games attempting to use the event to propagandize its cause of 'Aryan racial superiority'.

   • Ask your students to research the Olympic Games, highlighting historic moments related to the cause of human rights. Should the Olympic Committee have allowed Nazi Germany to host the Games? The **U.S. Holocaust Memorial Museum** website includes several Nazi era propaganda posters, photographs of the 1936 Olympic Games and a clever "Program of the Olympics" from the November 1935 issue of *Arbeiter Illustrierte Zeitung* that satirizes the Nazi regime by listing fictional Olympic events.

   • **The film, Hitler's Pawn** follows the story of Greta Bergmann, a German Jewish athlete considered one of the world's top high jumpers, who was barred from competing in the 1936 Olympic Games in Berlin. Her captivating story is told in this riveting documentary which uses archival footage along with recreations. The video is great for teaching about anti-Jewish legislation and its impact on the whole of German society, including sports.

7. **Books and Films on the Hitler Youth:** Alfons Heck recalls his childhood in the Hitler Youth in a hauntingly powerful short film, **Heil Hitler:**

Confessions of a Hitler Youth. The video provides a good overview of the changes that occurred in Germany between 1933 and 1939 from the perspective of a young boy who once actively supported Hitler's propaganda. **Parallel Journeys,** juxtaposes the childhoods of Alfons Heck and Helen Waterford, a young Jewish girl who grew up near Alfons in Germany. It is a good complement to the video mentioned above. We suggest selecting various chapters of the book to be read in class or assigned with follow-up class discussion for high school age students. The book is too dense and too graphic for middle school students. **The Borrowed House** is a good fictional account of a young German girl's indoctrination into the Hitler Youth and her subsequent revelations about the atrocities committed by the Nazi Party. It is an appropriate read for upper elementary and middle school students as it avoids grisly details.

Resources for Teaching

Art of the Third *Reich*. Written by Peter Adam and published by Harry N. Abrams, New York, 1992. *Adam Peter includes hundreds of examples of officially sanctioned artwork that demonstrate how the Nazi regime used fine arts including film, painting and architecture as manipulative propaganda tools.*

The Borrowed House. Written by Hilda van Stockum and published by Farrar, Straus, Giroux, New York, 1975. *A good fictional account of a young German girl's experiences in the Hitler Youth and her subsequent revelations about the atrocities committed in the Nazi era. It is an appropriate read for upper elementary and middle school students as it avoids grisly details.*

The Garden of the Finzi Continis . Released by Columbia Tri-Star Pictures, 1971, 94 minutes. *Set in northern Italy at the outbreak of World War II, this classic film tells the story of an old, aristocratic Jewish family who maintain their isolated, idyllic ways within the stone walls of their lush estate while Mussolini imprisons Jews outside.*

Heil Hitler: Confessions of a Hitler Youth. Produced by HBO, 1992, 30 minutes. *A hauntingly powerful glimpse into the Hitler Youth movement as recalled by Alfons Heck.*

Hitler's Pawn. Produced by HBO Sports, 2004, 60 minutes. *Follows the story of Greta Bergmann, a German Jewish athlete considered one of the world's top high jumpers, who was barred from competing in the 1936 Olympic Games in Berlin.*

Parallel Journeys. Written by Eleanor Ayer with Helen Waterford and Alfons Heck and published by Atheneum Books for Young Readers, New York, 1995. *The author juxtaposes the stories of two World War II youth, Alfons Heck, a patriotic*

Hitler Youth and Helen Waterford, a young Jewish girl, both of whom grew up in war torn Germany.

The Pianist. Directed and produced by Roman Polanski, 2002, 150 minutes. *A Polish Jewish musician struggles to survive the destruction of the Warsaw ghetto of World War II.*

A Teacher's Guide to the Holocaust. Website site: http://fcit.coedu.usf.edu/ holocaust, produced by the Florida Center for Instructional Technology, College of Education, University of South Florida. *Includes Nazi era propaganda posters and cartoons depicting antisemitic references.*

U.S. Holocaust Memorial Museum. Website: www.ushmm.org/museum/ exhibit/online/olympics. *Includes several Nazi era propaganda posters, photographs of the 1936 Olympic Games and a clever "Program of the Olympics" from the November 1935 issue of* Arbeiter Illustrierte Zeitung *that satirizes the Nazi regime by listing fictional Olympic events.*

Resources for Further Learning

Destruction of the European Jews. Written by Raul Hilberg and published Holmes & Meier Publishers, New York, 1985. *Widely considered the landmark study of the Holocaust, Hilberg's study focuses on the perpetrators of the Nazi death machine— civil servants, military personnel, Nazi Party functionaries, SS men, and representatives of private enterprises.*

The Emigrants. Written by W. G. Sebald, Michael Hulse, and W. G. Sebald and published by New Directions Publishing Corporation, New York, 1997. *Although it is a fictional work, this novel profoundly blurs the line between fiction and non-fiction. The novel is composed of four compelling portraits of Jewish émigrés during World War II.*

Nazi Germany and the Jews: Volume I: The Years of Persecution, 1933–1939. Written by Saul Friedlander and published by Harper Collins, New York, 1997. *Friedlander describes and interprets the increasing anti-Jewish persecution in Germany after Hitler's rise to power in 1933.*

The War Against the Jews: 1933–1945. Written by Lucy Dawidowicz and published by Holt, Rinehart and Winston, New York, 1975. *Several chapters provide illuminating overviews into this time period, particularly the chapters entitled, "The Jews in Hitler's Mental World", "Anti-Semitism in Modern Germany", "Phase One: Anti-Jewish Legislation, 1933-1935", and "Between Freedom and Ghetto: The Jews in Germany, 1933-1938."*

Women in the Holocaust. Edited by Dalia Ofer and Lenore J. Weitzman and published by Yale University Press, New Haven, 1998. *The chapter entitled,*

"Keeping Calm and Weathering the Storm: Jewish Women's Responses to Daily Life in Nazi Germany" by Marion Kaplan provides an excellent overview of this time period from the perspective of women.

EMIGRATION EFFORTS

Sol and Henrietta Meyer, and their son, Harvey, pose at their railcar window, as they leave Germany for the United States, in 1939. USHMM, courtesy of Kurt & Jill Berg Pauly.

Realizing that Hitler is about to take over his country, an Austrian Jew goes to a travel agent. The travel agent takes out a globe and begins to go over the various places the Austrian Jew might find refuge. One by one, each country on the globe is eliminated as a place to go—each has a different excuse for not wanting to take in any Jews. Finally, in desperation the Austrian Jew asks, "Haven't you got another globe?"

This joke illustrates one of the greatest tragedies that befell the Jews of Europe in the years leading up to and following World War II—nearly every country in the world turned its back on the vast majority of Jews seeking refuge, refusing to allow them to immigrate. Palestine, as it was then called, was the one place that seemed to be a viable safe haven since Jews both lived in and yearned for the Land of Israel for millennia. This connection to the Holy Land is integral to the Jewish people's master story.

Thousands of European Jews tried to escape Nazi persecution by immigrating to the Land of Israel. Palestine was under the control of Great Britain whose Jewish immigration policies rapidly escalated from inconsistent to violently unreceptive, and the Arabs who lived in the land at the time vehemently resisted the influx of Jewish immigrants. The story of Jewish immigration to Palestine during the Holocaust era is, subsequently, controversial and emotional.

The State of Israel contains a complicated history in terms of its creation on the heels of the Holocaust, the British government's capricious policies vis-à-vis Jewish immigration, and members of the Arab community living in Palestine who feared and resisted the arrival of Jews in the land. Rabbi Michael Lerner writes, "Jews did not return to their ancient homeland to oppress the Palestinian people, and Palestinians did not resist the creation of a Jewish state out of hatred of the Jews."[33] During the Holocaust era, as Jewish refugees desperately tried to escape the inferno in Europe, the Arab people in the Middle East were in the midst of their own struggle to free themselves from colonialism. "They viewed the Jews who came to Palestine not as desperate refugees but as Europeans introducing European cultural assumptions, economic and political arrangements, and thereby extending the dynamics of European domination."[34] Lerner continues, "The Jews thus became the embodiment for many Palestinians of the worst impacts of the global capitalist market, and opposition to their presence in Palestine was a way of expressing (albeit irrationally) the anger that people were feeling at the changes that the new global order was imposing. No surprise, then, that many Palestinians were opposed to and deeply resented the increased presence of Jews in Palestine."[35]

What you make of this complicated history is wholly dependent on your own stance and educational objectives, the context in which you teach and your students. This chapter traces Jewish immigration to Palestine as a result of escalating persecution during the Holocaust era. It is not intended as a primer on teaching about the Middle East, but rather as a door into the history of European Jews.

The big ideas of this chapter are that:

- While immigration to Palestine was difficult and dangerous, it represented a possibility for survival for countless Jews during the Holocaust.
- Immigration quotas set up by the British were determined by complicated and even contradictory political agendas, prohibiting the vast majority of Jews from seeking refuge in the Land of Israel.

[33]Rabbi Michael Lerner, *Healing Israel/Palestine: A Path to Peace and Reconciliation* (San Francisco: Tikkun Books, 2003), xiii.
[34]Ibid, p. xiv.
[35]Ibid, p. 18.

Key terms of this chapter include: *aliyah, olim,* Balfour Declaration, *Aliyah Bet,* White Papers, *Yishuv, Mossad, Haganah,* the Struma, *Atlit, Palmach, Kielce Pogrom, Bricha,* Abba Kovner, American Jewish Joint Distribution Committee, Exodus 1947, displaced persons (DP) camps, *She'erit HaPletah,* War of Independence, and *landsmanschaft.*

Modern Waves of *Aliyah*

Immigration to the Land of Israel is commonly referred to as **aliyah**, literally meaning to go up, and those who immigrate are called **olim** (those who go up). Substantial waves of Jewish immigration to Palestine were often the result of Jews seeking refuge from persecution. In modern times, the first waves of Jewish immigration began in the late 1800s following antisemitic riots in Russia. Most of the *olim* at this time were young people inspired by socialist ideals. They formed *Degania,* the first *kibbutz* (cooperative community); *Ha-Shomer,* the first Jewish defense organization; and revived the Hebrew language as the modern spoken vernacular. These young pioneers laid the foundation for what became the modern State of Israel.

Great Britain wrested Palestine from the Ottoman Empire in 1917, and on November 2nd of that year, the British government announced that it would endorse the establishment of a Jewish homeland in Palestine. The decision was made public in a letter from Lord Arthur James Balfour to Lord Rothschild, the contents of which became known as the **Balfour Declaration**. It reads, in part, "His Majesty's Government views with favor the establishment in Palestine of a national home for the Jewish people, and will use their best endeavors to facilitate the achievement of this object, it being clearly understood that nothing shall be done which may prejudice the civil and religious rights of existing non-Jewish communities in Palestine, or the rights and political status enjoyed by Jews in any other country." The Balfour Declaration, along with ensuing pogroms in Russia, Poland and Hungry, triggered another wave of *aliyah* comprised mostly of young *halutzim* (pioneers) from Eastern Europe. These new immigrants built roads and towns, formed political organizations, expanded agricultural settlements and established the first industrial enterprises.

Another wave of immigration was triggered when the Polish government enacted a series of anti-Jewish laws in the 1920s and then when the Nazis rose to power in Germany in the early 1930s. From 1933 to 1936, 175,000 Jews settled in Palestine. Unlike previous waves of *aliyah,* many of these immigrants were middle-class professionals. They established small businesses and industrial enterprises that strengthened the economic development of the fledgling country.

Beginning in the early 1930s, the Arab community in Palestine, which had been established centuries earlier, began protesting the influx of Jewish immigrants by staging violent attacks against them. Great Britain relied heavily on oil supplies from the Arabs and did not want to jeopardize its lucrative economic relationship. As a result, the British government imposed a series of increasingly strict restrictions on Jewish immigration that eventually made it 'illegal' for Jews to immigrate. These events triggered ***Aliyah Bet***, a wave of clandestine immigration focused on rescuing Jews from Nazi persecution in Europe. As the second letter of the Hebrew alphabet, *Bet* signified that this was a secret or unofficial immigration. The term *Aliyah Bet*, therefore, conveyed both the historically sacred notion of going up to the Holy Land with the caveat that immigration was considered 'illegal' by the British.

The British restrictions on Jewish immigration to Palestine were issued through a series of reports called **White Papers** that, in addition to restricting Jewish immigration, also repudiated the Balfour Declaration. The 1922 White Paper was the first official addendum to the Balfour Declaration. Although the White Paper stated that the Balfour Declaration could not be amended and that the Jews were in Palestine by right, it reduced the area of the Balfour mandate by excluding the area east of the Jordan River. The document also established the economic absorptive capacity of the land as a criterion for determining Jewish immigration quotas.

The 1930 White Paper further restricted immigration by stating that if Jewish immigration prevented the Arab residents from obtaining work, then the British government would curtail Jewish immigration significantly or even terminate it altogether. In 1934 the first shiploads of 'illegal' Jewish immigrants arrived in Palestine. These immigrants were members of *He-Halutz*, a Polish Zionist youth movement.

In 1939, the third White Paper (also known as the MacDonald White Paper, after the British colonial secretary, Malcolm MacDonald,) completely negated the Balfour Declaration's commitment to the creation of a Jewish state and instead called for the creation of an independent state to be established within 10 years. That White Paper further limited Jewish immigration to 15,000 per year for five years. Thereafter, all Jewish immigration would be contingent on both the country's economic absorptive capacity and Arab consent. Even before the 1939 White Paper, however, the British only approved roughly one-third of the requests for immigration to Palestine, which resulted in various clandestine immigration attempts. The **Yishuv** (organized Jewish community in Palestine) saw the 1939 White Paper as a direct threat to Jewish rights and Jewish survival. As a result, *Aliyah Bet* became a resistance tool of the *Yishuv.*

Great Britain further restricted its immigration policies by declaring that ships carrying immigrants attempting to enter the Haifa port would be sent back to their ports of embarkation in Europe. Upon arriving back in Europe, many were forced into ghettos or concentration camps. However, some Jews were able to reach Palestine, smuggled into the country by Jewish resistance organizations.

The *Aliyah Bet* operations were complicated, risky and costly. Private entrepreneurs, Zionist groups, and the *Yishuv* orchestrated and financed the missions. The Jewish communities in Europe and Palestine also created immigration organizations including *Mossad l'Aliyah Bet* (Organization for *Aliyah Bet*, known as **Mossad**) and **Haganah** (the defense in Hebrew; a Jewish paramilitary organization). It is important to recall that not all Jewish organizations and Zionist movements were supportive of *Aliyah Bet*. Some believed that cooperating with Great Britain was the best way to realize mass immigration, while others argued that *Aliyah Bet* was the only way to save Jews.

The onset of World War II adversely affected the number of Jewish refugees who could be smuggled out of Europe and into Palestine. The war limited the *Yishuv's* ability to communicate with the resistance movements in Europe and to obtain ships for transport. Even when passage could be arranged, the dangers of maritime travel under wartime conditions were undeniable.

As a result, most *Aliyah Bet* operations halted for several years during the war, with a few notable and sometimes tragic exceptions. Dr. Baruch Confino, a wealthy member of the Zionist movement in Bulgaria, is credited with having financed the passage of 3,000 immigrants until one of his boats sank in a storm, drowning 220 passengers. Berthold Storfer, a Jewish philanthropist from Vienna, provided passage for nearly 2,000 immigrants. However, when his ships arrived at the Haifa port, they were impounded by the British and their passengers were transferred to ships bound for Mauritius off the coast of Africa. *Haganah* sabotaged one of these ships in attempt to prevent its departure, but a miscalculation caused the boat to sink, drowning 267 of its passengers. The British Navy deported the survivors to Mauritius for the duration of the war.

Another tragedy befell immigration attempts in early 1941 when 769 Jews boarded a rickety cattle boat named **the Struma** in the port of Constanta, Romania. The boat was barely seaworthy, heavily overcrowded and without sanitary facilities. The Struma was to sail to Istanbul where the passengers hoped to obtain immigration visas for Palestine. After one-hour at sea, the Struma's engines gave out and the boat was towed to Istanbul. For 10 weeks, the Turkish authorities kept the Struma's passengers docked under quarantine until their fate could be decided. Meanwhile, the British exerted pressure on the Turks to return the Struma and its passengers to Romania while the Turkish Jewish community pleaded with the British government to grant immigration visas or to at least allow the children to disembark in Istanbul. British authorities reluctantly granted immigration visas to the 50 young children on board the ship. Catastrophe struck before the children could disembark. On February 23, 1942, the Turkish police inexplicably towed the Struma into the Black Sea, though its passengers had no food or water on board and the ship had faulty engines and no fuel. Within a few hours, the Struma was struck by a torpedo and sunk. Only one passenger survived.

Who sunk the Struma remains a mystery to this day. However, recent evidence spreads blame across many countries, positioning the Struma's passengers as the unwitting victims of international politics. England sabotaged the ship's engine in an effort to keep Jews out of Palestine, while Turkey towed the Struma out to sea because it did not want to jeopardize its relationship with Germany by becoming a 'highway for Jewish refugees.' Recently declassified Soviet documents indicate that the Struma may have been sunk by a Soviet submarine and that Stalin waged a secret war in the Black Sea from 1941 to 1944, destroying ships in order to disrupt a lucrative chromium trade between Turkey and Germany.

Despite these setbacks, the *Mossad* resumed its secret immigration operations in 1944. By that time, the 'Final Solution' had been implemented, and many were convinced that immigration to Palestine was the only viable, albeit dangerous, escape from certain death. Before the end of the war, the *Mossad* successfully brought another 3,000 immigrants to Palestine. That number, however, represents a small fraction of those who attempted to immigrate. Only a few of the 66 ships that attempted immigration managed to penetrate the British blockade and bring their passengers ashore. Great Britain kept the gates of Palestine tightly closed, stranding hundreds of thousands of Jews in Europe, many of whom perished as a result.

During this time, British troops also incarcerated thousands of Holocaust survivors who attempted to circumvent the British coastal blockade in the Illegal Immigrant Detention Camp at *Atlit*, south of Haifa. Members of various Jewish underground organizations in Palestine who were resisting the British were also imprisoned at *Atlit*. In the fall of 1945, the **Palmach** (the elite striking force of *Haganah*) liberated over 200 Jews from *Atlit* in a daring operation commanded by Yitzhak Rabin. The refugees were secreted away at night and hidden at *Kibbutz Bet Oren* and other nearby settlements. British troops were besieged and overtaken by masses of people from the area when they tried to recapture the refugees.

Post-War

When World War II ended, survivors not only had to contend with the knowledge that they had lost children, parents, siblings, spouses, aunts and uncles, grandparents, friends, colleagues, neighbors, homes and communities, they had to contend with their own physical and emotional devastation as well as the knowledge that they were unwanted in virtually all of the countries they had once called home. Thousands who attempted to return to their former homes were met with lingering antisemitic violence. Prior to the war, for example, Kielce, Poland was a flourishing city with some 28,000 Jewish inhabitants. After the war, approximately 400 Jewish survivors returned there, hoping to find surviving relatives or friends, hoping to reclaim their homes and whatever property remained, and wanting to start their lives anew despite the devastation they had lived through. Forty-two of these people were brutally murdered on July 4, 1946, accused of the Medieval antisemitic myth of blood libel. Approximately 50 more Jews who had been recovering at a home for returning survivors were attacked the same evening, and 20 more were murdered on the outskirts of Kielce. Polish Cardinal August Hlold blamed the Jews for the **Kielce Pogrom**, claiming that because the Jews of the area had supported the Communists and the Communists had occupied Poland, Polish Jews had brought this on themselves. The bishop of Kielce agreed, suggesting that Jews had actually orchestrated the riot to persuade Britain to hand Palestine over to them. Only the bishop of Czestochowa condemned the killings, and was then reprimanded by his colleagues for doing so. In all, some 2,000 Jews were murdered in Poland alone in antisemitic pogroms between 1945 and 1947, catalyzing large numbers of Polish survivors to flee.

The British continued to refuse survivors of the Nazi regime to find sanctuary in Palestine. In June 1946, President Harry S. Truman urged the British government to allow 100,000 Holocaust survivors to enter Palestine. Britain's Foreign Minister, Ernest Bevin, replied sarcastically that the United States wanted displaced Jews to immigrate to Palestine because they did not want too many of them in New York. *Aliyah Bet's* efforts rose dramatically due to increased demand from Holocaust survivors and burgeoning political support.

Bricha (the Hebrew word for flight or escape) was the name given to the post-war mass movement of about 250,000 Holocaust survivors attempting to emigrate from Eastern Europe into the Allied-occupied zones and Palestine. *Bricha* began in 1944 with groups of Jewish partisans who initially had no contact with one another. Convinced that they could not carry on life in their former homes, places which had become Jewish graveyards, they organized first separately and later together to reach Palestine. Partisan and poet, **Abba Kovner**, was one of the *Bricha's* early leaders. In time, the loosely organized movement became highly efficient, with funding from the **American Jewish Joint Distribution Committee** (commonly referred to as "the Joint"), leadership from the officers of the Jewish Brigade of the British army, and operatives from *Haganah*.

A dilapidated ship named **Exodus 1947** became a symbol of the Jewish struggle for freedom in Palestine once it was recognized as the most notorious postwar immigration attempt. In November 1946, a Jewish immigration agency acquired an American ship with a capacity to hold 400 passengers. The plan was to smuggle Holocaust survivors from Europe into Palestine. On July 11 of the following year, the ship sailed from the port of Site, near Marseilles, France, carrying 4,515 immigrants, including 655 children. The Exodus was under British surveillance as soon as it left France. Seven days later, before it entered Palestine's territorial waters, the British rammed the ship, boarded it and towed it to the Haifa port. British troops forced the passengers off the ship. The refugees resisted defiantly, and three Jews were killed, 30 more, wounded. The British then forced the refugees onto deportation vessels bound for France. Upon arrival at *Port-de-Bouc* in southern France, the emotionally and physically exhausted Holocaust survivors again refused to disembark, organizing a hunger strike to call the world's attention to their plight. They held out for 24 days despite abominable conditions including a scorching heat wave, poor sanitary conditions and overcrowded quarters. French authorities refused to acquiesce to British demands that they force the refugees off the ships.

The British then decided to return the refugees to camps in Germany. When the ships arrived in the port of Hamburg, the refugees were forcibly removed by British soldiers. With hundreds of journalists from all over the world reporting on the event, public opinion turned virulently against the British. As a result, the British government acceded, though only slightly. From then on, 'illegal' immigrants were not sent back to Europe, but instead transported to **displaced**

persons' (DP) camps on the Mediterranean island of Cyprus. Members of the United Nations Special Committee on Palestine were so outraged by the British government's actions that they issued a report recommending that a Jewish state be established in Palestine. Eventually, the majority of the Exodus' passengers settled in Israel, though most were detained in Cyprus until after the founding of the state.

The fate of the Exodus' passengers galvanized world public opinion in favor of a Jewish state in Palestine. The *Mossad* and other Jewish organizations banded together with *Bricha*. Together they organized and provided passage for more than 70,000 Holocaust survivors. These rescue operations, though well intentioned, were extraordinarily complicated and mostly unsuccessful. While western European countries including Italy and France provided support for *Aliyah Bet*, some eastern and southern European countries either prohibited Jews from leaving at all or made it exceedingly difficult, requiring that Jews pay hefty sums in order to leave.

Until the establishment of the State of Israel, the British government continued to intern in Cyprus those they caught in displaced persons (DP) camps. Another 200,000 Holocaust survivors were interned in DP camps in Germany, Austria and Italy until their fate could be decided. The DPs were mostly Jews from Eastern Europe, as most of the survivors from Western Europe were able to return to their countries of origin.

Displaced Persons Camps

The British army was responsible for both the administration and security of the DP camps and ran them as though they housed prisoners of war rather than victims of atrocity. In many of the camps, those in charge did not distinguish between German prisoners, Nazi collaborators and Holocaust survivors, grouping them together. Conditions were harsh. The tents and barracks were overcrowded and unsanitary. Disease spread through the camps.

Eventually, the British ceded oversight of the DP camps to Jewish relief organizations that immediately improved medical and welfare services. Jewish organizations also set up a bureau at the camps to assist survivors in searching for missing relatives. The displaced persons themselves were given some authority to manage their own affairs. They organized under the name, **She'erit HaPletah** (surviving remnant). *She'erit HaPletah* actively worked towards securing immigration to Palestine and towards establishing a Jewish state there. Zionist parties and non-Zionist religious movements also became active in the DP camps. They created an intensive political and cultural life that included publishing more than 70 newspapers in Hebrew and Yiddish and developing school systems, most of which taught agricultural topics to prepare survivors for immigration to Palestine.

By 1947, the number of survivors in the camps increased substantially as Jewish refugees continued to arrive from Eastern Europe, but the fate of the survivors hung in political limbo. The camps became inhumanly crowded. Finally, world public opinion exerted enough pressure on the British and American governments to find a homeland for Holocaust survivors. That said, the last DP camp did not close until 1954.

Statehood

Many Holocaust survivors who immigrated to Palestine found themselves fighting another battle when the Israeli **War of Independence** broke out in 1948. Some survivors recall literally being handed guns as they stepped off the ships having just arrived at Haifa's port. Hundreds of Holocaust survivors died in battle, an unknown number of whom before any of their family members even knew they had survived the Holocaust.

In the years following statehood, Israelis faced the challenges of repeated wars, immigrant absorption, austerity, and a longing for normalcy. There seemed to be no time, space or inclination to come to grips with the Holocaust. Specifically, there was no room in the emerging Israeli national self-image for victimization; Israelis at that time cultivated a sense that the new nation and its new citizens were strong, independent, militarily adroit and hyper-masculine. Not coincidentally, the victimization of the Holocaust and the bravery of the War of Independence became symbolically linked, the latter trumping the former. The War of Independence seemed to redeem Holocaust victimization under the new banner of Israeli heroism. As a result, in the years immediately following statehood, the Holocaust was largely ignored by the Jewish communities in Israel and abroad. Though Holocaust survivors spoke about their experiences within their survivor circles, their *landsmanschaft* (or communities from the "Old Country"), many were shamed into secrecy in the public arena. Survivors in Israel found that, aside from those who came from 'over there,' people were unwilling or unable to listen to stories about their catastrophic experiences. Some survivors even endured ridicule in Israel, being called names (like 'soap') because their victimization was seen as an embarrassment in the newly formed state.

In the years since, Israeli society has learned to confront its vexed relationship to Holocaust suffering. Since the end of World War II, Holocaust memory in Israel has evolved and matured and interest in the events of the Holocaust has risen at an unprecedented rate. Whereas the first few decades immediately following the Holocaust might be considered the years of guilt and shame, the last few decades may be characterized as years of interest, even reverence. Over the last few decades, the Holocaust has become a major facet of Israeli identity. Indeed, throughout the western world, interest in the Holocaust has increased, testimonies of survivors have been collected, and Holocaust remembrance has burgeoned.

Teaching Ideas

1. **Personal Biographies**: First-hand accounts and personal biographies can transform historical facts into compelling stories, revealing individual perspectives on personal, social, cultural, religious, political and historical issues. Divide your students into groups of two or three and ask each group to trace the life of someone who immigrated to Palestine during the Holocaust or immediately thereafter. You can access biographies from various websites including the **U.S. Holocaust Memorial Museum**'s (ushmm.org). Ask your students to familiarize themselves with the person's journey including his/her country of origin, what daily life was like for him/her prior to the Nazis' rise to power, where he/she spent the Holocaust years, how he/she came to attempt immigration, and what was the result. The goal of this research process is to illuminate the multiple paths that Jews took in seeking refuge. Therefore, we encourage you to select biographies that illuminate different origins, routes, implications and outcomes. Students can share the findings of their research with each other through maps, posters, photographs, and primary source material.

   After the presentations, lead a group discussion to deepen their learning: What were some commonalities among the ways people escaped from Nazi controlled Europe to Palestine? What were some of the differences between immigration attempts before, during and after the war? In what ways did British restrictions impact immigration attempts? What were some of the reactions to Jewish immigration by the Arab community in Palestine? Were those reactions justified? Why/why not? What choices do you imagine you would have made at the time? Would they be similar to or different from the choices made by the person you researched? Why/why not?

2. **Biblical Connections to the Land of Israel**: Tracing the Jewish people's connection to the Land of Israel can dramatize the symbolism and meanings of the land to the Jewish people throughout history, particularly during the Holocaust era.

   Several passages from Jewish Scripture have been set to music as songs that are familiar to many students. Engage in some creative text study by singing the songs with your students, and then explore the meaning of the passages as they relate to the Jewish people's deep yearning for the Land of Israel. Some of the more familiar of these texts include:

   - Psalm 126, commonly known as *Shir HaMa'alot* (Song of Ascent), is the pre-amble to *Birkat Hamazon* (Grace After Meals) that is customarily sung on the Sabbath, *Rosh Hodesh* (the new month) and *Yom Tov* (holy days). *Shir HaMa'alot* is part of a series of 15 *tehillim* (psalms) written by King David. Some scholars believe that the pilgrims chanted *Shir HaMa'alot* as they made *aliyah* to Jerusalem to celebrate the *Shalosh Regalim* – the three pilgrimage festivals. The words of *Shir HaMa'alot* convey that it will be like a dream when God restores the land of Zion.
   - Psalm 137:5 contains the infamous words, "If I forget you, O Jerusalem, let my right hand wither." The entire psalm has been set to music.
   - Isaiah 66:10 is a well-known verse and song, *Sisu et Yerushalyim*—Rejoice with Jerusalem.
   - Deuteronomy 26:9, this text has become perhaps the most popular song about the Land of Israel. The passage refers to God freeing the Israelites from slavery in Egypt: "God brought us to this place and gave us this land, a land flowing with milk and honey."

   Mapping is another method for your students to trace the Jewish people's connection to the Land of Israel. Ask your students to create color-coded maps that chart Jewish migration to the Land of Israel from Biblical times. Some helpful resources include: **Heritage: Civilization and the Jews**, a DVD video and DVD-ROM interactive multimedia collection organized into searchable, cross-referenced components. **The Atlas of the Jewish History** by Martin Gilbert provides hundreds of maps that trace world-wide Jewish migrations from ancient Mesopotamia to modern Israel.

3. **Books and Films:** Written by Carol Matas, **After the War** is a compelling adolescent novel about a teenage girl who emigrates from Poland to Palestine with the assistance of *Bricha*. There are several excellent films appropriate for young teens and older youth: Debbie's favorite is **The**

Struma, a new documentary that unravels the sordid web of international diplomacy that led to the sinking of the ship. **Displaced Persons** chronicles the fate of Holocaust survivors attempting to reach Palestine only to be turned away by the British blockade. **The Illegals** was filmed in 1948 by Meyer Levin who recorded survivors attempting passage into Palestine aboard an 'illegal' *Haganah* ship. Levin kept filming even as British soldiers boarded the ship and ultimately confiscated his film. The footage was later recovered and serves as a remarkable record of post war *aliyah* efforts. Two films based on Gila Almagor's autobiographical memoir reveal what life was like for Holocaust survivors in post-statehood Israel. **Under the Domim Tree** (also a novel) presents life in an Israeli youth village established to house orphan teenage survivors of the Holocaust. *Hakayitz shel Aviya* (The Summer of Aviya) tells the story of a girl in Israel in the early 1950s who must cope with the worsening mental illness of her mother, a Holocaust survivor. Simone's favorite is **The Long Way Home**, an Oscar-winning documentary that traces the tumultuous years between 1945 and 1948 as Holocaust survivors tried to rebuild their lives from the remnants of their destroyed worlds and took part in the creation of the State of Israel.

Resources for Teaching

After the War. Written by Carol Matas and published by Simon & Schuster Books for Young Readers, New York, 1996. *A fictional adolescent novel about a teenage girl who emigrates from Poland to Palestine after the war with the assistance of* Bricha.

Atlas of the Jewish History. By Martin Gilbert and published by William Morrow and Company, Inc., New York, 1992. Provides hundreds of maps that trace world-wide Jewish migrations from ancient Mesopotamia to modern Israel.

Displaced Persons. Produced by the Israel Film Service, 1981, 50 minutes. *Through archival footage and interviews, the film chronicles the fate of Holocaust survivors attempting to reach Palestine only to be turned away by the British blockade.*

Hakayitz shel Aviya (The Summer of Aviya). Produced by Gila Almagor and Eitan Evan, 1989, 96 minutes. *In Hebrew with English subtitles, the film, based on Gila Almagor's memoir, tells the story of a girl in Israel in the early 1950s who must cope with the worsening mental illness of her mother, a Holocaust survivor.*

Heritage: Civilization and the Jews. *A DVD video and DVD-ROM interactive multimedia collection organized into searchable, cross-referenced components produced by* *the Educational Broadcasting Corporation and available through* www.thirteen.org *or* www.pbs.org.

The Illegals. Distributed by the World Zionist Organization, 1948, 56 minutes. *In 1948 Meyer Levin recorded survivors attempting passage into Palestine aboard an 'illegal'* Haganah *ship. He kept shooting even as British soldiers boarded the ship and ultimately confiscated his film. The film was later recovered by Levin and serves as a remarkable record of post war* aliyah *efforts.*

The Long Way Home. Produced by Moriah Films, 1997, 116 minutes. *Oscar winning documentary that traces the tumultuous years between 1945 and 1948, as Holocaust survivors tried to rebuild their lives from the remnants of their destroyed world and took part in the creation of the State of Israel.*

The Struma. Produced by HBO2, 2003, 90 minutes. *Filmmaker Simcha Jacobovici unravels the sordid web of international diplomacy that led to the sacrifice of nearly 800 Jews attempting to escape Nazi occupied Romania for Palestine in 1942.*

Under the Domim Tree. Produced by Jewish Television Production, 1996, 102 minutes. Book by Gila Almagor, translated by Hillel Schenker and published by Simon and Schuster, New York, 1995. *A powerful coming-of-age story based on the autobiographical memoir by Gila Almagor that presents life in an Israeli youth village established to house orphan teenage survivors of the Holocaust.*

U.S. Holocaust Memorial Museum. Website: www.ushmm.org. *Includes biographies and photos of Holocaust survivors who attempted to immigrate to Palestine.*

Resources for Further Learning

Commander of the Exodus. Written by Yoram Kaniuk, translated by Seymour Simckes and published by Grove Press, NewYork, 1999. *Biography of Yossi Harel, who defied the British blockade on four expeditions between 1946 and 1948 including the voyage of the Exodus.*

Exodus 1947. Written by Ruth Gruber and published by Times Books, Random House, Inc., New York, 1999. *A first hand account of an American journalist who was reporting from the Haifa port in 1947 about the Exodus. Includes more than 100 photographs by the author.*

Flight and Rescue: *Brichah.* Written by Yehuda Bauer and published by Random House, New York, 1970. *History of the mass movement of Jewish survivors of the Holocaust from Europe beginning in 1944 until the creation of the State of Israel.*

From Diplomacy to Resistance: A History of Jewish Palestine 1939–1945. Written by Yehuda Bauer and published by The Jewish Publication Society of America, New York, 1970. *An historic overview of the controversies surrounding the British mandates during the Holocaust era and its implications for European Jewry.*

GHETTOIZATION

Frightened Jewish families surrender to Nazi soldiers at the Warsaw Ghetto in 1943.
© Hulton-Deutsch Collection/CORBIS.

eaching about the Jewish ghettos of Nazi Europe can present special problems for educators: the problem of overgeneralization, the problem of historical determinism, and the problem of moral culpability. All of these problems can plague teaching about the Holocaust generally, but the problems emerge especially so with teaching this topic in particular.

The problem of overgeneralization refers to the tendency to teach about all ghettos as if they were the same, or as if they were mostly the same, whereas, the ghettos in Nazi-occupied Europe, while they shared many attributes, also differed from each other in substantive ways. There were large ghettos and small ghettos, ghettos that supplied slave labor to the Nazi war machine or German industries, and ghettos where that labor was useless and purely dehumanizing. Some ghettos were open, while others were closed, though all were relatively isolated. Of those that were closed, there were those that allowed some degree of movement outside the walls, and there were those that allowed practically none. **Lodz ghetto** was the most isolated. Fenced in with barbed wire, with exits watched over by armed guards, the Lodz ghetto allowed very little black-market trafficking in goods or supplies between the ghetto and the outside world as a result. By contrast, in the Warsaw ghetto, an entire aristocratic elite formed out of those who smuggled in and traded goods stolen or procured from outside. From some ghettos, the inhabitants could view the outside world, could gain information about how the war was progressing, or could see those who were deported from the ghettos being shot at point-blank range. In other ghettos, the lack of information was so profound as to allow wild rumors to circulate constantly (the war was about to end, the Allies had forfeited). Some ghettos are famed for their acts of heroic military resistance—Warsaw, Vilna, Minsk; others had none. There were even a few ghettos where Jews weren't systematically starved (Czestochowa and Sosnowice-Bedzin). Over time, too, the attributes of single ghettos changed as refugee populations were crowded in or as deportations to concentration camps cleared them out. One of the great challenges of teaching about the ghettos, then, is to make sure that your students don't leave thinking that all ghettos were able to mount large-scale, heroic resistance efforts, or that no ghettoized Jews knew what the Nazi plans for them entailed.

The problem of historical determinism involves the trap of teaching about the ghettos as though they were inevitable, as though they were simply a logical step in the progression of the Nazi plan. This pedagogical problem is especially acute in teaching about the ghettos because most of us consider the ghettos to be a kind of intermediary step in Holocaust history, the link between the expulsions of Jews from the fabric of civil society to their mass murder in the gas chambers. It is very difficult to remember, and more difficult to teach, in a way that recognizes that history is never inevitable, and that other decisions could have been made, that other paths could have been taken. When most of the ghettos were established, for example, the decision to mass murder the Jews of Europe had not as yet been made. It is likely, in other words, that when the first ghettos were established, the Nazis conceived of them as holding pens, places to centrally locate Jews while they figured out where to deport them to, not how to annihilate them. If we treat the ghettos as simply the fan belt of the Nazi juggernaut, we inadvertently strip history of its intricacies, its multiplicity of possibilities.

The third problem, **the problem of moral culpability,** also strips history of its complexities, specifically of its moral complexities. In teaching about the ghettos, teachers, especially in Jewish schools, may purposefully skip mentioning or teaching about the *Judenrate,* the Jewish councils (sometimes called the Council of Elders), whose job it was to execute Nazi demands, and, as much as possible, act on behalf of the ghetto inhabitants. Some historians have claimed that by obliging Nazi demands for goods, labor and ultimately lives, the *Judenrate* are to be condemned for feeding the Nazi machine's appetite and ultimately in aiding the destruction of the Jews. Other historians, though, have claimed that *Judenrate* members were acting in good faith, attempting to save their ghetto's inhabitants through whatever means possible, and in the worst cases, by sacrificing the few to save the many or by sacrificing the many to save the remaining. Though there was a range of responses among *Judenrate* leaders—which encompassed dedicated subterfuge, self-serving collaboration, and suicide—there can be no question that, as Yehuda Bauer writes, "However one views the *Judenrate*, the ultimate responsibility lies, of course, with the Nazis, not with those who were, at worst, but tools."[36] And yet, the aura of moral culpability surrounds the *Judenrate* to this day, complicating images of victimization and prompting teachers to avoid coverage of this topic in classrooms. We strongly advocate that you not make this same mistake.

The big ideas of this chapter are that:

- Ghettos varied tremendously from place to place, even while they shared certain basic features.

- Ghettos were not only places where Jews died of starvation and disease, but places where secular culture, religious life, and complex social and economic systems thrived.

- The roles of the *Judenrate* and the Jewish police forces are crucial components of Holocaust history, which students need to learn about.

Key terms of this chapter include: the problem of overgeneralization, Lodz ghetto, the problem of historical determinism, the problem of moral culpability, *Judenrate*, ghettos, Joint Distribution Committee, Janusz Korczak, Warsaw ghetto, Emmanuel Ringelblum, *Oneg Shabbat*, Jewish ghetto police forces, Chaim Rumkowski, and Adam Czerniakow.

Formation of the Ghettos

…On the afternoon of October 21, 1941, we received a registered, official envelope from the Gestapo offices in Hamburg: "You are ordered to appear on October 25, 1941, at the Sammelplatz for resettlement. Take only one suitcase per person." …After a long and distressing journey…we arrived in Lodz, Poland. The [Jewish] police lined us up, and we began to walk. Although we straggled and complained,

---

36 Yehuda Bauer, *A History of the Holocaust* (New York: Scholastic Books, 2001), 172.

there were no wagons or cars for the elderly or the children. Next to Mother walked a young man in the ghetto police uniform. They began talking in Polish, and …Mother…sounded relieved. I, however, saw only the dilapidated houses, the huts, and the filth around us. The shabbily dressed men and women of the ghetto stared at us through dull, unsmiling eyes. The cobblestone streets were in need of repair, the walkways were unpaved, and the open sewers were vile-smelling…. Four men and two women passed us, pulling a heavy, long, metal drum as though they were horses. Clad in reeking rags, they left an unbearable stink in their wake. I learned later that they received double rations for cleaning the outhouses.[37]

Lucille Eichengreen was deported to the Lodz Ghetto in 1941, almost two years after that ghetto was established. Like others forced into ghettos, she was to take only one bag on the journey, leaving her parents' home, furniture, estate and belongings to be confiscated by the *Reich*. The shock of her entry to the ghetto is palpable in this short excerpt from her memoir, *From Ashes to Life*; within a few weeks, however, she, too, would be hungry, and within a few months, orphaned.

Chaim Kaplan, one of the chroniclers of the Warsaw ghetto, wrote in his diary about the expulsions from the suburbs of Praga. "By the thirty first of October [1940] Praga must be empty of its Jewish inhabitants, who were rooted to its soil for hundreds of years. Most of them are poor. They have no money to move their belongings. And where would they move them to?" Kaplan went on to describe that their Polish neighbors in many cases, drove them out of their apartments "in advance, before the fixed date," wanting to plunder that which was left behind.[38]

Most **ghettos** were established in Poland between the years of 1939 and 1943, and mostly between 1940 and 1941. A few ghettos were erected elsewhere: in occupied USSR, Romanian territory, and briefly in Greece and Hungary. The largest were located in Warsaw, Lodz, Cracow, Lublin and Lvov, but smaller ghettos dotted the landscape as well. In all, there were approximately 400 ghettos established in Poland alone. Procedurally, to establish a ghetto, the poorest and most broken-down section of a city would be emptied of its non-Jewish inhabitants, and the Jews from the same city and from its surrounding villages would be funneled into these mostly fenced- or walled-in areas. In Warsaw, for example, the largest of all the ghettos established, the Jews of Warsaw were

---

[37]Lucille Eichengreen, *From Ashes to Life* (San Francisco: Mercury House, 1994), 34-36.

38 Chaim Kaplan, *Scroll of Agony: Hebrew Diary of Ch. A. Kaplan, September 1, 1939-August 4, 1942* (Tel Aviv: Yad Vashem, 1966).

forced to build the ghetto wall, which had shards of glass laid between bricks in order to discourage scaling the wall. As larger numbers of Jews came under Nazi dominion, the SS, under Adolf Eichmann, paid for their transport to ghettos by train, usually demanding funds from the displaced Jewish communities themselves to cover the costs. Jews rounded up from the Balkans, from Hungary and some of the other Eastern conquests, were mainly sent straight to concentration camps.

Life within the Ghettos

"The milk of the six cows in the [Kovno] ghetto must be handed over to the German Ghetto Guard."[39]

Document from November 4, 1942, Instruction from Lieutenant Miller to the Kovno Ghetto *Judenrat*.

"The water closet: Tanach [Jewish scriptures: Torah, Prophets and Writings] used for the first time, Heine's poems."[40]

—Oskar Rosenfeld's diary, kept in the Lodz ghetto.

Intense overcrowding plagued all of the ghettos, such that starvation and disease ran rampant. In the Warsaw ghetto alone, according to a Nazi report of 1941, the rate of "15.1"[41] people per room marked the average occupancy. The lack of water, sewage systems, food, medicine, clothing, fuel, and basic necessities all led inevitably to sweeps of epidemics: typhus, typhoid fever, 'spotted fever,' rickets, bed bugs, lice, and always starvation. In the Warsaw ghetto alone, over 13,000 Jews starved to death between the months of January and June, 1941. Both marriage and suicide rates soared within the ghetto walls as the young sought to live life as fully as possible while those who couldn't bear the transformations of the ghetto sought to end their miseries. Necessarily, the inhabitants of the ghettos hardened, surrounded as they were by needless and ever-present death. Oskar Rosenfeld, who kept a short diary while in the Lodz ghetto wrote, "One did not concern oneself with corpses. Warmth, laughter, humming in pure indifference to fate was unconstrained by a dead or dying neighbor. A pretty young girl shows her displeasure when someone carrying a corpse disturbs her in the moving of her lipstick across her lips."[42] Thus, while the poorest of the ghetto inhabitants, who were often the refugees to a ghetto rather than those Jews from its immediate environs, died most quickly, the wealthier Jews were able to apply lipstick, to start new businesses, to run cafes or frequent cafes, and to remain relatively healthy, at least for longer.

---

39 Avraham Tory (Ed.), *Surviving the Holocaust: The Kovno Ghetto Diary* (Cambridge, MA: Harvard University Press, 1990), 150.
[40]Alan Adelson and Robert Lapides (Ed.s), *Lodz Ghetto: Inside a Community under Siege* (New York: Penguin Books, 1989), 185.
[41]Bauer, 160.
[42]Tory, 182.

Within almost all of the ghettos, however, social welfare institutions sprang up to help those in need, and even the poor aided the poorest. From the Warsaw ghetto, for example, the survivor Mary Berg wrote about "spoon actions," where the families within neighboring buildings would each contribute one spoonful of an ingredient to be made into a single dish to be distributed on a Friday afternoon to the young and the old of that building.[43] In the Warsaw ghetto, too, food rations were taxed in order to garner funds to support the neediest. In addition, the American-based **Joint Distribution Committee** was able to collect monies from donors in New York and throughout the U.S., and through complex negotiations, to support practically single-handedly some of the welfare organizations within the ghettos. There were soup kitchens, hospitals, public baths, public laundries, delousing stations, fire brigades, clothing and utensil distributions, old-age homes, children's homes and orphanages. In one of the most famous acts of personal martyrdom, **Janusz Korczak** chose to accompany the children of his Warsaw ghetto orphanage when they were deported to Treblinka on August 12, 1942. A celebrated pediatrician, Korczak had been offered the chance to live. Instead, he carried one child in each arm, leading the rest, in their Sabbath clothes, as they sang and waved banners on their way to the train platform.

Within the ghettos, there were also thriving cultural institutions (theatres, orchestras, string quartets, choruses, ballets, photographic studios, painters, singers and storytellers,) religious institutions (*minyanim*—prayer quorums of 10), synagogues, *yeshivot* (places of study), rabbinic courts, and even butchers and *mohelim* (those who perform circumcision) and educational institutions (kindergartens, schools, high schools, universities, debating clubs, trade schools and even medical apprenticeships). Many of these organizations were underground ones, where Jews met in secret, voluntarily flouting Nazi orders in order to remain socially active. In the ghettos where education was forbidden by Nazi order, for example, students met in small groups in the homes of teachers or rabbis who were sometimes paid only a slice of bread in exchange for their work. There were newspapers, mail systems, burial societies and documentation organizations. In the **Warsaw ghetto**, **Emmanuel Ringelblum**, a young Jewish historian, encouraged those around him from a range of occupations—scientists, poets, artists, teachers—to document their day-to-day lives in the ghetto; his organization was code-named *Oneg Shabbat* (Delight in the Sabbath or the celebrations for Shabbat evening,) because the group met to discuss their activities on the Sabbath. Both the diary that Ringelblum himself kept and two thirds of

[43]Mary Berg, *Warsaw Ghetto: A Diary* (New York: L.B. Fischer Publishing Corp, 1944)

the works collected by the vast membership of the organization survived the war. Ringelblum, his family and the Polish family who hid them in the non-Jewish part of Warsaw as the ghetto was being decimated, were all summarily killed in 1942.

When people describe life within the ghetto walls, they enumerate the ways in which the illusion of normalcy was maintained through the flourishing of social institutions, but that image seems to be more about fulfilling wishes that life was somehow partially normal than about recognizing the reality that life was desperate, even for the wealthiest within the ghetto walls. For, common among ghettos were the following attributes, all of which made life perpetually anxiety-filled, terrifying and traumatic: All ghettos were required to supply forced labor in the form of quotas of workers demanded by the SS. All ghetto Jews were subject to Nazi harassment, which could take the form of random humiliation (an Orthodox Jewish man's beard being publicly shaven,) random shooting or random beating. All ghetto Jews had to wear identifying clothing (yellow stars pinned to the chest, back or wrapped around an arm) and had curfew imposed upon them. Escape from even open ghettos was exceedingly difficult and made more complicated by the feature that all ghettos were subject to mass reprisals; that is, the infractions of the few could cause collective punishment to be meted out. And, most importantly perhaps, once the Nazi policy decision was made to mass murder the Jews of Europe, ghetto Jews were forcibly deported *en masse* to concentration and 'extermination' camps.

Judenrate and the Jewish police

A grievous blow has struck the ghetto. They are asking us to give up the best we possess—the children and the elderly. …Yesterday afternoon, they gave me the order to send more than 20,000 Jews out of the ghetto, and if not—'We will do it!' So, the question became: 'Should we take it upon ourselves, do it ourselves, or leave it for others to do?' And, we reached the conclusion that…I must perform this difficult and bloody operation—I must cut off limbs in order to save the body itself! I must take children because, if not, others may be taken as well.[44]

Chaim Rumkowski, the leader of the Lodz ghetto Judenrate, addressing the ghetto, entreating them to give up children under 10 and elderly over 65.

(The transcriber's note reads "Horrible, terrifying wailing among the assembled crowd.") September 4, 1942

They are on a cart for the first time in their lives, a cart that will be pulled by a real horse, a proper horse. They are looking forward to a

---

[44]Alan Adelson and Robert Lapides (Ed.s), *Lodz Ghetto: Inside a Community under Siege* (New York: Penguin Books, 1989), 328.

gay ride. More than one of the little ones jumps for joy on the floor of the wagon as long as there is enough space. And at the same time his mother has almost gone out of her mind, twisting about on the ground and tearing the hair from her head in despair. It is difficult to overcome several thousand mothers. It is difficult to persuade them to give their children up willingly to death, as a sacrifice.[45]

Notes by Oscar Singer, following the deportation of the children from the Lodz ghetto: September 16, 1942

Yesterday, I lost Mucha, my sweet little daughter. I lost her through my own fault, cowardice, stupidity and passivity. I gave her up, defenseless. I deserted her, I left the 5-year old child, did not save her, and I could have done it so easily. ...The Germans were deporting, it was chaotic, like work round-ups, it was so easy to get away. ...Of course they were taking away the children. But it was possible to hide them, it was easy to do. I walked off with Anya, but left Mucha behind. Instead of hiding with her in the cellar or in the toilet, I put her in a clothes basket and she gave herself away with crying. Naked, barefoot, miserable—my dear child, it's me, your father, who betrayed you, it's me, driven by selfishness, who did nothing for your salvation, it's me who spilled your blood. ...I can't write... I can't concentrate and describe it all chronologically. I am broken, I feel guilty, I am a murderer... I killed Mucha.... How can it be that a father deserts his own child and runs away?[46]

Written in Yiddish, anonymously, Lodz ghetto, September 8, 1942

The appointments of the *Judenrate* (the plural of *Judenrat*, or Jewish Council) allowed the SS to manage the Jewish ghetto populations efficiently. On the one hand, the *Judenrate* deflected resentment against the Nazis themselves, and on the other hand, they carried out the complex tasks of running the ghettos. In actuality, however, the SS controlled the important boundaries of ghetto life, even as they had only small offices within or near the ghetto walls. As Rita Steinhardt Botwinick explains, the SS controlled all "supplies from the outside [such as:] food and water, electricity and waste disposal, medicines and telephones, postal service and cemetery space, ...the size of the ghettos, the number of blocks, houses, and available rooms."[47] The *Judenrate* were responsible, then, only for how these ever-limited resources and responsibilities would be distributed and met respectively. The councils were in the unenviable positions of overseeing the internal dynamics of the ghettos without nearly enough resources or provisions

---

[45]Yitzhak Arad, Yisrael Gutman, Abraham Margaliot (Ed.s), *Documents on the Holocaust* (Jerusalem: Yad Vashem, 1981), 286.

[46]Adelson and Lapides, 348-349.

[47]Rita Steinhardt Botwinick, *A History of the Holocaust: From Ideology to Annihilation* (New Jersey: Prentice Hall, 1996), 161.

while at the same time complying with Nazi orders for property, slave labor and, eventually, for lives. They were aided in their work, especially in the more oner- ous responsibilities, by **Jewish ghetto police forces**.

Importantly, Yehuda Bauer distinguishes between two stages in the ghettos: "before and after the first mass murders."[48] The first period, though horrendously complex for *Judenrate* leaders to negotiate, nonetheless paled in comparison to the leadership skills required in the second. In the first period, to comply with Nazi demands, the *Judenrate* leadership had to assess Jewish property within the ghet- tos, provide lists of laborers, and keep census tallies. In many cases, they taxed the measly food rations within the ghetto in the hopes of gaining more provi- sions for the needy. And, it's worth noting that the taxes they imposed were flat taxes, which discriminated against the poor, the wealthier ghetto inhabitants or smugglers being more able to pay the taxes for their rations. It was not until the second period that the *Judenrate* were ordered to supply lists of names for deporta- tion. Thus, while it was already impossibly difficult to serve as a *Judenrat* leader in the first stage, it nonetheless paled in comparison to the impossibilities of serving as a leader in the second. In many ghettos, the residents hated the Jewish police forces as it was their job, in the second phase, to round up people for deportation, to load them onto trains, sometimes compliant, other times, kicking and scream- ing, but never willingly. Like the *Judenrate*, people served on the Jewish police having been falsely promised that their families would be spared deportation.

The leadership styles that emerged among ghetto leaders varied, not only across ghettos, but across stages. And the *Judenrate* of single ghettos varied as well, since, if a *Judenrat* was found to be disobeying or flouting Nazi orders, its members could be murdered as a group and replaced by a newly appointed council whose members would be more compliant. Of the strategies *Judenrate* leaders chose to attempt to save their ghetto's inhabitants, there were those leaders who complied with Nazi demands for property and slave labor but who refused to supply names of those to be deported. There were those who provided all three in the hopes of saving the few. There were a few who infamously exploited their power, extort- ing sexual favors with the threat of deporting family members. And there were those who gave up their lives rather than serving at all. At two of the extremes, perhaps, were the Lodz ghetto *Judenrat* leader, **Chaim Rumkowski**, and the Warsaw ghetto *Judenrat* leader, **Adam Czerniakow**.

Rumkowski is infamous for having become an autocratic, megalomaniacal leader, riding through the ghetto in a carriage pulled by a white horse, having

---

[48]Yehuda Bauer, *A History of the Holocaust* (New York: Scholastic Books, 2001), 172.

money printed with his own image, being referred to as the 'ghetto king,' and having those who disagreed with his decisions deported. Rumkowski believed that complying with Nazi orders, no matter how repugnant they were (as in the handing over of children under 10,) was the best way to ensure the survival of the few, and he is much reviled historically for this position and for the brutality with which he pursued it. And yet Rumkowski, in the earlier stage of his leadership, through the same brutality, had made Lodz a highly efficient ghetto, organized by workshops that repaired Nazi uniforms damaged on the Soviet front and produced other goods such as armaments that the German war effort needed. In part because of this productivity, the Lodz ghetto was the last ghetto to be (in Nazi terminology) 'liquidated.' In fact, as Bauer points out, by July of 1944, the Soviet army had conquered territory within 3 days' march of the Lodz ghetto, and had the USSR continued to move in the direction of Lodz, it might have liberated the 69,000 Jews there. Unfortunately, in August, most of these Jews were sent to Auschwitz, and when the Soviets finally did arrive in January of 1945, only 870 Jews remained in the ghetto.

Adam Czerniakow, by contrast, is usually remembered as a hero, as the possessor of an ethical compass well-tuned despite the ravages of the immoral world he was forced to lead. Though the Warsaw ghetto inhabitants blamed him and the other 23 members of the *Judenrate* for the horrors of their lives, the diary he kept survived the war and attested to his struggles to lead the ghetto intelligently and ethically, inasmuch as either was possible. As Czerniakow wrote in his diary on July 8, 1942, "Many people hold a grudge against me for organizing play activity for the children, for arranging festive openings of playgrounds, for the music, etc. I am reminded of a film: a ship is sinking and the captain, to raise the spirits of the passengers, orders the orchestra to play a jazz piece. I had made up my mind to emulate the captain."[49] Unlike Rumkowski, Czerniakow in the end refused to aid in the mass deportations from the Warsaw ghetto. The entry of July 22, 1942, in Czerniakow's diary was his last, and it said the following:

> It was announced to us that the Jews, without regard to sex or age, apart from certain exceptions, would be deported to the East. Six thousand souls had to be supplied by 4 o'clock today. And this (at least) is how it will be every day....
>
> Sturmbannfuhrer Hofle (Beauftragter—[person in charge]—of the deportation) called me into the office and informed me that my wife

---

[49] As quoted in Bauer, 180.

was free at the moment, but if the deportation failed she would be the first to be shot as a hostage.[50]

Faced with this impossible decision, Czerniakow killed himself, swallowing cyanide with a glass of water. He left two letters on his desk, one an informational letter for the remaining members of the *Judenrate*. It said, "They are demanding ten thousand for tomorrow, after that seven thousand."[51] For Czerniakow, of course, there was no end in sight to what they would demand of him. The other letter contained an apology to his wife, asking for her forgiveness for leaving her.

Teaching Ideas

1. **Primary Documents Discussions:** There are many heartbreaking collections of documents about particular ghettos. We especially recommend the two books, **Surviving the Holocaust: The Kovno Ghetto Diary**, edited by Avraham Tory, and **Lodz Ghetto: Inside a Community Under Siege**, compiled and edited by Alan Adelson and Robert Lapides. These compilations include diarists' notes and photographs, Nazi documents and historians' observations, all arranged in chronological order. Online, there are many websites with vast stores of archival information as well. Among them, the **Jewish Virtual Library** has documents about the Bialystok, Kovno, Lodz, Warsaw and Vilna ghettos as well as a map of all ghettos in occupied Poland. The website called **Shtetlinks** (a project of the Jewish Genealogical Society) has similar reservoirs of information. The most thorough website, however, is the one at the **U.S. Holocaust Memorial Museum**, where you can view rare film footage of Adam Czerniakow.

Having students read through a selection of documents can be exceedingly useful as every page of these volumes and every artifact represented contain vivid illustrations of life within the ghettos. Consider the following brief diary excerpts as points of departure for discussions:

May 26, 1942

…Relief work doesn't solve the problem; it only keeps people going a little while. The people have to die anyway. It lengthens suffering but cannot save them; if it [the Jewish Self-Help] really wanted to do anything, it would have to have millions of zloty at its disposal every

---

[50]Yitzhak Arad, Yisrael Gutman, Abraham Margaliot (Ed.s), *Documents on the Holocaust* (Jerusalem: Yad Vashem, 1981), 281.
[51]Ibid.

month, and it does not have them. It remains a proven fact that the people fed in the soup kitchens will all die if they eat nothing but the soup supplied and the dry rationed bread. The question thus arises whether it would not serve the purpose better to reserve the available money for selected individuals, for those who are socially productive, for the intellectual elite, etc. But the situation is such that, first of all, the numbers even of such select individuals is quite considerable, and there would not be sufficient even for them. Secondly, the question arises why should one pronounce judgment on artisans, laborers and other useful persons, who were productive people back in their small towns, and only the ghetto and the war have turned them into non-people, into scrap, into human dregs, candidates for mass graves. There is left a tragic dilemma: What shall one do? Shall one [hand out the food] with little spoons to everybody, and then no one will live, or in generous handfuls to just a few...?[52]

Notes from the Warsaw Ghetto: The Journal of Emmanuel Ringelblum

September 8, 1942

The Council has issued an announcement about the ban on pregnancies in the Ghetto. From now on, the Germans declare that any pregnant woman will be killed on the spot.[53]

Surviving the Holocaust: The Kovno Ghetto Diary

September 20, 1942

Rabbi Shapiro has announced that, on the Day of Atonement, workers must appear to work. [Avraham Tory, who took down the final wording of this announcement from Rabbi Shapiro, later recalled that anyone seeing the profound expression of pain on the face of the elderly rabbi would have been brokenhearted.][54] Jews had been murdered previously for not appearing for work on Jewish holidays.

Surviving the Holocaust: The Kovno Ghetto Diary

2. **Listing Reasons:** While this doesn't sound like an innovative or interesting activity, we've found that it's quite useful for students, in small groups, to try to list as exhaustively as possible, reasons that explain some of the complex behaviors of ghetto inhabitants. Ask them to tackle a single ques-

---

[52]Yitzhak Arad, Yisrael Gutman, Abraham Margaliot (Ed.s), *Documents on the Holocaust* (Jerusalem: Yad Vashem, 1981), 232.
[53]Tory, *Kovno Ghetto Diary*, 132.
[54]Ibid, 135.

tion at a time: why, for example, did the *Judenrate* members serve? Why did the larger Jewish ghettos have their own police forces and jails? Why were resistance movements so hard to operationalize? Why was it so difficult to escape from a ghetto?

3. **Mock Trial**: Once your students have considerable information about the *Judenrate* in general, and at least one *Judenrat* in particular, consider staging a post-war trial of that ghetto's *Judenrat* leader. Modeled on the post-war trials of *Judenrate* leaders who survived, you may have your class role play the parts of defendants, prosecutors, and tribunal judges. We strongly encourage you to use primary source material in helping prepare your students for such an event. Had Chaim Rumkowski survived, for example, how would your class judge him?

4. **Plays and Play Excerpts**: There are a few Holocaust-based plays, which, while mainly fictional nonetheless bring to life some of the terrible dilemmas faced by ghetto inhabitants. Meant for adult audiences, they need to be used selectively in classrooms with young adults. The text of Joshua Sobel's famous play, *Ghetto*, can be found in a fabulous volume called **Art from the Ashes**, edited by Lawrence Langer. This play is utterly provocative, perfect in some ways for teenagers, as it makes the Nazi officer in charge of the Vilna ghetto humorous, charming and likeable. The dialogue is interesting, and the plot is fast paced. In Volume 1 of **The Theatre of the Holocaust**, edited by Robert Skloot, there are two plays set in the Lodz ghetto: *Resort 76*, by Shimon Wincelberg, and *Throne of Straw*, by Harold and Edith Lieberman. Both of these plays use sophisticated language and references, but nonetheless have short scenes that can be used as excerpts to prompt discussion.

5. **Films**: When showing films to illustrate life within the ghettos, there are a number of excellent resources to choose from. There is of course **Schindler's List**, which contains a marvelous scene about the formation of a ghetto. The scene follows a single, upper-class Jewish family as they are expelled from their home in a matter of minutes, as their home is then occupied by Schindler, and as the family is joined in an already crowded and furniture-less apartment by a large Hasidic family. (This excerpt is especially useful in discussing the pejorative views of Eastern European Jews, so-called **Ost-Juden** that assimilated, Western European Jews sometimes held. The scene positions the viewer in the place of the later rather than the former.) In **The Pianist: The Extraordinary True Story of**

One Man's Survival in Warsaw, 1939–1945, a number of scenes depict the class distinctions among Jews incarcerated in the Warsaw ghetto. There are also a number of great documentaries about specific ghettos (and the ghetto-like camp, Terezin). These titles include: **Lodz Ghetto, Warsaw Ghetto, Terezin Diary**, and **Theresienstadt: Gateway to Auschwitz**. **Partisans of Vilna**, which is a little too long and which focuses on the organization of the resistance movements in Vilna, has some marvelous sections to be used in classrooms (like the moment where Abba Kovner describes refusing his mother and sister entrance to the sewer systems as he was escaping from the ghetto, knowing this meant he was condemning them to likely death). **Diamonds in the Snow** is also excellent, interweaving the stories of three female survivors. **A Day in the Warsaw Ghetto: A Birthday Trip in Hell** is short, which is good, and it contains great photographs, but it's stilted. **The Story of Chaim Rumkowski and the Jews of Lodz** focuses almost exclusively on Rumkowski.

Resources for Teaching

Art from the Ashes. Edited by Lawrence Langer and published by Oxford University Press, Oxford, 1995. *This collection of works is extensive and useful. Contains poetry, plays, memoir excerpts, all of which are acute examples of their genres.*

A Day in the Warsaw Ghetto: A Birthday Trip in Hell. Produced by Jack Kuper, 1992, 30 minutes. *A German Sergeant in 1941 spent his birthday touring the Warsaw ghetto and taking pictures of its inhabitants. This documentary, based on those photographs, includes ghetto diarists' entries.*

Diamonds in the Snow. roduced by Mira Reym Binford, 1994, 60 minutes. *In this documentary, three women who survived the Holocaust retell their stories. Useful especially in excerpted form, to give students a personalized view of ghetto life.*

Ghetto Diary. By Janusz Korczak, with an introduction by Betty Jean Lifton and published by Yale University Press, New Haven, 2003. *Another heartbreaking diary.*

Jewish Virtual Library. ebsite: http://www.us-israel.org/. *Has an impressive array of primary and secondary documents about the Bialystok, Kovno, Lodz, Warsaw and Vilna ghettos as well as a map of all ghettos in occupied Poland.*

Lodz Ghetto. Produced by Alan Adelson, 1989, 118 minutes. *This film is divided into four parts for easier use in classrooms. Documents the Lodz ghetto's establishment, the leadership of Rumkowski, the cultural life within the ghetto and its destruction.*

Lodz Ghetto: Inside a Community Under Siege. Compiled and edited by Alain Adelson and Robert Lapides and published by Penguin Books, New York, 1989. *Fabulous resource book with memoirs, documents, color photographs, etc.*

Notes from the Warsaw Ghetto: The Journal of Emmanuel Ringelblum.
Written by Emmanuel Ringelblum and published by Schocken Books, New York,
1974. *Heartbreaking history from inside the ghetto.*

Partisans of Vilna. irected by Josh Waletzky, distributed by Capitol Entertainment,
133 minutes, 1986. *Truly separates enthusiasts from academics, this film gets a little mired
in the minutia of the partisan movements of Vilna. With Hebrew, English and Yiddish interspersed, it's sometimes hard for students to read along fast enough. That said; it has some
fabulous excerpts for classroom use.*

**The Pianist: The Extraordinary True Story of One man's Survival in
Warsaw, 1939-1945.** Written by Wladyslaw Szpilman and published by Picador
USA, New York, 2000. *This is the book on which the movie,* The Pianist, *was based.*

Schindler's List. Directed by Steven Spielberg and produced by Amblin
Entertainment, 1993. *Needs very little introduction for most teachers, though fewer and
fewer students have seen it as time passes.*

Shtetlinks. Website: http://www.shtetlinks.jewishgen.org/Lodz/. Maintained by the
Jewish Geneological Society. *This is the address for their site with documents about the
Lodz Ghetto, but they have reservoirs of other documents as well. Simply cut off the "Lodz/"
part of the address to redirect.*

The Story of Chaim Rumkowski and the Jews of Lodz. Produced by Poj
Filmproduction, AB, Sweden, 1982, 55 minutes. *This documentary focuses primarily on
Rumkowski.*

Surviving the Holocaust: The Kovno Ghetto Diary. Written by Avraham
Tory, edited and with an introduction by Martin Gilbert and published by Harvard
University Press, 1990. *An excellent resource book with memoirs, documents, photographs
and maps about the Kovno ghetto.*

Terezin Diary. Directed by Dan Weissman, produced in 1990, 88 minutes. *Uses
one Terezin survivor, Helga Kinsky, to discuss the strange dilemmas of living as children in
Terezin, a 'model ghetto.' Children like Kinsky had a theatre, art supplies, their own magazine and opera, and yet it was all 'for show.'*

Theater of the Holocaust. Edited by Robert Skloot and published by University of
Wisconsin Press, Madison, 1982. *Four Holocaust plays with an introduction by Skloot*

Theresienstadt: Gateway to Auschwitz. Available from American Film and
Video Association, 1993. *Theresienstadt (or Terezin), though called a "concentration camp"
was more like a model ghetto. In this film, survivors of the ghetto discuss their incarceration
there as children.*

U.S. Holocaust Memorial Museum. Website: http://www.ushmm.org. *For the
impressive film footage of Adam Czerniakow, follow the links through the "Introduction to*

the Holocaust" section to the section entitled, "Ghettos," and then to "Judenrate." *There are exceedingly useful stores of information, documents and teaching ideas on the website as well.*

The Warsaw Diary of Adam Czerniakow. Edited by Raul Hilberg and published by Madison Books, 1982. *This is a compelling read for adults. Hilberg is a master at making the heart-breaking diary of Czerniakow meaningful beyond the ghetto.*

Warsaw Ghetto. Produced by BBC, 1967, 51 minutes. *This documentary, while it feels dated, is nonetheless exceptionally informative.*

Resources for Further Learning

A History of the Holocaust. Written by Yehuda Bauer and published by Scholastic Books, New York, 2001. *A fabulous and thorough textbook. Useful as a reference text.*

A History of the Holocaust: From Ideology to Annihilation. Written by Rita Steinhardt Botwinick and published by Prentice Hall, Saddle River, New Jersey, 1998. *A history of the Holocaust in summary form. Useful as background information.*

Children with a Star: Jewish Youth in Nazi Europe. Written by Deborah Dwork and published by Yale University Press, New Haven, 1991. *This book, though not only about ghetto life, nonetheless includes great information about children's lives within ghettos.*

From Ashes to Life. Written by Lucille Eichengreen and published by Mercury House Press, San Francisco,1994. *This memoir is especially useful for classrooms both because it documents a woman's experiences and because it is broken into short chapters. Eichengreen served as a secretary in the Lodz ghetto bureaucracy.*

In the Ghetto of Warsaw: Heinrich Jöst's Photographs. Written by Günther Schwarberg and published by Steidl Verlag, Berlin 2001. *An astonishing array of photographs.*

Judenrate: The Jewish councils in Eastern Europe under Nazi occupation. Written by Isaiah Trunk and published by Stein and Day, New York, 1977. *This book, though somewhat out-of-date, is notable still, given that it stands as the authoritative work on the Judenrate.*

On Both Sides of the Wall. Written by Vladka Meed and published by Holocaust Library, New York, 1993. *Meed has written her memoir of being a smuggler between the 'Aryan' side of Warsaw and the Jewish ghetto. As part of the Warsaw resistance movement, Meed helped smuggle in supplies and weapons.*

THE CAMPS

A watchtower stands near a silhouetted barbed wire fence at Auschwitz, the largest Nazi concentration camp and extermination camp in operation during World War II. © Michael St. Maur Sheil/CORBIS.

Among the questions that are put to us," wrote Primo Levi, "one question is never absent; indeed, as the years go by, it is formulated with ever increasing persistence and with an ever less hidden accent of accusation." The question Levi refers to is actually a three-part question: Why did you not escape? Why did you not rebel? Why did you not evade capture before they got to you?

Levi describes what happened when he spoke to a group of fifth graders in an elementary school:

> An alert-looking boy, apparently at the head of the class, asked me the obligatory question: 'But how come you didn't escape' I briefly explained to him what I have written here. Not quite convinced, he asked me to draw a sketch of the camp [Auschwitz] on the blackboard indicating the location of the watchtowers, the gates, the barbed wire, and the power station. I did my best, watched by thirty pairs of intent eyes. My interlocutor studied the drawing for a few instants, asked me for a few further clarifications, then he presented to me the plan he had worked out: here, at night, cut the throat of the sentinel; then, put on his clothes; immediately after this, run over there to the power station and cut off the electricity, so the search lights would go out and the high tension fence would be deactivated; after that I could leave without any trouble. He added seriously: 'If it should happen to you again, do as I told you. You'll see that you'll be able to do it.' [55]

While this vignette may provide ample evidence that fifth graders are too young to learn about the Holocaust, it also illustrates one of the real problems in teaching about the concentration camps in particular. Because the camp system encapsulates industrialized dehumanization, it is easy to inadvertently forget the humanity of the victims while focusing on the machinery of death. It is easy, on the one hand, to ascribe to the victims power they did not have, as the fifth grader in Levi's audience did. (As a side note, a high school student Simone once interviewed made the same assumption that the fifth grader did, saying to Simone, "I still don't understand how y'all let yourselves get gassed like that."[56] Both the fifth grader and the high school student assumed that those incarcerated in concentration camps had agency, choice, options, and the rugged individualism to overcome the obstacles of imprisonment.) On the other hand, the images of concentration camp inmates make it hard to imagine them as anything other than utterly debased, unthinking, barely functioning, and stripped of everything human. As a recent study by Mary Juzwik revealed, even the language we use to describe what happened puts victims grammatically in subordinate positions, locating them as direct objects rather than subjects of sentences.[57]

---

[55]This summary of Primo Levi's encounter appears in Sam Wineburg, *Historical Thinking and other Unnatural Acts: Charting the Future of Teaching the Past*, (Philadelphia: Temple University Press, 2001), 23. The original exchange appears in Primo Levi, *The Drowned and the Saved* (New York: Vintage Books, 1989), 150-151.

[56]Simone Schweber, *Making Sense of the Holocaust: Lessons from Classroom Practice* (New York: Teachers College Press, 2004), 56.

[57]Mary Margaret Juzwik, *Towards a Rhetoric of Teaching: An Investigation into Teaching as Performance in a Middle-Level Holocaust Unit* (Unpublished Dissertation, University of Wisconsin-Madison, 2003).

A central tension in teaching about the concentration camps, then, is to portray the psychological and physical machinery of the camps in enough detail for students to understand why the victims could not simply 'cut the throat of the sentinel' or 'leave without any trouble,' while at the same time rendering the wide range of responses and activities among those trapped within the camps in order to ascribe to them the humanity that victims always deserve. By humanity here, however, we don't mean saintliness. To ascribe to them their full humanity is to reveal how debased they were, how the systems of torture rendered the victims capable of despicable, cruel, and desperate acts that they wouldn't have done in other circumstances. In short, students need to learn enough about the concentration camp universe for them to distrust their very capacity to understand it[58] and for them to gain humility in the face of atrocity.

Another central tension in teaching about the concentration camps stems from their symbolic importance; the concentration camps occupy the symbolic center of the Holocaust. Because they represent the technological efficiency associated with this murderous campaign, they stand in for the Holocaust as a whole. Recognizing their central importance is thus inescapable. And yet, we cannot teach towards that understanding. Or, put differently, that understanding needs to be put aside in teaching about the concentration camps, for their symbolic importance shouldn't shroud their actual place in Holocaust history. While they may represent the story of the Holocaust as a whole, they do not tell the story of the Holocaust as a whole.

The big ideas of this chapter are that:

- The so-called 'Final Solution' was implemented in stages.

- The concentration camps are the symbolic center of the Holocaust.

- In teaching about the concentration camps, it's important to continually articulate the humanity of the victims by showing the complexities of the camp system.

- For students to understand the concentration camps, they need a tremendous amount of information about them and, just as importantly, many opportunities to discuss them. Otherwise, they can't imagine the limitations of "living" through such a system.

Key terms of this chapter include: Wannsee Conference, 'Final Solution,' transition camps, labor camps, concentration camps, 'death camps', Auschwitz,

---

[58]For more on this central concept of history education, see Wineburg, above.

Belzec, Chelmno, Majdanek, Treblinka, Sobibor, Zyklon B, *Haftlinge*, 'death marches', and liberation.

Plans for the 'Final Solution'

On a cold winter day in January 1942, 15 high-ranking Nazi officials gathered at a lakefront villa in Wannsee, a posh suburb near Berlin. The **Wannsee Conference**, as it came to be known, was a defining moment in the history of the Holocaust. The topic of discussion was the coordination and implementation of the so-called '**Final Solution**'—the code name for the Nazi campaign to murder all of European Jewry. Those in attendance unanimously approved the plan.

At the meeting, Chief of the Security Police, Reinhard Heydrich reported that "the *Reich* Marshal had appointed him delegate for the preparations for the final solution of the Jewish question in Europe and pointed out that this discussion had been called for the purpose of clarifying fundamental questions."[59] He gave a brief report of the 'accomplishments' that had been carried out to date against the Jewish 'enemy.' These included "the expulsion of the Jews from every sphere of life of the German people [and] the expulsion of the Jews from the living space of the German people."[60] Heydrich assured the attendees that the 'Final Solution' would ultimately bring about an end to the estimated 11 million Jews residing throughout Europe.

While the Wannsee Conference was historically paramount in its significance, it did not mark the beginning of the implementation of the 'Final Solution.' Already in June the *Einsatzgruppen* had begun mass murdering Jews in the Soviet Union. Following on the heels of the regular army, these mobile killing units had been rounding up Jews and shooting them at point-blank range. And, just five weeks earlier, at Chelmno, special, hermetically sealed trucks had gone into operation. The trucks had been outfitted to funnel their exhaust pipes back into the sealed truck beds; they could thus serve as small, mobile, gas chambers. Beginning on December 8, 1941, the Jews deported to Chelmno had been asphyxiated that way. In short, the decision to mass murder Jews had already been made; at Wannsee, the resources of the regime were put towards that end, and the different arms of the Nazi octopus were coordinated to work towards it. The minutes of the Wannsee Conference reveal the euphemistic language that characterized all Nazi documents but here described the concentration camps

---

[59]John Mendelsohn, ed., *The Holocaust: Selected Documents in Eighteen Volumes Vol. 11: The Wannsee Protocol* (New York: Garland Press, 1982), 18-32.
[60]Ibid, p. 18-32.

for the first time. As Heydrich put it, "Separated by sex, the Jews capable of work will be led into these areas in large labor columns to build roads, whereby doubtless a large part will fall away through natural reduction." Those who were not murdered through overwork, "the residual final remainder which doubtless constitutes the toughest element, will have to be dealt with appropriately since it represents a natural selection which, upon liberation, is to be regarded as a germ cell of a new Jewish development."[61]

The Concentration Camps

According to Yehuda Bauer's authoritative history of the Holocaust, there were essentially four preconditions that paved the way for the camp system to emerge.[62] First, the Nazis had realized that mass deportation of Jews would be unfeasible, especially as larger and larger numbers of Jews came under their dominion with the conquering of more and more European nations. Second, it was clear that most countries worldwide were indifferent to the plight of Jews and other victim groups persecuted by the Nazi regime. By 1940, for example, neither the U.S.A. nor the Vatican had protested the treatment of Jews. Third, the invasion of the Soviet Union, which was planned as an all-out ideological war against the 'Jewish Bolshevik' state, would allow for the cover-up of mass murder, and not only of Jews. The invasion, in other words, could form the curtain for atrocities committed behind it. Finally, there may or may not have been a direct order from Hitler mandating the genocide of all European Jews. According to the commander of the *Einsatzgruppen*, the 'Commissar Directive' required that all Soviet POWs who were found to be Jewish or communist officials (or both), were to be killed rather than taken into custody. Whether this order included only Soviet Jews or all European Jews doesn't matter. Indeed, whether such a direct order was issued by Hitler or by his underlings, whether committed to paper or not, don't matter much either. Certainly by the time that the Wannsee Conference occurred and the gassings at Chelmno had begun, the goal of murdering all of Europe's Jews was already in place.

Before the decision for the 'Final Solution' was made, three types of camps had existed throughout occupied Europe: **transition camps, labor camps** and **concentration camps**. In the wake of the Wannsee Conference, so-called **'death camps'** (sometimes called 'extermination camps' or 'killing centers') were built, all in or near the General Government section of Poland, all near rail

---

[61]John Mendelsohn, ed., *The Holocaust: Selected Documents in Eighteen Volumes Vol. 11: The Wannsee Protocol* (New York: Garland Press, 1982), 18-32.

[62]Yehuda Bauer, *A History of the Holocaust* (New York: Scholastic Books, 2001), 209-212.

lines. While victims were worked to death, starved, beaten, brutalized and murdered in all four of these camp types, the 'extermination camps' were specifically designed to mass-produce corpses. These were: **Auschwitz** (which had already been in operation as a concentration and labor camp), **Belzec, Chelmno, Majdanek, Treblinka** and **Sobibor**. The death camps all functioned similarly, though with various rates of 'efficiency' and different technologies. (Rudolf Hoss, the commandant at Auschwitz, was proud that he designed his camp to work more 'efficiently' than Treblinka, which he had visited during his planning stages.)

Forced to board trains from all over Europe, Jews traveled to these camps for days and nights, usually arriving at the platforms filthy, exhausted, demoralized, desperately hungry, thirsty, weak and suffocated. The old, the sick, and the very young didn't live through the trips. Those who made it to camps that were combined concentration/labor and death camps could be 'selected' for hard labor upon arriving, if they were strong, healthy, fit, and neither too old nor too young. Separated by sex, their body hair was shaved, their clothes and whatever possessions remained were taken, given striped uniforms, ill-fitting shoes, and assigned to a barracks. At Auschwitz, prisoners were tattooed with numbers. In her memoir, Lucille Eichengreen describes the feeling of having her hair shorn:

> The Kapo …pulled my long, brown hair upward and proceeded to shave, running the clippers from the nape of my neck to the top of my head, onto the forehead and back again, repeating the motion several times until my hair slid past my naked shoulders and onto the floor. Bits and pieces covered my feet and stuck to my damp toes. I stared at the brown curls, then at the SS woman. …Pure hatred, mixed with fear and pain swirled in my brain until I silently screamed and swore revenge. As if reading my thoughts, the SS woman slapped my face hard with the back of her hand. My head reeled back, but the Kapo kept on clipping. As she shaved my armpits and all other body hair, I concentrated on my hatred: hatred for her, hatred for the Germans who had reduced me to this sweating, naked creature, without hair, without dignity. I was no longer a human being to them, just an expendable Jew. …I wanted to scream, to kick, to scratch. Instead, I stood in silent rage.[63]

Eichengreen's notion of an 'expendable Jew' was utterly precise. Given starvation rations, the pointless labor that victims were forced to do was designed to

---

[63]Lucille Eichengreen, *From Ashes to Life* (San Francisco: Mercury House, 1994), 94.

annihilate them, through work. Roughly translated from the German, the term that described the process was 'annihilation through work.' While sometimes serving German factories—by making rockets, quarrying rock, or synthesizing rubber—at other times, the labor victims were forced to perform was utterly unnecessary, moving boulders from one place to another and back again. At the end of their obscenely long workdays, marching back to their barracks, those 'lucky' enough to have been assigned to work might pass by the Auschwitz string quartet where prisoners were playing Beethoven. In her chilling memoir of "a Holocaust girlhood," Ruth Kluger remembers her mother suggesting that, together, they kill themselves on their first night in Auschwitz by running into the electrified barbed wire that surrounded the camp. While not an act usually associated with mothering, Kluger casually remarks on both the depravity and reasonableness of the suggestion. It was proof, in a way that her mother understood the camp system more quickly than she, as a child, had.[64]

Those who arrived at the 'death camps' could not be selected for labor. They were simply processed for death. At Belzec, Treblinka and Sobibor, they would stop at a 'reception area,' where they were forced to strip, where the women's hair was shorn, where they discarded their last possessions. Then, told that they were going to be showered in preparation for 'work,' they were shunted through walkways, beaten and whipped along the way, and finally forced into hermetically sealed rooms where the exhaust of diesel engines poured in, depriving them of oxygen. They suffocated, sometimes slowly. Their bodies were then burned in vast, open pits. When the majority of Polish Jewry had been decimated, these three camps were disassembled in attempt to hide their evidence of mass murder. Belzec, Sobibor and Treblinka I (its 'killing center') were dismantled in 1943; Treblinka II, the forced labor camp, was closed in July, 1944.

Though known for the murderous efficiency of its death camp—in only two of its five crematoria, 2,500 people could be murdered in one half hour alone—Auschwitz functioned as a labor camp, a concentration camp and a 'death camp.' It was, in effect, a system of camps, built by many German companies who bid on the exceedingly lucrative contracts for cement, wood, potatoes, the ovens and the Prussic Acid (called **Zyklon B**) used to asphyxiate victims in the gas chambers. Built originally as a concentration camp for Soviet POW's and Polish prisoners, it became a death camp in 1941/42, primarily for Jews.

Within Auschwitz, as within most of the concentration and labor camps, an intricate, fearsome and desperate economy among prisoners took shape. Those

---

[64]Ruth Kluger, *Still Alive: A Holocaust Girlhood Remembered* (New York: Feminist Press, 2001).

with smaller numbers who had been incarcerated longer had lived brutally enough to amass more privileges. They had garnered connections and jobs that provided them with perks like shelter, non-manual labor, extra food, access to cigarettes or power over other prisoners; they were thus able to survive the frequent shootings, hangings, beatings and starvation for longer periods. At Auschwitz, for example, the job of unloading the trains of new arrivals was lucrative. Called the Canada-Kommando, the prisoners who served there sometimes found foodstuffs to eat or jewelry that could be traded, small objects that could be scurried away without the SS seeing. Staffed mostly by women, the Canada-Kommando were allowed to grow their hair out, a seemingly trivial luxury, but one which symbolized their status. At the so-called 'hospital' at Auschwitz, Levi explains that the nurses' jobs were exceedingly profitable as well:

> The nurses …make huge profits from the trade in spoons. The Lager [barracks] does not provide the new arrivals with spoons, although the semi-liquid soup cannot be consumed without them. The spoons are manufactured in Buna, secretly and in their spare moments, by Haftlinge [ordinary prisoners] who work as specialists in the iron and tin-smith Kommandos: they are rough and clumsy tools, shaped from iron-plate worked by hammer, often with a sharp handle-edge to serve at the same time as a knife to cut the bread. The manufacturers themselves sell them directly to the new arrivals: an ordinary spoon is worth half a ration, a knife-spoon three quarters of a ration of bread. Now it is a law that although one can enter [the hospital] with one's spoon, one cannot leave with it. At the moment of release, before the clothes are given, the healthy patient's spoon is confiscated by the nurses and placed on sale in the Market. Adding the spoons of the patients about to leave to those of the dead and selected, the nurses receive the gains of the sale of about fifty spoons every day.[65]

The lurid economy of the camp system supported both the German war machine and many private industries even after the end of the war. Auschwitz, for example, provided slave labor to many German factories; ones both privately owned and set up by the SS, among them, I.G. Farben, Siemens, and Volkswagen. Even the corpses of victims served German interests. The gold teeth extracted from victims' dead bodies were melted down and sent to the coffers of the *Reichsbank*, and ashes from the crematoria were used as fertilizer. The individual SS members who ran the camps profited enormously, too. Jewelry, watches, gold, foreign currencies, precious objects—anything of value that the

---

[65]Primo Levi, *Survival in Auschwitz*, (New York: Simon & Schuster, 1996), 85.

Jews of Europe brought with them—made it into the pockets and lockers of the SS men first, sent home to their wives and sweethearts, children and relations later. Moreover, as the *Haftlinge* (the regular inmates) desperately tried to stay alive from day to day and hour to hour, the SS controlling the camp had access to every imaginable luxury: French cognac, Russian caviar, a gymnasium, and a brothel (staffed by female prisoners). The hundreds of concentration camps throughout Nazi occupied Europe, each with their satellite labor camps, thus profited not only the SS men, the female prison guards and their families and connections; they also enriched the German economy as a whole.

As the allied armies closed in on Greater Germany, (the British and American forces from the west, the Soviet armies from the east,) the SS wanted to cover up the existence of the concentration camps and to prevent their prisoners from being liberated. As a result, in the final months of 1944 and the first months of 1945, the SS forced large numbers of concentration camp inmates on what came to be called '**death marches**.' Emaciated, weakened, sick, lice-ridden, typhus-ridden, diarrhea-stricken, and practically delirious, the surviving remnants of the concentration camp populations were forced to run in long columns, in the dead of winter, towards the interior of Germany. Some of the 'death marches' were hundreds of miles long. The SS guarding the prisoners shot anyone who fell out of line or who couldn't continue; it was the job of prisoners to bury the dead and those who fell by the wayside as they progressed.

The **liberation** of the concentration camps occurred as the Allied armies overran them. While the retreating SS had destroyed camp records, burned buildings and attempted to hide the evidence of their crimes, they nonetheless left enough human evidence to attest to the atrocities. At Auschwitz, for example, the Soviet armies found a 14,000-pound pile of human hair as well as hundreds of remaining prisoners. Ernie Hollander, who, along with some other victims, had managed to drift away unnoticed from the 'death march' he was on, hid in the cupboards of a farmhouse evacuated by retreating Germans. When a troop of Japanese American soldiers liberated them a few days later, he and his friends were terrified. Mistaking the Americans for Japanese soldiers, they were sure that the food offered to them was poisoned and they refused to eat it. That mistake may indeed have helped save Ernie's life. Many thousands of concentration camp inmates, upon liberation, were offered or found foods that their starved bodies could not digest, that their emaciated bodies could no longer stomach. Thousands died even after liberation as a result.

Teaching Ideas

1. **Wannsee Conference Investigation:** An original document of the top-secret minutes of the Wannsee Conference was found after the war. It can be downloaded in English from several websites including the **Simon Wiesenthal Center, A Teacher's Guide to the Holocaust, U.S. Holocaust Memorial Museum,** and **Brigham Young University**. Like most Nazi documents the minutes of the Wannsee Conference are filled with euphemistic language. Ask your students to read the minutes and to track the euphemisms. Assign various perspectives to your students and then ask them to interpret the meaning of the minutes. What would Holocaust deniers say about this language? What would Holocaust historians? How do you think Holocaust survivors would understand the notes from this meeting? How do you imagine these notes were used in the post-war trials of Nazi officials attending?

   The Wannsee Conference was significant to the Holocaust not only because of the detail in which the 'Final Solution' was discussed, but also because the attendees at the conference represented high-ranking officials from various political and cultural entities in the Nazi bureaucracy. While it's important not to glorify the role that each attendee played in operationalizing the 'Final Solution,' it is educational to understand how each leader in attendance operated. Ask your students to research the attendees at the Wannsee Conference, paying particular attention to the roles that each played in orchestrating the 'Final Solution.'

2. **Camp Testimonies**: A number of excellent resources exist online for students to hear testimonies from survivors of concentration, labor and death camps, and as the number of survivors who are alive, willing and able to speak in schools decreases; such resources are becoming increasingly important. The three best are the **U.S. Holocaust Memorial Museum's** website, where film excerpts can be played alongside transcripts of survivors from very different camps at very different times and with very different experiences. In the Holocaust Learning Center area of the website, there are numerous excerpts to choose from. The **Shoah Visual History Foundation**'s website is also marvelous. (This is the organization Steven Spielberg set up with the proceeds from *Schindler's List*, which helps explain its visual artistry.) A third website with tremendous resources is housed at the **Fortunoff Archives of Yale University**. One of the first organizations to collect Holocaust testimonies, Yale loans out its videotaped

testimonies for a small fee. The testimony by Edith P. is especially riveting for students.

While Elie Wiesel's **Night** is the most widely read memoir, there are a number of other excellent memoirs and realist fictional works that can serve as testimonial literature. Most are beautifully written, spare, informative and emotionally gripping. A few of our favorites are: Sara Nomberg-Przytyk's **Auschwitz, True Tales from a Grotesque Land**, and Tadeusz Borowski's book, **This Way for the Gas, Ladies and Gentlemen**. Both these works have short, easily excerpted sections that can be used in class to pack powerful punches. A few longer memoirs that engross teenage readers are: **All but my Life**, by Gerda Weissman Klein, (especially popular with teenage girls) and **Maus**, by Art Spiegelman (popular with all readers).

3. **Camp Scenarios**: Have your students discuss the following scenarios, asking about them what they reveal about the concentration camp system. How might each scenario affect the thinking, the attitudes, and the humanity of *all* of the parties involved?

   - A young man, an inmate at a concentration camp, breaks down when told of the death of his family. He decides that in the morning he will commit suicide by attacking an SS officer. Because of the Nazi practice of mass reprisal, this act will cost the lives of all 400 men in his barracks. If the young man cannot be convinced to change his mind, should he be killed by members of the camp inmate underground in order to protect the welfare of the other barracks members? (Bear in mind that the policy of mass reprisal was a constant feature of concentration camp life.) According to a famous Jewish quotation, "One who saves a single life, it is as if he had saved a world entire" (*Pirke D'Rav Eliezer*, chapter 48). Because every person contains, like Adam, a whole multitude of descendents, saving even one life is considered utterly sacred. How does this text help you understand the camp scenario (or not)?

   - A male concentration camp inmate desperately needs certain medicines to survive. Medicines can be obtained by giving in to the sexual desires of a particular SS officer who has access to these medicines. Should a friend of the man from the same barracks try to obtain the medicines if this is the only way to get them?

   - In most concentration camps, women who gave birth were automatically sent with their newborn children to the ovens. A decision can be made to save such a mother by making her newborn infant stillborn. The Talmud teaches that if an unborn fetus threatens the life of the mother, terminating the pregnancy is permitted because the fetus is considered a *rodef*—a pursuer of the mother's life. Should the decision to kill the infant to save the mothers be made?[66]

- Rabbi Meisels, from Hungary, was interned at Auschwitz when, on the evening of *Rosh Hashanah* (Jewish New Year), 1944, a selection occurred to find all of the boys under 18 years of age left in the camp. Approximately 1,400 were rounded up and enclosed in a locked block guarded by *Kapos*. All of these boys were slated for death. The condemned boys could be exchanged for other boys who were not already on the list, but in order to make such a substitution, a new boy had to be literally handed over, whereupon the *Kapos* would release one of the locked boys. Knowing that it is against Jewish law (*halakha*) to substitute one life for another, a man approached the rabbi to ask, given the circumstances, whether he could make such a substitution to save his own son. What should the rabbi's answer be? (As Michael Berenbaum documents in his book, *Witness to the Holocaust*, Rabbi Meisels refused to answer the question, which was, in itself, the answer. The man understood that he was forbidden to ransom his son. After the war, Rabbi Meisels wrote a volume of responsa entitled *Mekaddeshei HaShem* in which he described that incident and many others. "All that day of Rosh Hashanah, he walked around talking to himself, murmuring joyfully that he had the merit to sacrifice his only son to God, for even though he could have ransomed him, nevertheless he did not because he saw that the Torah did not permit him to do so; and that his sacrificial act should be considered by God like the binding of Isaac which also occurred on Rosh Hashanah. ...I have no doubt that his words caused a great commotion among the celestial host; and the Holy One, blessed be He, gathered together all the host of heaven and was, so to speak, very proud."[67])

4. **Explaining Survival:** A number of thinkers have attempted to explain why it is certain inmates survived the concentration camp experience and others did not. Ask your students by way of introduction whether they think there were reasons some survived or whether it was the result of

---

[66]These three scenarios come directly from an excellent Holocaust curriculum which is sadly no longer in print: Harry Furman, ed. *The Holocaust and Genocide: Search for Conscience.*

[67]Michael Berenbaum, *Witness to the Holocaust*, (New York: HarperCollins, 1997), 209-214.

pure chance or luck. Are there particular attributes (such as courage, a willingness to take risks, wealth, deviousness, brutality, a dedication to remembering or carrying on a family, a whole-hearted religious belief system)—that enabled some to survive?

- Viktor Frankl, a psychologist who survived Auschwitz described that his consciousness, his search for meaning, allowed him to survive. While consumed by the desperate need for food, the all-consuming fear of dying, the cunning involved in outlasting death at Auschwitz, he one day became disgusted with his own thoughts, their triviality and irrepressibility. Through force of will, he imagined himself lecturing to a group of students about the psychology of the concentration camp, and that leap of imagination allowed him to recast his thinking, allowed him a measure of distance from his own suffering that enabled him to survive. It was this insight that drove his philosophy of psychotherapy post-war. In short, according to Frankl, all people need to make meaning of their lives. In his words, "...meaning must be found and cannot be given."[68]

- Terrence Des Pres argued that it was the very humaneness of the survivors that sometimes kept them alive. "The survivor's experience is evidence that the need to help is as basic as the need for help, a fact which points to the radically social nature of life in extremity and explains an unexpected but very widespread activity among survivors. In the concentration camp, a major form of behavior was gift-giving. Inmates were continually giving and sharing little items with each other, and small acts like these were enormously valuable both as morale boosters and often as read aids in the struggle for life." Des Pres cites the following example: "One evening we were served a soup made with semolina. I drank this with all the more relish since I often had to forgo the daily cabbage soup because of my bowels. Just then I noticed a woman, one of the prostitutes, who always kept very much to themselves, approaching my bunk, holding her bowl out to me with both hands. ...She emptied her bowl into mine and went without food that day."[69]

---

[68]Viktor Frankl, *The Unconscious God: Psychotherapy and Theology.* (New York: Simon and Schuster, 1975), 112. (This book was originally published in 1948 as *Der unbewusste Gott*, and republished in 1997 as *Man's Search for Ultimate Meaning.*)

[69]Terrence Des Pres, *The Survivor: An Anatomy of Life in the Death Camps* (Oxford: Oxford University Press, 1975), excerpted with permission in Donald Niewyk, *The Holocaust* (New York: Houghton Mifflin, 1997), 59-66. Indeed, it is to Niewyk's comparison we owe the debt of catalyzing this teaching idea.

- For Primo Levi, the famous Italian memoirist of the Holocaust, there were two categories of people among the concentration camp inmates—"the saved and the drowned. Other pairs of opposites (the good and the bad, the wise and the foolish, the cowards and the courageous, the unlucky and the fortunate) are considerably less distinct, they seem less essential, and above all they allow for more numerous and complex intermediary gradations."[70] Within Auschwitz, in other words, there were simply those who were going to make it if it all possible, those who had learned to function "desperately and ferociously alone," and those who were doomed, those who became the walking dead.

- In her lovely book, **Hasidic Tales of the Holocaust**, Yaffa Eliach retells stories of Hasidic survival and loss during the Holocaust. In one vignette, for example, the Grand Rabbi of Bluzhov, Rabbi Israel Spira, describes the kiss a father gave to his son when turning him over to the Grand Rabbi's care in the midst of the Lvov ghetto, saying that from that moment on, this man [the rabbi] would be his father. For the rabbi, that kiss protected both him and his orphaned son throughout Bergen-Belsen concentration camp and beyond. And, in another vignette, his love for his rabbi inspired a group of followers to light a *Hanukkiah* in Bergen-Belsen. In short, according to Eliach's impressive collection, *hasidut*, the practices and beliefs associated with Hasidism itself, enabled some to survive.[71]

5. **Bystanders**: As Gordon Horwitz documents, most of the concentration camps and death camps, built near populated areas, were purposefully shielded from the sight of local residents. At Treblinka, for example, leaves were woven into the wire surrounding the camp such that local farmers couldn't see in easily. Nonetheless, the sights, smells and evidence of murder were inescapable. Moreover, as Horwitz explains, those who lived on the outskirts of the camps not only profited personally from the camps' activities, but actively avoided 'seeing' what was visible in them. "In 1941, [for example,] a woman whose farm lay on a height above the rock quarry in **Mauthausen** [a concentration camp in Germany] filed an anguished request with the police after witnessing bodies of inmates who had been shot and left in the open. Indicating that the sight of inmates lying dead at the rock quarry was burdensome to her nerves, she was compelled to ask

---

[70]Levi, 88.

[71]Yaffa Eliach, *Hasidic Tales of the Holocaust* (New York: Vintage Books, 1982).

that the killing be halted or at least done elsewhere and out of sight. ... [A] priest from Ebensee [another camp] who arrived at the end of the war to enter the liberated camp wrote in 1946 that he had spoken with residents of the town, discovering not only women whose nerves suffered because of the unavoidable sights and sounds of persons being beaten, but also farmers who avoided working certain fields too near the camp, and mountaineers who went out of their way just in order to avoid coming into contact with such 'horrifying events.'"[72] We know that those bystanders who helped round up the rare Jews who escaped from the concentration camps were collaborators or perpetrators; does Horwitz' analysis make the entire category of bystander suspect? What does it mean to be a bystander?

6. **Mapping**: A staggering activity is for students to overlay maps printed on transparencies, which allow them to visually comprehend the interplays of various systems. For example, maps of the location of the ghettos, the death camps, the concentration camps, the satellite labor camps, the transit camps, and the railroad system, when overlaid, provide a crystallized key to this history. Martin Gilbert's excellent book, **Atlas of the Holocaust**, has fabulous maps with brief editorial descriptions needed to understand them. The **U.S. Holocaust Memorial Museum**'s website has a section entitled Mapping the Holocaust. Alternatively, the website associated with **A Teacher's Guide to the Holocaust** has a great assortment of maps, all on one page, including one map with a pronunciation guide for camp names. Once students see all of these maps superimposed on each other, it is easier for them to consider the question of who knew what was going on at that time.

7. **Liberation**: is usually imagined as a beautiful moment, a heroic time, a release, a victory. At the very least, the word is associated with positive movements in education, politics, and theology. Nonetheless, the liberation of many concentration camp inmates didn't have happy endings. Some groups were simply incarcerated again upon liberation. Homosexuals in Germany, for example, were liberated from the concentration camps and rearrested for breaking homophobic German laws post-war. The Sinti and Roma faced continued racism and discrimination throughout Europe post-war. And some Soviet citizens who were either Jews or POWs who had the good fortune of surviving concentration camps during the war were arrested after their return to Russia, on suspicion of having spent so much time away from the USSR. Many of these people were then sent to Soviet

---

[72]Gordon Horwitz, *In the Shadow of Death: Living Outside the Gates of Mathausen* (New York: The Free Press, 1990), 35.

prison camps, some in Siberia. As an introduction to this bleak coda, ask your students to freely associate the word "liberation." Is there perhaps a better word to describe the end of the Holocaust?

8. **The Importance of a Story:** In Nomberg-Przytyk's collection of stories about the concentration camp universe, one story, "The Revenge of a Dancer" had legendary status in Auschwitz. As Nomberg-Przytyk relates it, the story centers on a beautiful dancer who, when commanded to strip naked, refused, grabbing the pistol of an SS guard, shooting him, wildly shooting around him and finally shooting herself. Based on an actual event that occurred in October of 1943, this story appears in many, many survivors' testimonies as though it were actually observed by all of them. In actuality, it is likely that this event was observed only by a few. Why do you suppose this story would have such power among concentration camp inmates that it would appear in many of their testimonies as if witnessed? Does such a trend compromise the integrity of all survivors' testimonies, as Holocaust deniers might want? Why and why not?

9. **Legos and Concentration Camps**: The Polish artist Zbigniew Libera designed a series of seven "Lego sets," one of which was a kit for building a "Lego Concentration Camp." The Legos company donated the building blocks (as they do to artists worldwide), unaware of Libera's plans (or perhaps unwilling to be aware of them given the possible legal ramifications). Libera constructed models of concentration camps out of the blocks, photographing the model and putting the photograph on the cover of a "Legos" kit replica. Libera's claim is that the work is meant to provoke thought; questions such as what "reality" are children's toys fabricating? What kind of work, child-rearing work and construction work, went into the building of the real concentration camps? Were there elements of "play" in the SS's perceptions of the camps? Relatedly, a best-selling videogame features an escape-from-Auschwitz scenario. After describing these "toys" or showing images of them, ask your students whether, in their opinions, such images demean the reality of the camps or spur people's thinking about their meanings. How would they have felt had they been assigned to build a model of the camp? Is there a difference between building in Styrofoam vs. building in Legos?

10. **Poetry:** Theodore Adorno is famous for having claimed that after Auschwitz, to write poetry is barbaric. Variously interpreted, his argument is worth discussing. Is it barbaric to write any poetry after Auschwitz or

especially that poetry about Auschwitz, or by extension, about the machinery of death in the Holocaust? What should be the role of art in the wake of atrocity? Is it "barbaric" to beautify the world through poetry and other forms of art when alongside such efforts, places like Auschwitz continue to exist? What are artists' responsibilities vis-à-vis *tikkun olam*, the repairing of the world? Have your students examine a few works of Holocaust poetry. Are they beautiful? Do they exploit the ashes of the concentration camps or do they do something else altogether? Your students might research: Dan Pagis, Abraham Sutzkever, Paul Celan, or Nelly Sachs. They may even want to write themselves.

To serve as an entry point, here are some excerpts of a single poem, entitled, *Death Fugue*, written by Paul Celan. (Incidentally, it's the poem that prompted Adorno to retract his statement.)

> *Black milk of daybreak we drink it at sundown*
> *we drink it at noon in the morning we drink it at night*
> *we drink it and drink it*
> *we dig a grave in the breezes there one lies unconfined*
>
> *A man lives in the house he plays with the serpents he writes*
> *he writes when dusk falls to Germany, your golden hair Margarete*
> *he writes it and steps out of doors and the stars are flashing he whistles his*
> * pack out he whistles his Jews out in earth has them dig for a grave*
> *he commands us strike up for the dance*
>
> *He calls out stab deeper into the earth you lot you others sing now and*
> * play*
> *he grabs at the iron in his belt he waves it his eye is blue*
> *stab deeper you lot with your spades you others play on for the dance*

11. **Films: The Last Days**, produced by the Shoah Foundation, is an excellent documentary which weaves together the stories of five Hungarian Holocaust survivors, describing their various experiences during the war and afterwards. Claude Lanzmann's famous nine and a half hour documentary, **Shoah**, is too long to show in full in a class, but it contains moving segments that illuminate camp experiences and the actions of the bystanders. The BBC, in cooperation with KCET of Los Angeles has produced a tremendous documentary entitled **Auschwitz**. This documentary, though too long to show in full, has riveting sections that discuss the building of the camps, the profits it generated as well as the human tolls it extracted.

Resources for Teaching

From Ashes to Life. Written by Lucille Eichengreen with Harriet Hyman Chamberlain and published by Mercury House, San Francisco, 1994. *A lesser known memoir with some appeal. The chapter entitled, "The Scarf" is especially useful for discussing the way gender affected concentration camp experiences. ("The Scarf" recounts an incident where a German guard was intending to rape Lucille, but desisted.)*

Atlas of the Holocaust. Compiled and edited by Martin Gilbert and published by William and Morrow, New York City, 2002 *A phenomenally useful resource for the classroom.*

Auschwitz, True Tales from a Grotesque Land. Written by Sara Nomberg-Przytyk and published by University of North Carolina Press, Chapel Hill, 1985. *A volume of short vignettes from Auschwitz, this book is fabulous for classroom use. The language is direct, the images horrendous.*

Brigham Young University, Harold B. Lee Library. Website: www.lib.byu.edu/estu/eurodocs. *Links to European primary historical documents translated into English including the Wannsee Protocol,* Einsatzgruppen *Archives, and documentation of the mass murder of Lithuanian Jewry by the* SS Einsatz *'Action Groups' from a secret* Reich *letter.*

The Fortunoff Archives at Yale University. Website: http://www.library.yale.edu/testimonies/excerpts/index.htm. *The testimonies at this website are very brief and very powerful. For longer, but still edited versions, contact the archives directly and borrow the videotapes. We recommend Edith P.'s testimony especially.*

Hasidic Tales of the Holocaust. Written by Yaffa Eliach and published by Vintage Books, New York City, 1982. *A remarkable collection of Holocaust experiences, perfect for classroom use, the stories raise questions of belief, experience, and God's role in history.*

The Last Days. Directed by James Moll and produced by Survivors of the Shoah Visual History Foundation, 1998, 87 minutes. *Beautifully produced, this film follows five Hungarian survivors, showing how their lives were transformed after the invasion of Germany in 1944. A great film for classroom use.*

Simon Wiesenthal Center. Website: www.wiesenthal.com. *The Simon Wiesenthal Center's Digital Archives includes primary source materials and images from the Holocaust which are available to users to access, browse and download at a low-resolution level.*

Survivors of the Shoah Foundation. Website: http://www.vhf.org/testimonyviewer/. *The testimonies on this site are categorized by the nature of the experience: pre-War, hiding, ghettos, camps, liberation, post-war.*

A Teacher's Guide to the Holocaust. Website: http://fcit.coedu.usf.edu/ Holocaust/resource/gallery/maps.htm. *Run by Florida's Center for Instructional Technology. A great selection of maps, also contains primary source material including the minutes of the Wannsee Conference and lessons plans on teaching about the Holocaust.*

U.S. Holocaust Memorial Museum. Website: www.ushmm.org. *The most exhaustive collection of primary source materials that includes photographs, maps, documents, reports, files, plans, speeches, and directives from high-ranking Nazi officials.*

This Way for the Gas, Ladies and Gentlemen. Written by Tadeusz Borowski and published by Penguin Books, New York, 1992. *Like Nomberg-Przytyk's collection, this book, too, has short vignettes that are perfectly suited to classroom usage. Borowksi's text is written from the perspective of a non-Jewish prisoner.*

Witness to the Holocaust. Written by Michael Berenbaum and published by HarperCollins, New York, 1997. *This text contains illustrations and documents from a variety of perspectives and is exceedingly useful both as a classroom resource and as a basis for in-class activities and discussions.*

Resources for Further Learning

All But My Life. Written by Gerda Weissman Klein and published by Hill & Wang, New York, 1995. *This memoir recounts Klein's experiences from 1939-1945 and beyond. Astonishingly, the man who liberated her became her husband.*

Historical Thinking and Other Unnatural Acts. Written by Sam Wineburg and published by Temple University Press, Philadelphia, 2001. *Though not about the Holocaust, this book is an excellent resource for teachers interested in academic studies on the teaching and learning of history.*

A History of the Holocaust. Written by Yehuda Bauer and published by Watts Publishers, New York, 1999. *This is a good overall textbook to use as a reference text. Written in clear prose, it intersperses primary documents as well as pictures and diagrams.*

In the Shadow of Death: Living Outside the Gates of Mauthausen. Written by Gordon Horwitz and published by The Free Press, New York, 1990. *An excellent and provocative account of bystanders.*

Landscapes of Memory: A Holocaust Girlhood Remembered. Written by Ruth Kluger and published by Bloomsbury Press, New York, 2003. *This brilliant memoir breaks stereotyped notions of survival. Taken first to Terezin at age 11, and then surviving two other camps, Kluger discusses embarrassing and even shameful aspects of hers and her mother's survival. Not recommended for young audiences.*

Masters of Death: The SS Einsatzgruppen and the Invention of the Holocaust. Written by Richard Rhodes and published by Alfred Knopf, New York, 2002. *A masterly text on the* Einsatzgruppen, *the book lays out in gruesome* *detail how the mobile killing units functioned. We don't suggest it for use in class, but rather as a resource for teachers.*

Man's Search for Meaning. Written by Viktor Frankl and published by Washington Square Press, New York, 1997. *This book is considered a classic, though it's not particularly useful in the classroom.*

Shoah. Directed by Claude Lanzmann, and produced by Films Aleph, Historia Films, 1985, 566 minutes. *Extraordinarily long, this documentary is difficult for kids to watch. The layers of translations and the slowness of the pacing put students off. That said, there are numerous sections of the film, which, if discussed with students before watching, can be exceedingly powerful.*

Survival in Auschwitz. Written by Primo Levi and published by Simon and Schuster, New York, 1986. *One of the most brilliant memoirs written about a concentration camp experience, it is sometimes too sophisticated or analytical for students in high school. We recommend it without reservation as a great book to provide you with background, though.*

The Survivor: Anatomy of Life in the Death Camps. Written by Terrence Des Pres and published by Oxford University Press, Oxford, 1980. *This book, like Frankl's, is considered a classic. Better for background knowledge than for reading in class, though.*

HIDING

Dit is een foto, zoals
ik me zou wensen,
altijd zo te zijn.
Dan had ik nog wel
een kans om naar
Holywood te komen.
Anne Frank.
10 Oct. 1942

(translation)
"This is a photo as I would wish
myself to look all the time. Then
I would maybe have a chance to
come to Hollywood."
Anne Frank, 10 Oct. 1942

Anne Frank, October, 1942. © Bettmann/CORBIS.

When Paul Schwarzbart, *Braking the Silence: Reminiscences of a Hidden Child* (Authorhouse, 2004), was seven-years-old, he was taken into hiding. He was a Belgian Jew, living with his mother. His father had been taken away by the Nazis a few years earlier, and the situation for Jews was worsening. His mother had obtained forged papers that allowed her to clean houses under an assumed 'Aryan' identity, but she had very little money, and she was exceedingly worried about how to care for her young son. She was especially afraid that he would betray their Jewishness somehow. One day, as the two were sitting at a train station, watching the trains come and go for free entertainment, a priest approached Paul's mother. He very quietly informed her that he could take care of her son for the duration of the war if she would entrust Paul at that moment to his care. As Paul would recount for young audiences much later in his life, he remembered vividly the decision his mother had to make instantaneously. He was sure that his mother would turn down this unknown stranger, sure that she would hug Paul close to her and shun the priest's offer. Instead, wordlessly, she kissed her son on the top of the head and left him on the bench. Paul recalled gripping his mother's arm tightly, desperately hoping she would stay or at least change her mind, terrified to lose his mother, having already lost his father. And yet, though only a child, Paul had been forced to grow up quickly enough to know not to scream or cry, not in any way to draw attention to himself. He watched his mother leave, and he traveled with the priest to a school for boys in Belgium where he survived, pretending to be Catholic, eventually even becoming an altar boy.

Paul's story is dramatic in and of itself, but it is also dramatically different from Anne Frank's, the story which has become one of the quintessential Holocaust stories and certainly the quintessential hidden child's. The differences between their stories indicate the enormous range of hidden children's experiences. Whereas Paul's mother had practically no warning, barely any time to consider her options, knew neither the priest nor where he would take her child, Anne Frank's parents planned for months in advance, considered their options carefully, knew their rescuers and even owned the attic in which they hid. Paul was hidden alone in plain sight, passing for 'Aryan'; Anne hid with her family, out of view. Though Paul's story is relatively unknown, despite being similar to the story of hiding portrayed in the French movie, *Au Revoir Les Enfants*, Anne Frank's became the governing portrait of Holocaust victims.[73]

Bruno Bettleheim, a famous psychologist who, it turned out had fabricated elements of his own story of Holocaust survival, was one of the first to analyze why Anne Frank's story became so wildly popular in the United States. Bettleheim explained that, especially as represented in the play by Goodrich and Hackett, "Her seeming survival through her moving statement about the goodness of men releases us effectively of the need to cope with the problems Auschwitz presents. ….[Her comment] explains why millions loved play and movie, [and we would add diary and girl,] because while it confronts us with the fact that Auschwitz existed, it encourages us at the same time to ignore any of its implications."[74] Because Anne's diary ends before her life does, because her narrative does not describe the concentration camps, because her ideas are very much ideals, Anne Frank has come to represent hope despite tragic circumstances, faith amidst inhumanity, life despite murder. She has come to symbolize the

---

[73]The opening of this chapter is modeled on the opening of the second chapter of Deborah Dwork's book, entitled, "Into Hiding." Dwok's book is: *Children with a Star: Jewish Youth in Nazi Europe*, (New Haven: Yale University Press, 1991).
[74]Bruno Bettleheim, *Surviving and Other Essays* (New York: Vintage Books, 1960), 247.

Holocaust, in reality representing what we prefer not to see over that which we ought to confront.

This interpretation of Holocaust memory highlights one of the pitfalls of teaching about hiding; it's not only possible, but easy to minimize the hardships people faced in hiding, whether they were hidden in plain sight or out of view. Just as Anne Frank's story of adolescence, hope and humanity served as a kind of screen, occluding the harsher realities of antisemitism, mass murder and Auschwitz, so the stories of Jews in hiding can be used as a way to screen out what are assumed to be the generally harsher experiences of Jews in ghettos, concentration and death camps.

This is another example, however, of where applying a hierarchy of suffering simply doesn't make sense. Consider, for example, the story of a Holocaust survivor, Louis de Groot, who grew up only a few blocks away from where Anne Frank lived in Holland. Like Paul's mother, Louis' parents were able to have him hidden only under the condition that he go alone, without them. Unlike Paul's mother, Louis' parents paid various non-Jews to hide him, never fully knowing the condition he was in. Louis, utterly beholden to a series of strangers, terribly anxious at all times, was hidden for a few months in a grave-site, literally within a cavity dug out of the ground: alone, with no light, not always enough air, no ability to move around and no one to talk to, a meager, daily meal was secreted to him in the dark of night. When he emerged from that hiding place to go to another, his leg muscles had atrophied and his eyesight had been compromised. Of course in some abstract sense, Louis was lucky to survive, even though he lost his entire family. (After the war, he was cared for in a home for Jewish orphans; he 'illegally' immigrated to Palestine, fought in the War of Independence, after a while, immigrated to the U.S.A. and was almost immediately drafted to fight in Vietnam.) On another level, though, Louis' story points out the idiocies of hierarchies of suffering. It is impossible and unnecessary to rank or sort survivors' experiences by their degrees of trauma; it is far more compassionate and useful to consider each experience as having its own nuances and layers of complexity: physical, moral, emotional, and otherwise.

The big ideas of this chapter are that:

- That there was an enormous range of experiences among those hidden during the Holocaust. Anne Frank's story is only one of them and an atypical one at that.

- That hiding itself is important to know about in considering the many avenues victims sought out to try to survive themselves or to save their families and friends.

- Though it is easy to teach about "hiding" as a way *not* to address the concentration, ghetto and death camp experiences, each of these pieces is integral to the historical puzzle of the period.

Key terms of this chapter includes: hiding out of view, and hiding in plain sight.

Dimensions of Hiding

In her fascinating book, *Children with a Star: Jewish Youth in Nazi Europe*, Deborah Dwork argues that there were essentially three ways Jews could go into hiding during the Holocaust. First, they could use their own "informal" networks of friends, family and connections to find locations to hide, or false identity papers to hide under. Edith and Otto Frank fit this model of hiding. Second, and more typically, Jews could rely on organizations that sprouted up to help hide them and others being hunted. Paul's story exemplifies this option, considering that the man posing as a priest was in reality a resistance worker who was part of a large organization dedicated to saving Jewish children. The third option Dwork describes as the most uncommon, where a child, "operating independently" went into hiding of his own volition.

Of ways to hide, there were primarily two: **hiding out of view** or being **hidden in plain sight**. Anne Frank and her family, Louis de Groot in the grave site, hid out of view; Paul, as a student in a Catholic boarding school for boys, and those Jews who could "pass" as 'Aryans,' hid in plain sight. Both options involved excruciating emotional trade-offs.

While Dwork doesn't specify sub-types, there is more than one way to hide out of view. During this period, Debbie's father hid in an abandoned castle with nearly 100 other children, ages three to 16, in a remote forest outside of La Hille in Southern France. The children subsisted on wild potatoes and radishes, occasionally arranging with the local farmers to work in exchange for food and supplies. (Of those who were hidden out of plain view, then, there were those who fended for themselves and those who couldn't.)

Those who hid like Anne Frank or Louis de Groot were utterly dependent on their rescuers. They depended on them for food, clothing, shelter, diversions (when possible). They were at once thankful for those provisions and fearful about their being discontinued. At any time, those in hiding could be found out, glimpsed through a window by a stranger or passer-by, turned in by someone providing ration cards or someone who heard a strange noise in the apartment next door, or even turned in by a member of the hider's family in exchange for a kilo of sugar or a much-needed favor. This means that for those in hiding, anxiety—intense anxiety—was a fact of life. Not knowing where your family members were, when you would see them again, if you would, where you yourself might be hidden next, and the constant fear of discovery wove the fabric of experience. Only to those too young to understand fully what was happening to them, was hiding, perhaps, less anxiety-laden, though even young children learned not to cry very early on, an indication that this kind of anxiety pervaded even babies who were pre-lingual.

Dwork quotes from the testimony of an adolescent girl who was hidden by a coal merchant and his wife:

> Once he changed coal for a very nice velvet dress for me. I was very happy with it. I remember I had it on and I was upstairs and he came to me and I said, 'I'm so happy with my dress,' and he embraced me and took me close and close and close and I was suddenly afraid. I thought, 'What's he doing?' It happened two more times that he came and said, 'I'm so glad because we have no children and you are a bit like my daughter.' He put his arms around me and he put me against him and I didn't feel safe.... I started to hate to be there because he always came upstairs, and he never did it when his wife was there.[75]

Being wholly dependent on those who were hiding her put this young woman in an exceedingly precarious position, clearly.

If hiding in full view, the complexities of life were also seemingly insurmountable. First, one had to buy, steal, forge or find false identity papers that would fool anyone who might examine them. Usually, this entailed adopting an entirely new, false identity (not simply holding onto the papers). Even small children hiding this way would need to memorize new birthdates, new names, new parents' identities, new religious rituals, new social practices, etc. Imagine a Jewish child who grows up in a city being hidden in a Catholic home in a small village in the countryside. Such a transition could involve new foods, new farm work, and new religious rituals. Sometimes, those hidden were worked ludicrously hard, forced to do backbreaking labor for long hours with little social interaction or emotional support. Like the young woman hidden at the coal merchant's house,

---

[75]Dwork, 80.

there was no recourse in such cases. One woman who worked at her rescuers' farm reflected on her experience this way:

> How did I feel during all this? …I had never thought, 'How do I feel?' It's just lately that I finally came to the conclusion what I thought; I didn't think. And I didn't feel… I certainly did not cry when my parents were taken, because I was so busy getting myself into a place, into a safe place for survival. I don't think I cried one tear during those entire years. From the day my parents were taken until liberation, I don't think I cried one tear. I don't remember ever mourning…. I know I did not mourn my parents. I just didn't have time, I didn't have energy. All my energy went into planning to survive and to day-to-day; we did one day, let's see about the next day. And there was no time, no room for any other emotion.[76]

Hiding in a Catholic school required Paul to go to confession, to say Grace, to learn Mass in Latin, to hold his cutlery in a new way, and always, to hide the fact of his having been circumcised. As he tells his story, though, he was quite lucky; he was fair-skinned and blond-haired as a boy, physical traits that made his hiding in plain view a little easier than it might have been otherwise. Because he was old enough to remember his mother and the address of his home in Belgium, Paul returned there after the war. Though his father was murdered in a concentration camp, his mother had survived, and they were reunited.

Teaching Ideas

1. **Philosophical Dimensions of Hiding**: It's interesting to consider that for most of us studying about Jews who went into hiding during the Holocaust; their act was not in any way shameful; it was simply a strategy for survival. The shameful part was that they were forced to go into hiding in the first place. And yet, consider how going into hiding in order not to serve in the American armed forces during the Vietnam War seemed to many at that time or how soldiers who refused to return to fighting in Iraq were viewed by some. Why is it that hiding in order to avoid being drafted was deemed shameful while hiding during the Holocaust is not? Compare those situations to that of Jews in Spain who were forced to convert or die and then hid or passed as Catholic *Conversos*. Or, consider the *Hanukkah* story of the remarkable Maccabbees, who chose to fight rather than hide. Can your students establish sociological guidelines around the concept of

---

[76]Dwork, 95.

hiding, formulating, for example, when it is shameful to hide and when it isn't? Why it is considered shameful in certain circumstances and not others? Why would some Jews believe it would be shameful to hide while others wouldn't?

Your students might want to hear from Jews who believed it was better to die as Jews than live as Christians, since this orientation may be more foreign to them than sacrificing anything to live. In her collection of interviews with children who survived the Holocaust, Claudine Vegh captures such beliefs. As one survivor remembers, "Hiding… was still a refusal to accept ourselves as Jews. …We were Jewish, that was our fate, and we had to accept it!"[77] Child survivor Annette Baslaw-Finger put it this way: "My parents said we had been born Jews, and we would do our best to survive as Jews. If need be, we would die as Jews, but Jews we were, and Jews we would remain."[78]

2. **Online Exhibition:** If you have access to the Internet in class, the U.S. Holocaust Museum has a phenomenal online exhibit about hidden children which works well to tour as a class. The site, **Life in Shadows: Hidden children and the Holocaust** has films of survivors who were hidden children talking about their experiences, transcripts of especially traumatic moments, artifacts from hiding, and a wealth of other materials. It's important as you tour the site (or afterwards,) to pose the question: in what ways do you imagine the experience of hiding was different for children than for adults?

3. **Poetry:** While it is obviously impossible for your students to truly know what it was like for Holocaust survivors and victims to hide, it is sometimes illustrative to allow them the opportunities to imagine what it might have been like. Rather than having students simply write poems, however (though some will be good at that), we encourage you to have them write poetry in response to a prompt. For example, tell your students Paul's story up until the moment the priest sat by them, and have them write poems from the perspectives of Paul, his mother, the priest and a passer-by or even the train conductor. Collect the poems, shuffle and redistribute them, and then have the students read aloud the poem they receive. Reading these fabricated, multiple perspectives aloud should enable your students, at least briefly, to view the complexities of single, small-scale, historical transactions. One of Simone's favorite poems written by a Holocaust survivor is

[77]Claudine Vegh, *I Didn't Say Goodbye* (New York: Dutton, 1984), 90.
[78]Jane Marks. *The Hidden Children: the Secret Survivors of the Holocaust.* (New York: Bantam Books, 1998), 202.

exceptionally good for this kind of exercise. The second part of the poem *Bashert*, by Irena Klepfiscz, is included at the end of this chapter. You can read it to your students up until the line, "And then she turns," allowing the students to complete the poem. Her students were always stunned to hear the actual ending of her poem once they had written their own.

4. **Ethical Dilemmas:** For a number of rich, ethical dilemmas rescuers encountered in hiding their charges, see the activity in the Rescue chapter in the Teaching Ideas section about Abraham Foxman, Alicia Appleman Jurman and Marion Pritchard. There are of course numerous ethical dilemmas that those in hiding faced, too, for example: who should eat the one wild radish dug up in the woods—the small child, the sick mother or the hardier teenager? Why? Whose door should be knocked on for refuge—the wealthy neighbor or the poor friend, neither of whom knew your family was Jewish? When was it acceptable for an Orthodox Jew in hiding to eat the un*kosher* food served to her? Is it necessary to feel guilty if you prefer your "wartime mother" to your real mother? (This feeling is described in a powerful scene from Sarah Kofman's slim volume, *Rue Ordener, Rue Labat*.) Even the question of whether to go into hiding at all was an ethical dilemma, the answer to which depended in part on your socio-economic status. If you were wealthier, you might well have more contacts in the non-Jewish world who may, or may not, be able to help you in finding places to hide. If you feel your students have learned enough basic information, ask them to come up with ethical dilemmas they imagine that those in hiding must have faced. The excerpt from Irena Klepfiscz's poem (included at the end of this section), lists a number of dilemmas faced by a mother hiding by passing in a single morning.

A post-war dilemma: Jean Marie Lustiger was a French Jew born in 1926 who converted to Catholicism during the war. While he speaks Yiddish with rabbis, says *Kaddish* every year for his mother who died in Auschwitz, signs his name in Hebrew in correspondence with Jewish friends and considers himself to be a Jew, he was ordained into the Catholic priesthood in 1954 and acted as archbishop of Paris from 1981 until 2005. His assertion that he is still Jewish has stirred quite a controversy among Jews. Does the fact that he converted as a strategy to 'pass' mean that his conversion wasn't sincere? Should he be considered Jewish? Why and why not?

5. **Anne Frank Revisited:** After having studied the considerable complexities of hiding during the Holocaust, ask your students why they think Anne

Frank became such a popular American and international icon. You might read them the quotation from her diary,

> It's a wonder I haven't abandoned all my ideals, they seem so absurd and impractical. Yet I cling to them because I still believe, in spite of everything, that people are truly good at heart. It's utterly impossible for me to build my life on a foundation of chaos, suffering and death. I see the world being slowly transformed into a wilderness, I hear the approaching thunder that, one day, will destroy us too, I feel the suffering of millions. And yet, when I look up at the sky, I somehow feel that everything will change for the better that this cruelty too shall end, that peace and tranquility will return once more (July 15, 1944.)[79]

Was Anne Frank transformed into an icon because she was optimistic? Because she served as a screen for Holocaust horrors? Because she was young, hidden with her family? Because her Jewishness was understated in the first play productions which worked well for Jewish Americans interested in assimilating into a Christian culture in the 1950s? Why else? For more information about Anne Frank's story, see **Anne Frank Center, USA,** the official website dedicated to preserving her memory.

6. **Films:** Showing a single short excerpt or a compilation of excerpts from movies about hiding is a good way both to heighten your students' engagement with this topic and to show them the array of problems those in hiding faced. For such use (or for showing in full,) we especially like **The Pianist** and **Europa Europa**, both of which are excellent. (Europa Europa is a little better for young audiences because it centers on the experiences of a young Jewish teenager, Solomon Perel, passing as a non-Jew in the Hitler Youth of all places; the story, however, is a little more complex to understand when Perel ends up in the Soviet Union. The Pianist, because it takes place almost wholly in Poland is a little easier to follow.) The documentary, **Courage to Care,** has a compelling, seven-minute excerpt where a Jewish woman discusses what it was like to hide in France as a young child.

7. **Books:** There are many books that document or describe hiding and passing during the Holocaust. While many of them are excellent, there are a few in particular that lend themselves to especially easy classroom use. Ida Fink's writing, almost all of which is about the experience of hiding and

---

[79]Anne Frank translated from the Dutch by B.M. Mooyaart with an introduction by Eleanor Roosevelt, *The Diary of a Young Girl*, (New York: Doubleday, 1993).

its repercussions in people's memories, is useful because her scenes are brief and poignant. See, for example, her short story called, "The Hiding Place." Other books that compile the stories of many people hidden include: **The Hidden Children,** by Howard Greenfeld, which is especially good for those who have difficulties reading; **The Hidden Children: the Secret Survivors of the Holocaust,** by Jane Marks, and **Hiding to Survive: Stories of Jewish Children Rescued from the Holocaust,** by Maxine B. Rosenberg.

Resources for Teaching

After Long Silence: A Memoir. Written by Helen Fremont and published by Delacorte Press, New York, 1999. *Having been raised Catholic; Helen Fremont found out as an adult only that her parents were not only Jewish but Holocaust survivors. It's a page-turner of a memoir that high school students like.*

Anne Frank Center, USA. Website: http://www.annefrank.com/. *A great selection of links and documents can be found at this website.*

Child in Two Worlds. Directed by Willy Lindwer and produced by Ergo Media, 1995, 60 minutes. *Though this film is Dutch (and only has sub-titles), it paints an interesting portrait of five war orphans hidden in Christian foster homes and the difficulties of post-war attempts to reclaim or reinvent cultural roots.*

Diamonds in the Snow. Directed by Hank Heifetz and produced by Cinema Guild, 1994. *The film shows three women from the same Polish town sharing how they survived in hiding and afterwards. The comparison is wonderful.*

Europa, Europa. Directed by Agnieszka Holland and produced by Orion Home Video, 1992, 107 minutes. *Oscar-nominated feature-length movie was based on a true story and stays pretty closely to it. Includes sub-titles.*

Hidden Children: Forgotten Survivors of the Holocaust. Written by Andre Stein and published by Penguin Books, New York, 1994. *Like the entry below, this book documents 10 survivors' tales of hiding.*

The Hidden Children: The Secret Survivors of the Holocaust. Written by Jane Marks and published by Ballantine Books, New York, 1993. *The book uses vignettes from a range of hidden children to layer a rich and complex understanding of hiding. Twenty-three survivors recount episodes from their survival and its aftermath. Highly readable and useful for classroom jigsaws.*

Life in Shadows: Hidden children and the Holocaust. Website: http://www.ushmm.org/museum/exhibit/online/hidkid/. *U.S. Holocaust Memorial Museum's online exhibit about hidden children.*

Resources for Further Learning

Anne Frank and the Future of Holocaust Memory. Written by Alvin H. Rosenfeld and published by the U.S. Holocaust Memorial Museum, Washington, DC, 2004. *This is one of a series of occasional papers that the Holocaust Museum publishes and distributes for free (upon request). This paper is a thought-provoking analysis of the uses of the Holocaust (as of 2004).*

Children with a Star: Jewish Youth in Nazi Europe. Written by Deborah Dwork and published by Yale University Press, New Haven, 1993. *This book is well written and well documented. It was one of the first and remains one of the best nonfiction resources on the topic.*

The Nazi Officer's Wife: How One Jewish Woman Survived the Holocaust. Written by Edith Hahn Beer with Susan Dworkin and published by Perennial, New York, 2000. *While the title of this work is sensationalistic, the story is sensational. A quick read about an adult strategy for survival, this book is also good for high school students.*

Who Owns Anne Frank? Written by Cynthia Ozick and published in *The New Yorker*, October 6, 1996. *This article was exceedingly controversial when it first appeared, and it remains assigned reading in most college courses on Holocaust representation. It's very engaging, and excerpts from it can be used to generate discussion in middle and high school classes.*

Your Name is Renee: Ruth Kapp Hartz's Story as a Hidden Child in Nazi-Occupied France. Written by Stacy Cretzmeyer and published by Oxford University Press, Oxford, 1999. *Focused on the early childhood of Hartz, the story conveys not only the hardships of living as a non-Jewish French girl, but also the difficulties of reconciling a hard-won identity with the newness of finding out she was Jewish.*

Bashert, Part 1: Poland, 1944: My mother is walking down a road.

(This poem is difficult to obtain as it is out of print. We have therefore reprinted this part of it here with permission.)

> My mother is walking down a road. Somewhere in Poland. Walking towards an unnamed town for some kind of permit. She is carrying her Aryan identity papers. She has left me with an old peasant who is willing to say she is my grandmother.
>
> She is walking down a road. Her terror in leaving me behind, in risking the separation is swallowed now, like all other feelings. But as she walks, she pictures me waving from the dusty yard, imagines herself suddenly picked up, the identity papers challenged. And even if she

were to survive that, would she ever find me later? She tastes the terror in her mouth again. She swallows.

I am over three years old, corn silk blond and blue eyed like any Polish child. There is terrible suffering among the peasants. Starvation. And like so many others, I am ill. Perhaps dying. I have bad lungs. Fever. An ugly ear infection that oozes pus. None of these symptoms are disappearing.

The night before, my mother feeds me watery soup and then sits and listens while I say my prayers to the Holy Mother, Mother of God. I ask her, just as the nuns taught me, to help us all: me, my mother, the old woman. And then catching myself, learning to use memory, I ask the Mother of God to help my father. The Polish words slip easily from my lips. My mother is satisfied. The peasant has perhaps heard and is reassured. My mother has found her to be kind, but knows that she is suspicious of strangers.

My mother is sick. Goiter. Malnutrition. Vitamin deficiencies. She has skin sores which she cannot cure. For months now she has been living in complete isolation, with no point of reference outside of herself. She has been her own sole advisor, companion, comforter. Almost everyone of her world is dead: three sisters, nephews and nieces, her mother, her husband, her in-laws. All gone. Even the remnants of the resistance, those few left after the uprising, have dispersed in the Polish countryside. She is more alone than she could have ever imagined. Only she knows her real name and she is perhaps dying. She is thirty years old.

I am over three years old. I have no consciousness of our danger, our separateness from the others. I have no awareness that we are playing a part. I only know that I have a special name, that I have been named for the Goddess of Peace. And each night, I sleep secure in that knowledge. And when I wet my bed, my mother places me on her belly and lies on the stain. She fears the old woman and hopes her body's warmth will dry the sheet before dawn.

My mother is walking down a road. Another woman joins her. My mother sees through the deception, but she has promised herself that never, under any circumstances, will she take that risk. So she swallows her hunger for contact and trust and instead talks about the sick child left behind and lies about the husband in the labor camp.

Someone is walking towards them. A large, strange woman with wild red hair. They try not to look at her too closely, to seem overly curious. But as they pass her, my mother feels something move inside her. The movement grows and grows till it is an explosion of yearning that she cannot contain. She stops, orders her companion to continue without her. And then she turns.

The woman with the red hair has also stopped and turned. She is grotesque, bloated with hunger, almost savage in her rags. She and my mother move towards each other. Cautiously, deliberately, they probe past the hunger, the swollen flesh, the infected skin, the rags. Slowly, they pierce five years of encrusted history. And slowly, there is perception and recognition.

In this wilderness of occupied Poland, in this vast emptiness where no one can be trusted, my mother has suddenly, bizarrely, met one of my father's teachers. A family friend. Another Jew.

They do not cry, but weep as they chronicle the dead and count the living. Then they rush to me. To the woman I am a familiar sight. She calculates that I will not live out the week, but comments only on my striking resemblance to my father. She says she has contacts. She leaves. One night a package of food is delivered anonymously. We eat. We begin to bridge the gap towards life. We survive.

ADDITIONAL VICTIMS

Four Roma children pose for this photograph, probably in Rivesaltes internment camp in France, 1939–1942.
USHMM, courtesy of Elizabeth Eidenben.

One of the significant tensions involved in teaching about the Holocaust is the question of how much to teach about non-Jewish victims vs. Jewish victims of the Nazis and their collaborators. Given the centrality of Jewish victimization during the Holocaust and its central importance to understanding Holocaust history, many teachers tend to include non-Jewish victims in their units only as a kind of after thought or side note, mentioning the list of other groups persecuted, but not delving into the particularities of their stories. Teachers may say something like: "Of course not only Jews were persecuted, but also the **Sinti** and **Roma** (formerly known as 'Gypsies'), homosexuals, people with disabilities, the mentally ill, Jehovah's Witnesses, and other ethnic minorities." While this list is factually correct, the strategy of only listing groups is a pedagogical pitfall. It's an understandable mistake given that time is short in the classroom and outside of it, and that materials about non-Jewish victims are harder to come by than documentation of Jewish victimization during the Holocaust.

Nonetheless, it's exceedingly important to understand the Nazis' range of victims, the differences between their experiences, and what that range reflects about Nazi ideology and racial policy. Nazi policy distinguished between racial enemies of the state (Jews), racially inferior groups (such as Blacks and Slavic minorities), those who were considered 'hereditarily ill' (people suffering from diseases like Multiple Sclerosis, manic depressiveness, the deaf, blind), so-called 'asocials' (which included the Sinti and Roma, criminals, the homeless, and other non-conformists), political prisoners (anyone who opposed the regime), and other kinds of 'enemies' of the Nazi racial state: Jehovah's Witnesses (who refused to serve in the army) and homosexual men (who were seen as compromising the desired population growth of the Third *Reich*). Each of these groups was treated differently and in that way sheds light on the regime as a whole. As you read the chapter below, bear in mind that these groups' histories during the Holocaust are not only interesting because they contrast effectively with the experiences of Jewish victims; rather, they are important and informative in and of themselves.

A final note worth bearing in mind as you teach about this topic is that it is very easy to fall into the trap of talking about victim groups along a hierarchy of suffering. That is, it's easy to think that Jews had the "worst" experiences since they were the group targeted most viciously by Nazi racial policy and action. Here it is crucial to recognize that policy intentions don't map onto individual experiences. In other words, while Jews were the centrally targeted group, individual experiences ranged in profound and unsettling ways regardless of a person's group identity. It's worth considering, for example, that whether you lose a child to a machete blade or a gas chamber, to a bus bombing or a hit-and-run, losing a family member is a profound trauma, despite the differences in those types of loss. In terms of individuals' experiences, no hierarchy of suffering makes sense. We caution you to word your remarks carefully when you talk about different victim groups' experiences in light of this point.

In the interests of brevity, in this chapter the experiences of only three victim groups are summarized: those of the Sinti and Roma, Gays, and Jehovah's Witnesses. Please see the Teaching Ideas section for ways to incorporate other groups' experiences in being persecuted by the Nazi regime.

The big ideas of this chapter are that:

- Jews, though they were the main targets of Nazi policy and action, were not the only group persecuted.

- Groups persecuted by the Nazis were exceedingly diverse and treated in very different ways.

- It's important to humanize non-Jewish victim groups by telling individual stories as well as communicating statistics. It is not enough to list those groups.

Key terms of this chapter include: Sinti, Roma, *mischlinge,* 'asocials,' pink triangle, Magnus Hirschfeld, Ernst Rohm, *putsch,* martyrs, and *Erklärung.*

Sinti and Roma

Unlike Jews, who in the Weimar period of German history had attained a measure of equality in most realms of German society (except the army), Roma had no such status to lose during the Holocaust. Originally called 'Gypsies' (in English) because they were wrongly thought to have originated in Egypt, the Roma people actually came from Northern India to Germany in the late 1400s, and they were discriminated against in Germany and Europe throughout the 20th century. Bavarian laws, for example, allowed police to remove Roma caravans from a township without provocation, disallowed them from traveling with their own school-age children, and enabled police to send "gypsies and travelers over sixteen years of age who are unable to prove regular employment …to workhouses for up to two years… on the grounds of public security."[80] In a kind of warped logic, local police, local inhabitants or some combination thereof, often hounded Sinti and Roma out of their towns, and yet claimed to persecute them on the grounds of their itinerant lifestyle.

After the Nazi ascension to power in 1933, the persecution of the 30,000 Roma living in Germany became centralized and systematized, though this didn't mean that Nazi racial policies towards the Roma were clearly expressed. What happened in the early stages of the regime, for example, was that Roma were included as targets of racialist policies even when their group wasn't specifically mentioned as such. Thus, while they were not mentioned specifically in the Nuremberg Laws of 1935, the laws were widely interpreted as applying to them nonetheless. As Michael Burleigh and Wolfgang Wippermann write, "Like Jews, [Roma] were 'carriers of alien blood,' and therefore could not be permit-

---

[80]Michael Burleigh and Wolfgang Wippermann, *The Racial State: Germany 1933-1945* (Cambridge, England: Cambridge University Press, 1991), 115.

ted either to marry or to have sexual relations, with those of 'German blood.'"[81] In short, Roma were considered racially impure, a potential defilement of the 'Aryan' national body. The *Reich* Central Office for the Fight against the Gypsy Nuisance, founded in 1936, coordinated policies and actions against them.

Interestingly, it was primarily mixed-race Roma, those men and women whose genealogy suggested intermarriage with other 'lesser races,' who were deemed most threatening to the regime. Because according to German racial categorizations, Northern Indian origin was subsumed under the category of 'Aryan,' only those Roma who had 'mixed blood' were considered to have 'criminal' elements. Given the long history of German persecution of the Roma, their genealogical records were easily available and for the most part well kept. Nazi racial scientists researched and interrogated Roma individuals in order to distinguish those who were 'pure' vs. those who were '*mischlinge*' ('mixed') 'Gypsies.' Not surprisingly, most of the Roma populations of Europe were deemed '*mischlinge*.' In the early part of the regime, these Sinti and Roma were to be 'resettled' or forcibly sterilized in order to contain the supposed racial threat they posed.

'Resettlement' often involved confining Roma to particular regions, usually ones that were filthy or undesirable in some way, which, as a side note, was particularly offensive to these people given their religious concerns with cleanliness. In preparation for the 1936 Olympics in Berlin, for example, the Nazis rounded up approximately 600 Roma, forcing them into an encampment alongside a sewage dump in Marzahn where the lack of water and basic amenities enabled disease to ravage the population. Though originally considered a short-term holding pen to 'clean up' Berlin's appearance for the Olympics, the camp at Marzahn and others like it became long-term prisons where Sinti and Roma suffered horrendous conditions until being deported out of Germany and Austria. It's worth noting, too, that many Roma by this time were already incarcerated in concentration camps like Dachau and Sachsenhausen, arrested as so-called '**asocials**,' the category which included criminals and vagrants.

By 1942, the so-called 'Final Solution' of the 'Gypsy Question' was in place, though it was less coordinated than efforts to mass murder Jews. The *Einsatzgruppen* advancing into the Soviet Union slaughtered Roma, and they were deported from Germany and the rest of Europe to Auschwitz. At Auschwitz, in a lager very near to the gas chambers and crematoria, they were housed as families (rather than separated by sex as Jews were). As Burleigh and Wippermann describe, this decision was motivated "chiefly to minimize the likelihood of the regime's

---

[81]Ibid, 116.

agents being knifed or torn apart while trying to separate extended families."[82] While the Roma were racial targets of Nazi policy just as Jews were, there was a critical distinction in their categorization. The historian Inga Clendinnen summarizes, "Gypsies were classified as genetic asocials: that is, as defective humans, not enemies of humankind [the classification of Jews]."[83] This accounted for the difference in their treatment at Auschwitz. While they were fed less than enough to survive, disallowed medicines and murdered through typhus, dysentery, smallpox, Noma and in some cases, medical experimentation, they were not subjected to brutal labor, but left mainly to themselves. Approximately 18,000 Roma lived at the family camp in Auschwitz, until the infamous night of August 2-3, 1944.

On that single night, almost 3,000 Sinti and Roma men, women and children were forced into the gas chambers. In fact, the SS had tried to 'liquidate' the 'Gypsy camp' already in May, but had given up when they faced Roma armed with iron pipes, pots and whatever weapons they had. The following day, Dr. Mengele enticed the children who had managed to hide into his car and personally drove them to be gassed. Burleigh and Wippermann summarize that "of the 23,000 [Sinti and Roma] who had entered camp B II e [the Gypsy camp], 20,078"[84] were murdered.

At the start of World War II, there were approximately 1 1/4 million Roma living on the European continent, the largest population being located in Romania. At the end of the Holocaust, 25-50 percent of the Sinti and Roma had been mass murdered. Their victimization in Europe, however, did not end in 1945. In fact, in Germany, because many of the same people who had dictated 'Gypsy affairs' during the Third *Reich* retained their positions after the war, 'security policies' against Roma persisted. Burleigh and Wippermann write, "The fact of Nazi genocide against Sinti and Roma was only officially acknowledged… in 1982, a fact which does not deter current deportations of eastern European 'Gypsies.'"[85] The German government did not disburse to Roma restitution payments until such time as many victims who would be eligible had died.

A final note: The Roma call the Holocaust, *Porraimos*, which translates as the Devouring. This is a recent term. Almost directly opposite of Jewish tradition, Roma tradition espouses a kind of forgetting, a dismissal of history in favor of "seizing the day." As Inga Clendinnen puts it, "they have chosen not to bother

---

[82]Ibid, 125.

[83]Inga Clendinnen, *Reading the Holocaust* (Cambridge, UK: Cambridge University Press, 1999), 7.

[84]Burleigh and Wippermann, 126.

[85]Ibid, 127.

with history at all, because to forget, with a kind of defiant insouciance…is the Gypsy way of enduring."[86] That said, each summer, European Roma hold a ceremony at Birkenau to commemorate the liquidation of the 'Gypsy Camp.'

Gay Men and Lesbians

The **pink triangle** is widely recognized in the U.S. today as the dominant symbol of gay pride. Gay men and lesbian women and their supporters don the pink triangle as earrings, t-shirts, bumper-stickers and flags. But this symbol has been reclaimed from its original status as a derogatory marker; in the concentration camps, prisoners arrested because they were gay were identified by pink triangles.

The persecution of gays in Germany both predates and extends beyond the period of the Holocaust. In fact, the law that made it a criminal offense for two men to engage in consensual sexual activity (Paragraph 175 of the 1871 *Reich* Criminal Code) was not repealed in East Germany until 1968 and in West Germany until 1969. This fact made it exceedingly difficult for gay male victims of the Nazi state to discuss their experiences openly; after all, the supposed crimes they had been incarcerated for during the Holocaust remained criminal offenses afterwards. Moreover, gay men were not officially recognized as victims of Nazism as long as homophobia was a legislative reality. There can be no question, however, that gay men suffered grievously under Nazism; approximately 50,000 were arrested during the Third *Reich*. Many served prison sentences for their 'criminal offenses,' only to be sent to concentration and labor camps thereafter, where they were subjected to back-breaking labor and to what might be considered 'perverse' labor—labor done just for the sake of doing it, e.g. moving boulders from one spot to another and back again.

Lesbians were not systematically persecuted during the Third *Reich* because they weren't viewed as a threat to Nazi racial policies. Thus, they were rarely arrested on the sole charge of their sexuality. That said, they were technically classified as 'asocials,' and their clubs, bars and businesses shut down.

During the Weimar Republic in Germany, sexual mores had loosened somewhat, especially in urban areas while the laws banning gay sex remained in place. **Magnus Hirschfeld**, a prominent Jewish leftist who pioneered the field of sexology, established a center to study sexual practices of both gay and straight Germans. Arguing for a liberalization of attitudes and legislation, Hirschfeld's work paved the way for a gay rights movement, which though progressing, was

---

[86]Clendinnen, 8.

still in its infancy when the Nazis came to power. In May, 1933, Hirschfeld's Institute for Sexual Science was ransacked and destroyed; the 12,000 books housed there were burned, a bust of Hirschfeld was symbolically hanged before being thrown on the pyre, and many of the SA men attacking the center sought out Hirschfeld, intending to "string him up or beat him to death."[87] Luckily, at the time, Hirschfeld was out of the country, being treated for malaria.

The most prominent symbolic act against gays occurred early in the Third *Reich* and is commonly referred to as the Rohm affair. **Ernst Rohm** was the leader of the Nazi thug group known as the SA, and as such, was a member of the Nazi leadership elite. He was also gay and outwardly so. He attended gay bars and parties and was a member of the League for Human Rights, a gay rights organization. In June of 1934, Heinrich Himmler, likely under orders from Hitler, had Rohm and his SA associates murdered, claiming that Rohm was planning a ***putsch*** (or takeover of power). As Burleigh and Wippermann write, "There is no evidence [to support that claim]. ...Nazi propaganda, however, justified Hitler's ensuing murder of his SA associates in terms of striking down a putative conspiracy, the restoration of 'law and order' against the anarchic gangsterism of the SA, and last but not least, as a cleansing operation against sexual 'deviants.'"[88] Many personal scores were settled during the "Night of the Long Knives."

According to Himmler, the 'sexual deviancy' of homosexual men was important insofar as it compromised the racial health of the Nazi state body as a whole. In other words, because gay men didn't procreate, they were shortchanging the number of Aryans who would otherwise be born during the Third *Reich*. As he stated in a speech to the SS, Himmler figured that there were approximately two million men "too few" who had been lost in WWI, and approximately two million men in Germany in 1937 who were gay. Thus, the Third *Reich* had, in effect, "a lack of about four million men capable of having sex, [which] has upset the sexual balance sheet of Germany." "...A people which has many children has the candidature for world power and world domination. A people of good race which has too few children has a one-way ticket to the grave," Himmler proclaimed. The "extinguishing of abnormal life" was an appropriate response.[89]

In 1935, the Ministry of Justice expanded the scope of criminal code, Paragraph 175, by the addition of Paragraph 175a, which not only disallowed private sexual behavior, but disallowed any behavior likely to be perceived as homosexual or to

---

[87]These were the words used by the perpetrators themselves as quoted in an eyewitness account. The excerpt appears in Burleigh and Wippermann, 190.

[88]Ibid, 188.

[89]Himmler's speech is excerpted in Burleigh and Wippermann, 192–193.

be perceived as an insult to 'public morality.' Under Himmler, this leeway in the law allowed arrests and attacks on gay German men to increase in frequency and brutality. By utilizing spies and informants, interrogating gay men with torture, by confiscating address books and organization lists, the SS were able to terrorize gay Germans. It is not known exactly how many gay men were incarcerated or murdered in concentration camps; estimates range between 10,000 and 15,000. What is known is that this class of prisoner was detested and mistreated not only by guards and *kapos*, but by other groups of prisoners as well. In some cases, gay men had medical experiments performed on them, which aimed to 'correct' their homosexuality through hormone implants or castration (as mentioned above). Those gay men who survived such brutalities lived to face the homophobia that characterized much of Germany, Europe, the United States and elsewhere until long after the Holocaust.

Jehovah's Witnesses

The language of Holocaust commemoration often refers to Jews murdered during the Third *Reich* as **martyrs**, people slaughtered on account of their faith or religion. The case of Jehovah's Witnesses as a victim group, though they comprised only a tiny minority of the German population, is fascinating from a Jewish perspective because their experience adds complexity to the notion of what it means to be a martyr. Unlike Jews, Roma, gays and most other victim groups, Jehovah's Witnesses could be released from concentration camps if they agreed to sign a document renouncing their faith. Upon signing, they could, literally, walk out the concentration camp gates. (The Nazis tended to trust Jehovah's Witnesses because they did not try to escape or attack their guards; instead they viewed their suffering as part of God's work.) The '*Erklärung*' or declaration stated the following:

1. I have come to know that the International Bible Students Association [what Jehovah Witnesses were called at the time] is proclaiming erroneous teachings and under the cloak of religion follows hostile purposes against the State.

2. I therefore left the organization entirely and made myself absolutely free from the teachings of this sect.

3. I herewith give assurance that I will never again take any part in the activity of the International Bible Students Association. Any persons approaching me with the teaching of the Bible Students, or who in any manner reveal their connections with them, I will denounce immediately....

4. I will in the future esteem the laws of the State, especially in the event of war will I, with weapon in hand, defend the fatherland, and join in every way the community of the people.

5. I have been informed that I will at once be taken again into protective custody if I should act against the declaration given today.

Very few Jehovah's Witnesses signed the document, though the precise numbers are hard to establish. Of the approximately 25,000 Witnesses living in Germany in 1933, approximately 2,000 were murdered in concentration camps. Moreover, because of their adherence to the principles of their faith, Jehovah's Witnesses resisted the Nazi regime from its inception. The strength of their convictions as a religious group prompted the Dartmouth Jewish Studies professor Susannah Heschel to write, "In considering the possibilities for Christian response to National Socialism, the Witnesses emerge as an important model of resistance against which other groups might be measured."[90]

Because the Witnesses do not pledge their allegiance to symbols (flags), people (leaders) or organizations (of a nation), they will not serve in armies, they do not vote and they don't support the financial apparatus of a state. All these aspects of their religion were an affront to the Nazis, who persecuted Witnesses for non-compliance. As early as 1933, Witnesses' meetings were disrupted, and Witness presses were destroyed in an effort to keep them from distributing the messages they thought of as apolitical. In 1936, for example, Jehovah's Witnesses printed and secretly circulated 200,000 copies of the Lucerne Resolution, which decried Nazism. Later in Germany, Witnesses were arrested and imprisoned, tortured and beheaded for their religious convictions. Often, men were shot at the behest of military tribunals for being what would now be called conscientious objectors, those who refused to serve in the army on the grounds of their convictions.

Simone Arnold Liebster describes in her memoir what it was like for a young Witness in France after the Nazi take-over. Liebster's mother became a Witness in 1938. Her father was baptized as a Witness that same year, though the *Reich* considered him Jewish, and she chose to become a Witness in 1941. Liebster's father spent nearly six years in five concentration camps. After he left, Liebster writes:

> At school I was under more and more pressure to *heil* Hitler. But I refused because in my heart I could never honor a man in this way as if here were a god who could save people. Several times the teachers

---

[90]Study Guide to *Jehovah's Witnesses Stand Firm Against Nazi Assault*, (Watch Tower Bible and Tract Society of Pennsylvania, 1996), 6.

stood me in front of the whole school and tried to force me to say '*Heil Hitler*.' One time, I was beaten unconscious, since I wouldn't do work to support the war. Finally I was expelled.[91]

Liebster herself was arrested when she was only 12-years-old and sent to be reeducated at a penitentiary school where her hair was washed only once a year. Her mother was sent to concentration camps. In the camps, the Witnesses, wearing purple triangles, were often cordoned off from other survivor groups in an effort to keep them from disseminating their teachings. They could receive letters and packages from outside. And they steadfastly refused to aid in military efforts of any sort or to conform even to military-like practices, the infamous roll calls. Many have written about the seeming calm of Witnesses facing persecution, that the courage of their convictions was inspiring. Regardless of this impression, however, it is clear that the Witnesses were also brutally treated, even if trusted by their Nazi captors. Indeed, they typically did not try to escape or resist. As an example, Liebster describes her reunion with her mother at the close of the war:

> As the war came to an end, my mother came to get me. Her face was cut and bruised. They told me it was my mother, but I just didn't comprehend it. Mother was told she needed a paper from the judge to secure my release. She took me by the hand and off we went to a building to get this paper. The judge was not in, so she went from office to office insisting on getting this document. It was when I saw her fighting for my freedom that I fully realized that this was my mother. I held her tight and cried.[92]

Teaching Ideas

1. **Additional Research:** The groups listed above do not comprise an exhaustive list of those victimized by the Nazis. Have your students do independent research on other, important groups of victims, such as: the Rhineland Blacks (referred to in Nazi terminology as the Rhineland 'bastards'), political prisoners, the 'hereditarily ill', so-called 'asocials,' or Poles, and other ethnic minority groups. The **U.S. Holocaust Memorial Museum's** website is a great place to start, as it has brief entries on each of these groups' experiences as well as video clips from individuals in each group.

---

[91]Ibid, 22.

[92]Ibid, 24.

2. **Ethical Dilemmas**: Consider some of the ethical dilemmas that different non-Jewish victims faced:

    -   In the concentration camps, gay prisoners could sometimes exchange sexual favors for material goods necessary for survival—medicines, food, clothing, etc. Consider the case of a gay inmate who knows of an SS officer who, for a sexual fee, will supply the inmate with insulin needed to save a fellow inmate. Given that there are no guarantees in the concentration camp universe; would this be worth the risk? Are you, as a student, more likely to agree to this kind of prostitution because the inmate is gay to begin with? What, if anything, does your answer to that question imply about how you think about gay men generally?

    -   Jehovah's Witnesses believe that all adherents of the religion must decide for themselves whether to join the faith. As a result, young children are schooled widely in the practices and beliefs of different traditions until such time as they are old enough to decide for themselves. Imagine being a Jehovah's Witness parent of a child 4-5 years old, someone too young to make that decision. By not renouncing your beliefs, you would be subjecting your child to unnecessary harm. Is that right?

    -   Some groups of non-Jewish victims incarcerated in the concentration camps could receive letters and packages from outside the camp. This allowed them, in theory, to act as rescuers within the camp, by giving away extra rations. Would you expect those groups receiving packages to share their rations? With whom and why?

3. **Restitution Role-Play:** After your students have studied the histories of Jewish and non-Jewish victims of the Holocaust, give them the following imaginary scenario. They are now policy makers for a restitution board representing Germany and all of its collaborating countries. Their job is to decide on guidelines for how to divide up the million dollars they have been allocated as restitution. Ask such questions as: How will you make the decision? Who will get the most money, and on what basis? Will you decide to divide the money evenly among the groups, unevenly by numbers of victims, or unevenly by losses suffered, or by the norms of the Nazi racial hierarchy? What documentation would you require of claimants, and what difficulties would this requirement pose? This activity can be used as a wonderful launch point from which to discuss hierarchies of suffering,

why they are so destructive and yet, why, too, they are sometimes politically unavoidable.

4. **Mosaic of Victims:** The U.S. Holocaust Memorial Museum refers to those persecuted under the Third *Reich* as a "mosaic of victims." First, discuss this term with your students. Why would the Holocaust Museum choose this term in particular? What are the benefits of this metaphor? Second, consider having your students design a memorial for victims of the Holocaust. How would they visually represent different victim groups and why? Would they use the idea of a mosaic? Third, have your students consider the dimensions of the assignment even. What would be implied if different groups persecuted by the Nazis had different memorials at the same camp, for example? Is it preferable to have separate memorials or a joint memorial, and why? What are the trade-offs involved in the decision?

5. **Films:** There are not nearly as many resources available on this topic as there are devoted to other topics related to the Holocaust. Some of the good ones, however, include: **Healing by Killing,** which is a documentary about the treatment of those considered the 'hereditarily ill.' It consists almost entirely of film footage from the period, which can be used to great effect by excerpting. **Stand Firm** and **Purple Triangles** are both devoted to Jehovah's Witnesses. Of the two, **Purple Triangles,** which was originally shown on British television, delves more personally into the topic. Both the films, **Persecuted and Forgotten** and **Porraimos** are excellent resources for highlighting the specific history of the Roma. **Persecuted and Forgotten** includes survivor testimony and indications of continued mistreatment of the Roma, but too little explanation about Sinti and Roma cultural practices. Directed by Alexandra Isles, **Porraimos** runs for a single hour and includes fabulous footage. **Carpati: 50 miles, 50 years,** is a little too long for easy showing in a single class session, but is the moving story of a Jewish ice cream seller from the Carpathian mountain region who returns to his hometown 50 years later. Because of his friendship with his Roma neighbors in that region, it has some usefulness in teaching about their experiences, too.

6. **Books: Dreaming in Black & White,** by Reinhardt Jung, tells the story of a boy with physical disabilities who dreams about what it would have been like if he lived in Nazi Europe in the 1930s. His "dream" character befriends a Jewish girl who is kicked out of school, and eventually he is sent to an institution because he is considered 'unfit' as an 'Aryan'. The "present

day" character ponders whether and how he fits into his own world. The book is especially good for middle school students. Tadeusz Borowski's masterpiece, **This Way for the Gas, Ladies and Gentlemen**, is a volume of short stories that a Polish (non-Jewish) concentration camp survivor wrote within a year of his release. The starkness of the language and the power of the images conveyed make it ideal for classroom use.

Resources for Teaching

Carpati: 50 Miles, 50 Years. Directed by Yale Strom, 1996, 80 minutes. *Though focused on a Jewish ice cream man living in the Carpathian Mountain Region of Ukraine, the film explores his friendships with the Rom of the region. A moving documentary narrated by Leonard Nimoy.*

Dreaming in Black and White. Written by Reinhardt Jung, translated by Anthea Bell and published by Phyllis Fogelman Books, New York, 2003. *Tells the story of a boy with physical disabilities who dreams about what it would have been like if he lived in Nazi Europe in the 1930s.*

Healing by Killing. Directed by Nitzan Aviram, distributed by New Yorker Films, 1998, 90 minutes. *Graphically details the Nazi euthanasia program from its inception through implementation and with its grisly applications to the 'Final Solution.'*

Stand Firm. Produced by Watch Tower Bible and Tract Society of Pennsylvania, 1996, 28 minutes (classroom version). *This documentary describes the ordeal of Jehovah's Witnesses in Nazi Germany. Includes testimony of survivors as well as historians' commentaries about their significance. The classroom version packs a powerful message.*

Purple Triangles. Directed by Martin Smith, Starlock Pictures Production for TVS and distributed by Watchtower Bible and Tract Society of New York, Inc. 1991, 25 minutes. *This video was originally made as a television show. It follows the experiences of one family of Jehovah's Witnesses, the Kusserows.*

Persecuted and Forgotten. Produced by EBS Productions, San Francisco, 1989, 54 minutes. *The film follows a group of German Roma who return to Auschwitz, explaining their experiences in the 'Gypsy Family Camp.' The documentary is moving, but he most illuminating parts deal with continued anti-Roma treatment.*

Porraimos. Directed by Alexandra Isles, and available from The Cinema Guild, 2000, 57 minutes. *This documentary is well produced, fascinating and fast-paced. Documenting the Sinti and Roma's experience of the Holocaust, the film includes many Sinti and Roma survivors. (The Cinema Guild's website is: www.cinemaguild.com.)*

This Way for the Gas, Ladies and Gentlemen. Written by Tadeusz Borowski and published by Penguin Books, New York, 1967. *A Polish concentration camp* *survivor wrote this short volume of stories within a year of his release. Written in simple prose, the stories are readable, excruciating and vivid, perfect for classroom use.*

U.S. Holocaust Memorial Museum. Website: http://www.ushmm.org/. *The Holocaust Museum's website has useful information about all groups persecuted by the Nazis.*

Resources for Further Learning

Days of Masquerade: Life Stories of Lesbians during the Third Reich. Written by Claudia Schoppmann, translated by Allison Brown and published by Columbia University Press, New York, 1996. *The first account of lesbians living through the Nazi era, Schoppmann's book reconstructs the lives of 10 women. An interesting read.*

Destined to Witness: Growing up Black in Nazi Germany. Written by Hans Massaquoi and published by William Morrow, New York, 1999. *If it had been edited a little more, this book would really be a fine read. As is, it is too long, but nonetheless interesting. Massaquoi was the son of the Liberian consul in Hamburg, and his mother was a native German.*

Facing the Lion: Memoirs of a Young Girl in Nazi Europe. Written by Simone Arnold Liebster and published by Grammaton Press, New Orleans, 2000. *A bit long, this book chronicles Liebster's experiences as a 12-year-old Jehovah's Witness. A helpful study guide for the book, the book itself, and an accompanying video are all available at no charge through the Watchtower Bible and Tract Society in Pennsylvania.*

Men With the Pink Triangle. Written by Heinz Heger and published by Alyson Publications, Boston, 1944. *Despite the title, making it seem as though it has a broad historical focus, this book is a memoir of an Austrian gay man's experiences in Nazi Germany. It is graphic, startling, and austere, well written and short.*

A Mosaic of Victims: Non-Jews Persecuted and Murdered by the Nazis. Edited by Michael Berenbaum and published by New York University Press, New York, 1990. *This is an excellent resource with entries from a number of different historians and scholars.*

The Other Victims: First-person Stories of Non-Jews Persecuted by the Nazis. Written by Ina R. Friedman and published by Houghton Mifflin, New York, 1990. *Friedman's interviews are interesting, if a little long for in-class usage. We recommend especially her interviews with church leaders.*

The Pink Triangle: The Nazi War against Homosexuals. Written by Richard Plant and published by Henry Holt, New York, 1986. *Discusses in* *great detail the treatment of gays under Nazism, the origins of anti-gay policy and its implementation.*

The Racial State: Germany 1933-1945. Written by Michael Burleigh and Wolfgang Wippermann and published by Cambridge University Press, Cambridge, 2000. *This book is one of the best all-encompassing histories of the Holocaust. It is concise, rich in detail, well-documented and written with a clear and occasionally caustic voice. Different chapters deal with different histories during this period, divided by group.*

Reading the Holocaust. Written by Inga Clendinnen and published by Cambridge University Press, Cambridge, 1999. *A sophisticated analysis of Holocaust writings, this book serves as a historiographical summary of writings on the Holocaust and debates among historians up to the date of its publishing. It is wise and poetic.*

PERPETRATORS, COLLABORATORS AND BYSTANDERS

German soldiers of the Waffen-SS and the Reich Labor Service look on as a member of an Einsatzgruppen prepares to shoot a Ukrainian Jew, Ukraine, 1941–1943. USHMM, courtesy of Library of Congress.

As part of a study about how the Holocaust is taught in various religious schools, Simone interviewed a group of eighth grade girls who attended an ultra-Orthodox *yeshiva* (religious school). One of the interview questions she asked was: "How do you understand the actions of the perpetrators?" In other words, she elaborated, "How do you think that the perpetrators were able to do what they did?" Using various phrases and wordings, almost all of the girls answered the same way, expressing the idea that understanding the perpetrators' actions is impossible. As one girl replied, "They were inhuman. You can't understand why they would do it." Reflecting almost exactly what they had been taught in their school, these girls simply considered murderous behavior to be beyond the human capacity to understand.

From our perspective, this orientation towards perpetrators is problematic. Not only does it make the perpetrators seem God-like—unknowable, all-powerful, beyond human reason—but it ignores some of the most useful lessons of this history. It denies the powerful Jewish teaching that God endowed all human beings with both a *yetzer ha-ra* and a *yetzer ha-tov*, the inclinations to do evil and good respectively, and that each human must make the choice, *bechira*, as to which inclination to follow at a given moment. Rather than teaching kids how not to perpetrate themselves, this orientation teaches students that it would be impossible for them to do so, blinding them to their own potential acts. By contrast, if we instill in students a deep understanding of what allows people to hurt each other, in both small and large ways, individually and collectively, randomly or systematically, that paves the way for them to make powerful decisions when confronted with such opportunities. Whereas victimization is essentially about being powerless to make decisions, having the range of decisions radically curtailed by circumstances, perpetrating is essentially about wielding power, shaping the circumstances in which others function. As naïve as it may sound, we do believe that if we as people could learn how not to perpetrate, no one would have to experience victimization. Making the actions of the perpetrators comprehensible to your students marks a local step in that global direction. Much harder than teaching about the experience of victimization, it is thus also that much more important.

Like the explanation that the perpetrators' actions are beyond comprehension, other flawed conceptions of the perpetrators circulate wildly: first, that the perpetrators were all evil, second, that they were all German, or third, that Hitler himself represents the perpetrators. These conceptions seem to follow from a kind of verbal or mental shorthand. Sometimes, for example, students will use Hitler's name to stand in for all perpetrators. We've heard lots of kids of all grades say something along the lines of "Hitler killed all the Jews." Likewise, they may say "the Germans" rather than "the Nazis," and they may forget altogether that the perpetrators included, were enabled and actively and passively helped by hundreds of thousands of collaborators and bystanders in every country they occupied: Poles, Lithuanians, Hungarians, French, Dutch, etc. Simone sometimes begins teaching about perpetrators with the simple statement that Hitler never fired a single bullet, which reminds students that he alone could never have achieved what he planned, and that he needed helpers, not only in Germany, but in every country, occupied and not. Moreover, of course, in order for the perpetration of large-scale atrocity, many more millions had to aid in more invisible ways.

Imagine a perpetrator during the Holocaust. What image comes to mind? When Simone answers this question, she immediately imagines 'field-killers', the men of the *Einsatzgruppen*, (the mobile killing units,) in their tall black boots, shooting naked women and children at point blank range. Even after years of studying the Holocaust, she has to remind herself that there were 'desk-killers' as well, women and men who ordered the tall black boots and rifles, who kept the trains running on time, who ordered the building supplies for the new concentration camps, who redistributed the properties left behind by deported Jews. Were such 'desk-killers' evil or human? Were they perpetrators or bystanders? To answer that they were all evil is to act as though they are beyond human comprehension, to act as though they were not as we are. While this is a psychologically comforting conclusion to draw, it's a terribly misguided one. The behavior of the Nazis and their collaborators as well as that of the bystanders was evil, unquestionably, but it is also fundamentally understandable. Only by making the actions of the perpetrators understandable, by teaching your students about the perpetrators' humanity, do you stand a chance of solidifying your students' own humanity, building the obstacles to their behaving in these ways.

In this chapter, we first describe the *Einsatzgruppen*, as an illustration of one class of perpetrators. We then discuss two categories of explanation for the perpetrators' behaviors: general social-psychological research that helps explain behavior, and a few specific historical studies that talk pointedly about Nazi atrocity. Neither category, though, addresses why the vast majority of people allowed the atrocities to occur nor how the systems of Nazi Germany worked together. Moreover, neither category addresses the very important concept that particular countries and whole institutions functioned as perpetrator countries, collaborating countries (or parts thereof) and bystanders. As a result, it is very important that you extend this chapter in your classroom, making sure to discuss examples of national collaboration and institutional negligence. As examples, war-time France and Pope Pius XII make great case studies, as do Switzerland's so-called neutrality and money laundering.

The big ideas of this chapter are that:

- The categories of perpetrators/collaborators/bystanders are complex, and thus, the lines between them are sometimes invisible, temporary or flexible.

- Not all Germans were Nazis and not all perpetrators were German.

- And, above all, the behavior of the perpetrators, though of course condemnable, is comprehensible. As such, there are multiple explanations for their behavior, and all are worth discussing, dissecting and debating.

Key terms of this chapter include: *yetzer hara* —evil inclination, *yetzer hatov*— good inclination, *Wermacht*, SS, *Einsatzgruppen*, Heinrich Himmler, *Babi Yar*, 'authoritarian personality,' Stanley Milgram, Philip Zimbardo, ordinary men, 'eliminationist anti-Semites,' Police Battalion 101, and Jedwabne.

The *Einsatzgruppen*

On June 22, 1941, Germany invaded Eastern Poland and the Soviet Union, and in the first few weeks of their advance, they conquered areas densely populated by Jews. Following orders from the SS officers who had planned out the 'Final Solution,' the *Einsatzgruppen* followed the **Wermacht** (the German army) as it moved west. The **SS** was an elite military organization within the Nazi ranks. The name SS came from the German term *Schutzstaffel*, meaning "defense unit." The *Einsatzgruppen* were a special division of the SS. The men in both divisions had to prove that they were 'racially pure' by providing records of their ancestry back to the 18th century. They were educated in special officers' schools, and they had their own court system, allowing them to disobey any German law. The SS swore complete obedience and loyalty to Hitler. Along with supervising the deportations and ghettoization of Jews, SS men managed the concentration camps. With the invasion of the Soviet Union in 1941, the *Einsatzgruppen,* the mobile killing units of the SS, took charge of murdering the Jews of the newly occupied areas.

The *Einsatzgruppen* at first attempted to incite the local populations to murder Jews, sometimes trying to make it look as though the riot had spontaneously erupted. But under SS commander **Heinrich Himmler**, the forces quickly began doing the murderous work themselves, helped along by the local populations. Himmler envisioned clearing out the Jews and repopulating the land with German soldier-farmers. In service of this aim, typically, the *Einsatzgruppen* would 'round up' the Jews of a township, gather them at a central location, march them to a field or forest where they were forced to dig a mass grave and strip naked. With their backs to their murderers, they were then shot, falling into the pit before them. In many instances, babies and small children survived the shootings, clutched by their mothers at the fronts of their bodies. But helpless, they suffocated slowly beneath the dirt of the mass grave or collapsed under the weight of the corpses above them. To circumvent this possibility, sometimes the children were separated from their parents and shot at the edge of their own mass grave. Occasionally too, adults survived, crawling out of the graves once night had fallen or the *Einsatzgruppen* had left the scene.

Sarra Gleykh kept a diary of her survival of one such massacre in far southeastern Ukraine. The Germans had invaded her town on October 8, 1941 and registered all of its Jewish inhabitants by the 10th. On the 18th, when the Jews of her town were commanded to turn in their riches, Gleykh's family submitted "three silver soup spoons and a ring."[93] By the 20th of October, Gleykh, her two sisters and one sister's son, were facing the pits. Her mother and father, and another sister, had left earlier on trucks and had already been slaughtered by the time she arrived:

> We were herded toward the trenches which had been dug for the defense of the city. These trenches served no other function than as receptacles for the death of 9,000 Jews. We were ordered to undress to our underwear, and they searched for money and documents. Then we were herded along the edge of the ditch, but there was no longer any real edge, since the trench was filled with people for a half kilometer. Many were still alive and were begging for another bullet to finish them off. We walked over the corpses, and it seemed to me that I recognized my mother in one gray-haired woman. I rushed to her and Basya followed me, but we were driven back with clubs. At one point I thought that an old man with his brains bashed out was Papa, but I could not approach him any closer. We began to say goodbye, and we managed to kiss… Fanya did not believe that this was the end: 'Can it be that I will never again see the sun and the light?' she said. Her face was blue-gray, and Vladya [her son] kept asking 'Are we going to swim? Why are we undressed?' Fanya took him in her arms, since it was difficult for him to walk in the wet clay. Basya would not stop whispering, 'Vladya, Vladya, why should this happen to you too? No one even knows what they have done to us.' Fanya turned around and answered: 'I am dying calmly with him, because I know I am not

[93]Richard Rhodes, *Masters of Death: The Einsatzgruppen and the invention of the Holocaust* (New York: Alfred Knopf, 2002), 188.

leaving him an orphan.' These were Fanya's last words. I could not stand it any longer, and I held my head and began to scream in a wild voice. I seem to remember that Fanya had time to turn around and say, 'Be quiet, Sarra, be quiet.' At that point everything breaks off.

When I regained consciousness, it was already twilight. The bodies lying on top of me were still shuddering; the Germans were shooting them again to make doubly sure that the wounded would not be able to leave. ...These people were buried alive since no one could help them even though they screamed and called for help....

When I had crawled out [from underneath the corpses], I looked around: the wounded were writhing, groaning, attempting to get up and falling again. I began to call to Fanya in the hope that she would hear me, and a man next to me ordered me to be silent. ...He was afraid that my shouts would attract the attention of the Germans. A small group of people were resourceful enough to jump in to the trench when the first shots rang out, and they were unharmed.... They kept pleading with me to be silent. ...An old woman called out in a singsong voice: 'Lieutenant, Lieutenant...' There was so much horror in this endlessly repeating word! ...By chance I overtook [an acquaintance]....The two of us, undressed except for our slips and smeared with blood from head to toe, set off to seek refuge for the night....[94]

One of the largest operations of the *Einsatzgruppen* occurred a month earlier on September 29-30, 1941, at **Babi Yar** in Kiev. The *Einsatz* killers ordered all of the Jewish townspeople to assemble in the town square where they were marched passed the Jewish cemetery and a ravine called *Babi Yar*. In a bloody, two-day massacre, the *Einsatzgruppen,* with help from Ukrainian auxiliary units, shot and killed 34,000 Jews. In the months that followed, nearly 60,000 more Jews, Roma and Soviet prisoners of war were killed at *Babi Yar.*

The 3,000 men of the *Einsatzgruppen* were carefully acclimated to their so-called work. As Richard Rhodes documents in his gruesome study of the mobile killing units, the *Einsatzkommandos* only shot adult men until they were utterly used to murdering, whereupon they shot women and children as well. For the most part, they were plied with excellent food and quantities of alcohol after the 'actions' in order to deaden the emotions of their 'accomplishments,' but this wasn't always necessary. Despicably, the superintendent of police of Slonim

---

[94]Ibid, pp. 189-191.

described (in post-war testimony) that a certain massacre was largely "the work of a special SS commando that carried though the exterminations out of idealism, without using schnapps."[95] After one massacre in Bialystok, the shooters were treated to strawberries and cream as a reward. And Himmler himself provided 'rest-homes' outside of Berlin for those who suffered breakdowns at the psychological stress of mass murdering; those who availed themselves of these treatment centers were transferred to other assignments as officers without repercussion. Still, the rates of psychological breakdowns of the shooters—along with the inefficiencies of the process—encouraged experimentation with more 'impersonal' and more 'civilized' forms of mass murdering, experimentation which led to the building of the gas chambers.

Explaining Perpetrators: Generalist Explanations

In the immediate aftermath of the Holocaust, a number of early psychological explanations for the perpetrators' behavior emerged. Among them was the idea that Germans, as a people, had had, throughout history, mostly authoritarian forms of government, which meant that they were used to following orders, habituated to not questioning. When the right charismatic leader arose, they simply followed in lockstep behind him, carrying out mass murder with ease and efficiency. In this notion, the German people were practically brainwashed by history. Another idea which briefly found an audience held that German family life mimicked that authoritarian governmental structure. The German people of the Nazi period had thus grown up in homes where they were metaphorically, psychologically, and physically beaten, making it easier for them to mass murder than it would be for other nation's peoples. A third conjecture theorized that an '**authoritarian personality**' existed among the German people, and that because of this personality predilection, they were the playground bullies on the world's stage.

All of these explanations, largely offered up by American academics, shared the underlying proposition that such large-scale, systematically murderous activity could not occur in the U.S.A. Amalgamated, the three theories could be woven together to form a storyline about the greatness of American democracy: we Americans have been a historically democratic people, democratic practically since our inception. Thus, we do not cultivate 'authoritarian personalities' in authoritarian homes. And, we are thus incapable of the kind of atrocity the Holocaust was. Needless to say, perhaps, Native Americans would of course be chagrined at this mainstream self-perception.

[95]Ibid, p. 169.

In July 1962, a year after the trial of Adolf Eichmann, **Stanley Milgram**, a Yale psychologist, set out to determine whether obedience to authority was a particularly German trait or a more universal, human one. Specifically influenced by the Eichmann trial, he wanted to know whether or not Eichmann and his million accomplices were just following orders. He devised a controlled experiment where at first Yale students, and later other New Haven residents, were recruited for a "study of learning." In the initial design of the experiment, an unwitting volunteer would enter Dr. Milgram's laboratory, thinking that the person sitting in the lobby next to him was a "man off the street," interested in being paid to participate in the study as well. The two would draw papers out of a hat to decide who would play the role of the "teacher" and who would play the role of the "learner." The unwitting volunteer would always be assigned the first role, that of "teacher." The other person in the lobby, assigned to be the "learner" actually worked for Milgram. The two were jointly explained the outlines of the experiment. Milgram pretended that the point of the experiment was to figure out how quickly people could be taught to learn unrelated strings of words and whether an instrument that delivered shocks, or negative consequences, could help them learn more efficiently. Thus, the "learner" would have some time to memorize the random list of words, and then the "teacher" would test the learner on his memorization. Both the "teacher" and "learner" were administered a 45-volt shock initially to see what it felt like (which, incidentally, is a very low-level shock, akin to a static electricity shock). Sitting in separate rooms and invisible to each other, the "teacher" was instructed to give the learner small shocks every time he got an answer wrong. And each time that occurred, the "teacher" was instructed to increase the voltage level of the shock by 15 volts. The range of switches in the "teacher's" cubby was marked off in categories: low, medium, high and dangerous in red.[96]

Unbeknownst to the participant in the study, the experiment actually was designed to study how obedient Americans are as measured by how far up each participant would go on the voltage scale in shocking another human being. The teacher would read aloud the string of words, ask for the next one, and the learner would supposedly respond. In actuality, the learner's responses at each shock level were fabricated and pre-recorded so that they were consistent across participants. In every experiment, the "learner" would make lots of mistakes, affording the participants opportunities to shock the learners at greater and greater voltages. When a participant wanted to stop giving the learner shocks, when, for example the "learner" cried out in pain, "I have a heart condition!

---

[96]Stanley Milgram, *Obedience to Authority: An Experimental View* (New York: Harper & Row, 1974), 13-43.

Stop!" Milgram would stand over the "teacher," urging him to continue, telling him that this was "science," and that the entire experiment would be compromised if the "teacher" didn't continue. At a later period on the voltage scale, the "learner" wouldn't respond, as though the shocks had possibly killed him. Even then, the "teacher" would be encouraged strongly to keep reading the meaningless lists of words and shocking the non-respondent "learner." Only if the participant utterly refused to continue or if the end of the shock meter had been reached did the experiment end. At that point, after an interview in which the participant was told about the true nature of the experiment was the actor playing the "learner" invited into the room to shake hands with the "teacher," in order to assuage his possible guilt.

Shockingly, the results of Milgram's experiments showed that 65 percent of participants would follow orders to increase the shock levels throughout the entire range of shocks, ending only at the 450-volt denomination. And, just as importantly, no subject in the experiment refused before the 300-volt level. At first, it was speculated that the Yale students who were participants might be more obedient than other college kids or their adult counterparts; after all, they wanted good grades, were used to getting them, believed in the institution of science, trusted men in white coats, etc. Repeating the experiment, though, Milgram found basically the same ratios among adults of different socioeconomic classes, professions, ethnicities, and genders. The rates changed somewhat when the experimental set-up was different. Milgram found that when the "teacher" could neither hear nor see any response from the "learner," obedience rates were greater, helping to explain 'desk-killers'. Obedience rates decreased when the "teachers" had to touch their "learners" to apply the shocks.

Milgram explained his findings in ways that help explain perpetrators everywhere. From his perspective, hierarchical situations organize all of people's lives; from family through school, in work and in military service, and that the rewards of obedience trump the punishments for disobedience. In this experiment the participants identified with the authority rather than sympathizing with the victim. And many factors, "cemented" that orientation—Milgram called these "cementing mechanisms" —etiquette, the hoped-for reward, the investment in the activity, anxiety over possible punishment. He concluded from these experiments that "men are led to kill with little difficulty."[97]

Simone once studied with a Stanford professor who had replicated Milgram's experiments in the 1970s, to test their scientific validity. The professor, David

[97]Ibid, 7, 177.

Rosenhan, found that out of the hundreds of subjects he tested, only one, a recently returned Vietnam veteran, objected to administering even the first shock.

While people may indeed follow authorities, there are other situations wherein they perpetrate violence, even situations where rightful authorities are absent or distant. **Philip Zimbardo**, who had been a graduate student at Yale, went on to elaborate the situational dimensions of perpetration, that is, those aspects of a situation that cause people to take on particular roles in particular situations. Asking what happens to good people when they are put in "bad" situations, Zimbardo's most famous experiment simulated a "bad" situation. In the summer of 1971, with the help of a group of graduate students, Zimbardo transformed the basement of the psychology department at Stanford University into a mock prison. Then, having screened out applicants who, based on a survey, seemed to have 'authoritarian personalities,' Zimbardo assigned roles to play to a group of students—the roles of "prisoner" or "prison guard." Those who were to be "prisoners" were arrested by the Palo Alto police, taken from their homes early in the morning, in full view of their neighbors, and transported to the local holding center. From there, Zimbardo's "guards" collected them and brought them to the improvised prison. Over the course of 36 hours alone, Zimbardo's "prison guards" began to behave brutally, and Zimbardo's "prisoners" felt themselves utterly dehumanized. One "prisoner" was released for symptoms associated with a nervous breakdown. Within six days, Zimbardo had to call off the experiment for fear of physical violence. Roughly one third of the "prison guards" were cruel, sadistic; a middle group was "tough but fair"; only a small minority were "good guards," allotting favors and small gifts to the "prisoners". Not urged on by any authority, not ruled by any commander, having been raised in a democratic country and having no personality disorders or medical conditions, the simulation of prison, the situation itself, brought out the sadistic behaviors, ones that presaged the Abu Ghraib prison scandals 33 years later.[98]

Many other experiments paved the way for Milgram's and Zimbardo's, and many have subsequently refined their findings. Notable within that list are Solomon Asch's experiments on conformity, which found that people, as social animals, will actually perceive their realities differently when alone or when pressured by peer groups. Albert Bandura's investigations into social modeling and the many ways people suppress their moral instincts are notable as well. While these two studies have certain flaws, they have been foundational for understanding perpetrator behavior in general and formed the basis for at least

---

[98]Philip Zimbardo, http://www.prisonexp.org/.

one historical study directed at understanding perpetrator behavior during the Holocaust.

Specific Historical Explanations

In addition to the psychological studies focusing on perpetrator behavior, in the last few decades, a number of historical works have tackled the same question, generating explanations from archival research. The most notable are Christopher Browning's thesis that social psychology can be used to explain why "**ordinary men**" could be induced to kill; Daniel Jonah Goldhagen's notion that Germans were "**eliminationist anti-Semites**" and thus "willing executioners"; and Jan Gross' recent research that Polish "neighbors" in a few cases acted almost independently of German orders. These three ways of seeing perpetrators' behavior are not comprehensive; each has its shortfalls. Taken together, however, they offer a portrait that illuminates situational, ideological and historical forces at play.

Of the three, Browning was the first to write and his book, *Ordinary Men*, published in 1992, has become a classic. By examining documents related to their post-war trial in Germany, Browning examined how a group of mostly older men who hadn't grown up under Nazism, weren't Nazi ideologues, and were mostly low-level bureaucrats and family men became accustomed to murder. As Browning puts it, these men were almost least likely to kill. None had wielded a gun before, and they were not selected for the job; instead, they were "available" to it. Members of **Police Battalion 101**, the group of approximately 500 men ended up with a 'body count' of roughly 83,000 Jewish lives. Serving behind the German lines in Eastern Europe, they were unexpectedly ordered to round up Jews and shoot them. Thirty-eight thousand Jews lost their lives that way. Another 45,000 were rounded up by members of the battalion and placed on trains that traveled to Treblinka. From his reconstruction of the first massacres this battalion instigated, Browning notes that 12 of the 500 declined to participate the first time. Countering the myths, there were no repercussions for withdrawing. None were punished for non-compliance. After the first experience of mass shooting, Browning describes the battalion members' reactions:

> When men arrived back at barracks in Bilgoraj, they were depressed, angered, embittered, and shaken. They were given generous amounts of alcohol, told that the responsibilities for the massacre lay with higher authorities, and they didn't talk about it further. "The entire mat-

ter was a taboo," as one participant recalled. Still, another policeman woke up firing his gun into the ceiling of the barracks that night.[99]

Browning explains that these men ultimately became efficient killers. Drawing on Milgram's and Zimbardo's experiments, Browning's study adds another list of factors to take into consideration. He reminds readers that in addition to the rampant antisemitic propaganda flooding the population at large, the Order Police had specific indoctrinatory lessons as part of their basic training. Moreover, like the statistics in Milgram's study, 80–90 percent preferred shooting over not conforming. They didn't want to leave the 'dirty work' of murdering to their comrades, didn't want to refuse their share of collective obligation. Theirs was a tight-knit unit, stationed amidst a hostile population. Simply put their notions of masculinity—being one of the guys, doing their fair share, chipping in—forced the majority over their initial disgust with mass killing. And over time, they became brutalized and desensitized through their actions.

Daniel Jonah Goldhagen's study, entitled *Hitler's Willing Executioners*, became a bestseller internationally when it was published in 1996. Using some of the same documents as Browning, Goldhagen argued that the Germans, not only the Nazis, were "willing executioners." Rather than having to overcome the disgustingness of murder, they embraced it. As Goldhagen summarizes:

> Germans' anti-Semitic beliefs about Jews were the central causal agent of the Holocaust. They were the central causal agent not only of Hitler's decision to annihilate European Jewry but also of the perpetrators' willingness to kill and to brutalize Jews. ...Not economic hardship, not the coercive means of a totalitarian state, not social psychological pressure, not invariable psychological propensities, but ideas about Jews that were pervasive in Germany and had been for decades induced ordinary Germans to kill unarmed, defenseless Jewish men, women and children by the thousands, systematically and without pity.[100]

Citing Police Battalion 309's genocidal work in Bialystok, Goldhagen describes that they were ordered merely to gather the Jews of the city at the assembly point. Instead, they 'played' sadistic games with their victims as pawns: making elderly Jewish men dance, lighting their beards on fire, urinating on them, packing 700 Jews into a barn, lighting it on fire and shooting the Jews attempting to

---

[99]Christopher Browning, *Ordinary Men: Reserve Police Battalion 101 and the Final Solution in Poland* (New York: HarperPerennial, 1992), 69.

[100]Daniel Jonah Goldhagen, *Hitler's Willing Executioners: Ordinary Germans and the Holocaust*, (New York: Alfred Knopf, 1996), 9.

jump from the windows. Goldhagen quotes letters home from German soldiers who were proud of their so-called work.

In short, unlike Browning, Goldhagen's claim is that the Germans were ideological warriors, driven to mass murder Jews because of an 'eliminationist' hatred, a specific hatred that spanned generations and was particular to Germany. For Goldhagen, the Germans are caricatured if they're portrayed as 'unwilling,' for even Nazi zealots disobeyed orders they disagreed with.

The most recent account is Jan Gross', whose book, *Neighbors*, published in 2001, surprised even Holocaust historians. Documenting the events in a small town in Poland, Gross' short volume upended a number of governing conceptions of Holocaust history. Gross' story focuses on the small East European town of **Jedwabne**. In July 1941, the town's Polish Christian population murdered the other half of the townspeople, some 1,600 Jewish men, women and children. All but seven of the town's Jews died. What was striking about Gross' history is that the German occupiers of the town did not order the Polish Christians to murder the Polish Jews. Moreover, the Poles of Jedwabne, Christian and Jewish, had lived together, side by side, as friends and neighbors, school chums and sweethearts, buyers and sellers, teachers and students for centuries. Thus, when the Jewish residents were clubbed, drowned, raped, plundered, burned alive and beaten trying to escape, they knew the names and faces of their murderers. They knew the barn they were burned in. When neighbors cut off the head of a young woman, kicking it around as though it were a soccer ball, the perpetrators knew she was the daughter of the learned Jew who had taught most, if not all of them, to read. The one group of Jews who survived the war were hidden by a Polish Christian family who ended up fleeing the town when they were incessantly harassed and beaten, *post-war*, for their selflessness.

The neighbors of Gross' text were not following orders. They were not German 'eliminationist anti-Semites', even if they were antisemitic. They were in many ways victimized themselves, Poland being brutalized by both Nazi and Russian occupations. Their story vividly illustrates that not all perpetrators were Nazis, nor were they all German. Not all were enabled to brutalize through dehumanization. Instead, a host of complicated factors crystallized throughout this genocide, allowing perpetrators to murder, 'desk-killers' to support it, and others, millions and millions of others, to stand by and observe.

Raul Hilberg, who might be considered the grandfather of the field of Holocaust historians, wrote a number of foundational works. His first addressed how the mass murder could be carried out. Focusing on the technical requirements of the genocide, Hilberg examined the railroad system alone, estimating that, for example, at least one million people who worked on or for the railroad system had to aid and abet the genocidal campaign. He summarized the process of destruction succinctly:

> As the Nazi regime developed over the years, the whole structure of decision-making was changed. At first there were laws. Then there were decrees implementing laws. Then a law was made saying, 'There shall be no laws.' Then there were orders and directives that were written down, but still published in ministerial gazettes. Then there was government by announcement; orders appeared in newspapers. Then there were the quiet orders, the orders that were not published, that were within the bureaucracy, that were oral. And finally, there were no orders at all. Everybody knew what he had to do.[101]

A more recent work of Hilberg's, entitled, *Perpetrators, Victims, Bystanders: The Jewish Catastrophe, 1933-1945,* was the seminal piece that funneled historians' thinking into those categories. That writing prompted him to end his speeches by commanding the members of his audiences and wishing for them never to be perpetrators, never to be victims and never to be bystanders. While it was moving to hear him and to be commanded by one so authoritative, that particular blessing also seemed to strike the wrong chord. At base, one of the features that defines atrocity is the slipperiness of roles, the speed and simultaneity with which people could change roles, completely or only temporarily.

The rescuer, who can no longer bear the pressure of hiding three Jewish charges, and who turns them in for a few kilos of sugar, the commandant who discovers that his maid is hiding Jews in his own basement and who refrains from turning her in, the German guard who stands at the door of the gas chamber but who allows someone to leave, the child who turns in his parents for anti-Nazi sentiments, the mother who murders her children in a concentration camp: these kinds of instances point to the fluidity of perpetration, collaboration and bystanding, indeed the impossibility of drawing clear boundaries between them for very long.

Teaching Ideas

1. **Survey**: As an introduction to perpetrators, have your students survey their friends, parents and neighbors, asking such questions as: Are wartime atrocities inevitable? Are children more obedient than adults? Are women

---

[101]Raul Hilberg, as quoted in *Facing Evil with Bill Moyers,* (New York: Public Affairs Television, Inc., 1994)

less likely to murder than men? What do you think of when you hear the word, 'mass murderer'? Do you think of Nazis as 'mass murderers'? Do you agree or disagree with the following propositions: People are essentially good. People will necessarily be cruel to each other to get ahead in life. Have your students analyze the results. What percentage of people answer in what ways? Who seemed to answer what? Did adults answer differently than children? Did men answer differently than women? Do you suspect that the answers to these kinds of questions would be different in different countries, such as Israel, Germany, Japan? Why/Why not?

2. **Compare and Contrast**: Beginning with a summary and excerpts of Browning, Goldhagen and Gross' claims, ask your students to compare and contrast the accounts. Which explanation appeals to them most and why? How do they contradict and complement each other? Which explanation seems to treat the category of victims/survivors with the most honor and in what ways? Which of the explanations seems to fit the perpetrators of the *Einsatzgruppen* best? Why would Daniel Jonah Goldhagen's book have become a bestseller, especially in Germany, while Christopher Browning's book has remained mostly unknown, even today? Ask your students which of the explanations seems best suited to explaining individual perpetrators' behaviors.

For an example of an individual perpetrator's mindset, you may want to reference Gitta Sereny's fascinating book, **Into that Darkness**, which was based on extensive interviews with one perpetrator, Franz Stangl, who had been the commandant at both Treblinka and Sobibor camps. Sereny probed and probed in the interviews with Stangl to find out where his humanity lay, what he did at the moments when his conscience surfaced. One exchange went as follows:

> "There were so many children [gassed at Treblinka], did they ever make you think of your children, of how you would feel in the position of those parents?
>
> 'No,' he said slowly, 'I can't say I ever thought that way.' He paused. 'You see,' he then continued, still speaking with this extreme seriousness and obviously intent on finding a new truth within himself, 'I rarely saw them as individuals. It was always a huge mass. I sometimes stood on the wall and saw them in the tube [on the pathway to the gas chambers]. But—how can I explain it—they were naked,

packed together, running, being driven with whips like...' the sentence trailed off.

'Could you not have changed that?' I asked. 'In your position, could you not have stopped the nakedness, the whips, the horror of the cattle pens?'

'No, no, no. This was the system. ...It worked. And because it worked, it was irreversible.'"[102]

3. **Weighing Culpability**: Raul Hilberg was the first to conceptualize and write about Holocaust history in terms of the roles that have now come to dominate Holocaust scholarship: perpetrators, victims, and bystanders. In the chapter about perpetrators from his book by the same name, *Perpetrators, Victims, Bystanders: The Jewish Catastrophe, 1933-1945*, Hilberg provided eight examples of perpetrator categories: Hitler himself, the establishment, old functionaries, newcomers, zealots, physicians and lawyers, non-German governments, and non-German volunteers. This list alone attests to the wide variety of roles included in the category. Those who pulled the triggers were clearly perpetrators, but were those who denied refuge to Jews seeking their help? Were those who worked at the offices of the Zyklon B gas manufacturing plant? Which were collaborators, which perpetrators, which bystanders, when were they each, and how do you know?

As an introductory activity on perpetrators, have your students rank order a list of perpetrators, deciding individually which crimes are most heinous, etc. Then, have them discuss their individual lists, explaining their criteria for ordering. Your list could include, for example: Hitler, a German who served in the SS, a Christian who moves into a home abandoned by Jews, a worker in the plant that produces Zyklon B, a train driver who takes the 'trainloads' to an death camp, a diplomat for the Nazi government who served in Argentina, a doctor who served on the 'health courts' determining who should be forcibly sterilized or killed, a concentration camp commander. Where would you draw the line between perpetrators and bystanders? This activity can be extended by visual mapping the explanations for individual behavior onto the operations of collectives (See Teaching Idea #5).

4. **Letters to Perpetrators**: Have your students write a letter, imagining that it is addressed to a young person, their age, whom they know is considering participating in a hate crime, an act of violence, at the very least, an act of

---

[102]Gitta Sereny, *Into that Darkness*, (New York: Vintage, 1974), 201-202.

profound indifference. What would they write to such a person, drawing on what they know about why people commit such acts? Consider shuffling the letters, reading them aloud, anonymously, and analyzing them as a group. What are the strategies the letters seem to take? Are they preachy and dull as a result? How convincing are they? Based on your discussion, have your students design a serious ad campaign that they think might work.

5. **Visual Mapping:** In small groups, have your students create a metaphor or an analogy for the complex reasons that people perpetrate violence, and have them draw that metaphor on a piece of butcher paper, illustrating it any way they want. For example, what does a garden grown on hate look like? What is in the soil that grows it, what is in the air that surrounds the plants, what do the bulbs themselves consist of and what gets poured on? In thinking of a metaphor, they should consider: Why do people perpetrate atrocity? Under what conditions? Why do others allow it to happen? What helps people make different kinds of decisions when faced with similar circumstances?

6. **Collective Culpability:** Studying the Holocaust is certainly incomplete without an investigation into how communities, institutions and nations participated as how individuals did. Collaboration and bystanding took many forms at this level. As research projects, have students, in small groups or alone, examine the following topics, answering the questions of how the particular individual or group participated in genocide, whether it should be considered perpetration, collaboration or bystanding, at what points, and why. Some examples include: the SS, the *Gestapo*, the *Wermacht*, Vichy France, Swiss banks, Hungary, the Catholic Church, German doctors, and the American State Department.

7. **Jewish Texts:** In thinking about perpetrators and their collaborators, there are many Jewish texts that apply. You may want to start by considering two Biblical passages whose messages about human agency are opposed. In Deuteronomy, God commands people in the following way, implying that they choose their actions in the world: "I have put before you life and death, blessing and curse. Choose life—if you and your offspring would live—by loving the Lord your God, heeding His commands and holding fast to Him" (Deuteronomy 30: 19-20). By contrast, in Exodus, the Torah speaks of God hardening Pharaoh's heart, suggesting that in certain instances, God does intervene to limit human choice, human action. How

might your students reconcile these competing notions of Jewish agency? Or, conversely, is it important to reconcile them? Are there times when people have agency and other times they don't? In short, how do your students navigate the dilemma between the omniscience of God and human free will? Why doesn't cause and effect work in the ethical world? How do the Rabbis limit God? How do you understand human free will? Are we really free to choose our paths? Why would God give us choice? What is wrong with destiny? To extend this activity, think of Noah, (the builder of the ark). Was he a bystander to genocide, a rescuer only to his family and the ark full of animals, a collaborator with God?

8. **Simulations:** Before Philip Zimbardo retired from Stanford University's faculty, he was famous for his usage of simulations in teaching. One year, for example, he had a graduate student pose as a gun-waving, epithet-screaming, vengeance-seeking outsider, who, without warning, burst into the back of a large lecture hall. Screaming at Zimbardo who was standing on the stage of the lecture hall, the pretend perpetrator took his time, walking down the aisle before "shooting" Zimbardo in the stomach. No one in the crowded auditorium stopped him. No one ran to alert the campus police (who had been forewarned by Zimbardo). All the students sat in their seats, stunned by the unexpectedness of the events. Only after a few minutes did Zimbardo rise, and dramatically remark to the crowd something to the effect of, "If any of you thought you would never be a bystander if faced with the possibility, think again."

We are not recommending that you perform any such simulation. Not only is it deceitful to your students, but in the aftermath of school shootings like the one at Columbine (which Zimbardo's simulation preceded,) it's an actionable offense that could result in being fired. That said, it is a remarkable story to use in your teaching. Why did the students in that auditorium fail to respond? Make sure to break down the answers to include specific factors like the anonymity of large groups, the perils of interceding, the unexpectedness, etc. If you were hurt on a sidewalk and needed help from unknown crowds walking by, what does this simulation about bystander behavior imply you should do? (Do not call out to all those walking by; instead, target someone individually, "You in the blue coat, call 9-1-1.")

A fabulous substitute for actually performing a simulation, Simone's favorite film to teach about perpetrator, collaborator and bystander behavior is **A Class Divided**, a documentary about the blue-eyed/brown-eyed simulation performed by Jane Eliot while she was teaching in Riceville, Iowa. A careful analysis of this film allows viewers of all ages (fourth grade through adult) to understand the social dynamics of atrocity.

9. **Films:** Interestingly, there are fewer solid films that deal with perpetrators than there are about other topics, perhaps a kind of sign that people tend to think of perpetration as incomprehensible. There are, however, a few gems. The short film, **Heil, Hitler!** is fascinating for discussing perpetrators. Describing the story of one young man's heartfelt involvement with the *Hitlerjugend* (Hitler Youth), it begs the question of whether children ought to be considered culpable. **Joseph Schultz** is a short and very powerful video about a Nazi army soldier who is ordered to execute a group a innocent Yugoslavian villagers and refuses. While it wrongly gives the impression that those who refused such orders were always themselves executed, it nonetheless highlights the difficulties of refusing to obey an unjust order. And it is based on actual fact. Interspersed throughout the film are black and white images of the event, taken at the time it transpired. It's especially a good film to juxtapose with Christopher Browning's opening chapters (which are very readable for middle and high school students). Why is it surprising that those who didn't follow orders to execute innocents were not punished? What does it show about our own values and hopes for human behavior? **The Democrat and the Dictator: A Walk through the 20th Century** is a little slow, but very informative, contrasting portraits of Roosevelt and Hitler.

Resources for Teaching

A Class Divided. Website: http://www.pbs.org/wgbh/pages/frontline/shows/divided/. *This website houses the Frontline film in which Jane Eliot divides her kids into blue-eyed and brown-eyed kids. It's moving and fascinating, and despite the fact that it looks somewhat dated (made in 1968), all kids get involved in it quickly.*

The Democrat and the Dictator: A Walk through the 20th Century. Produced by PBS Video, 58 minutes. *A little slow, but very informative, contrasting portraits of Roosevelt and Hitler.*

Facing Evil with Bill Moyers. Public Affairs Television, Inc., 1994, 88 minutes. *An excellent resource for teachers and useful for excerpting in the classroom. It features interview segments with many luminary historians and writers facing the questions of evil, philosophically and ethically.*

Heil Hitler: Confessions of a Hitler Youth. Produced by HBO, 1992, 30 minutes. *A hauntingly powerful glimpse into the Hitler Youth movement as recalled by Alfons Heck.*

Joseph Schultz. Produced by Wombat Productions, 1973, 13 minutes. *A short and very powerful film about a Nazi army soldier who is ordered to execute a group an innocent Yugoslavian villagers and refuses.*

Obedience to Authority. Written by Stanley Milgram and published by Perennial Books, New York, 1983. *The black and white film of Stanley Milgram's experiments, of the same title, was shot in 1962, and though it is hard to find, sometimes public school video centers have copies. Penn State University Media Sales produced the film.*

The Stanford Prison Experiments. Website: http://www.prisonexp.org/. *Philip Zimbardo has written extensively about the Stanford Prison Experiments he conducted. The site includes a comprehensive and compelling video and text-illustrated tour of the experiments that. For more information about Zimbardo's outrageous list of publications, see his own website:* http://www.zimbardo.com/.

Resources for Further Learning

The Destruction of European Jewry. Written by Raul Hilberg and published by Holmes and Meier Publishers, New York, 1985. *The latest edition abridges the original three volume set.*

Hitler's Willing Executioners. Written by Daniel Jonah Goldhagen and published by Alfred Knopf, a division of Random House, New York, 1996. *A voluminous book, it's hard to excerpt easily for classroom use. Argues that the Germans were 'eliminationist anti-Semites,' almost destined to mass murder Jews.*

Masters of Death: The Einsatzgruppen and the Invention of the Holocaust. Written by Richard Rhodes and published by Alfred Knopf, New York, 2002. *A tremendously informative but emotionally difficult book to read. Not for use in classrooms.*

Neighbors. Written by Jan Gross and published by Princeton University Press, Princeton, 2001. *The book reconstructs the murder of a single town's Jewish population, the town of Jedwabne, Poland. Both the hard cover and soft-cover editions serve almost as memorial books in that a lengthy section of photographs is included.*

The Neighbors Respond: The Controversy over the Jedwabne Massacre in Poland. Edited by Antony Polonsky and Joanna B. Michlic and published by Princeton University Press, Princeton, 1994. *This book discusses the controversies that erupted after the publication of Jan Gross' book. Most interesting were the responses of some Polish intellectuals.*

Obedience. Written by Ian Parker, this article and published in *Granta* magazine issue 71, Autumn, 2000 (http://www.granta.com). *Includes an interview with one of Milgram's volunteers and discusses modern interest in Milgram's studies.*

Ordinary Men: Reserve Police Battalion 101 and the Final Solution in Poland. Written by Christopher Browning and published by HarperCollins, New York, 1992. *Explains how 'ordinary men' became field shooters, who participated, who declined to, and what happened as a result. Exceedingly readable.*

Perpetrators, Victims, Bystanders: Jewish Catastrophe 1933–1945. Written by Raul Hilberg and published by Aaron Asher Books, New York, 1992. *Both theorizes and gives a huge range of examples of behavior in each category.*

A Problem from Hell: America and the Age of Genocide. Written by Samantha Power and published by Basic Books, New York, 2002. *This book is the best single volume that has been written to date that documents America's roles in genocide. It's stunningly well-written and researched.*

An Uncommon Friendship: From Opposite Sides of the Holocaust. Written by Bernat Rosner and Frederic C. Tubach and published by University of California Press, Berkeley, 2001. *A moving account of a perpetrator and victim's stories, along with how they became lifelong friends.*

RESISTANCE

Portrait of Sara Ginaite, a partisan, at the liberation of Vilna. The photograph was taken by a Jewish, Soviet Major who was surprised to see a female Jewish partisan, August 10, 1944. USHMM, courtesy of Sara Ginaite.

esistance to the Holocaust came in many forms and occurred in many places. Types of resistance ranged from armed to unarmed and from spiritual to symbolic. It occurred in concentration and death camps, ghettos and forests, villages and town squares, on the ground and even from the sky—in the case of the parachutists from Palestine. Resistance efforts happened everywhere and anywhere Jews were victimized.

In thinking about resistance, people often assume the success of an act should be judged solely by whether the resistor indeed survived or saved the lives of others. However, it's important to remember that victimization necessarily means that victims have few, if any, opportunities or resources available to them. Moreover, victimization blunts people's very ability to resist. As a result, in thinking about this topic, we encourage you to value resistance efforts, not merely in terms of physical survival, but as symbolic acts in themselves. In other words, any act of resistance, however small, however futile, however unsuccessful is to be admired, whether it saved lives or not.

While overt opposition to the Nazis and their collaborators was risky because of the danger of reprisals, there are numerous examples of both armed and unarmed resistance efforts. In this chapter, we summarize the Warsaw Ghetto Uprising, the single, most celebrated act of armed resistance. We discuss the partisan movement and the parachutists from Palestine who tried to assist the partisans. We also discuss unarmed resistance efforts including those aimed at documenting what was happening and communicating to the outside world, spiritual and religious observance in the camps, and other so-called symbolic acts.

The big ideas of this chapter are that:

- Resistance efforts took many forms depending on the resources (or lack of resources) available.
- Acts of resistance were acts of heroism, regardless of their outcomes.

Key terms of this chapter include: armed resistance, partisans, Hannah Szenes, parachutists from Palestine, Warsaw Ghetto Uprising, Mordecai Anielewicz, unarmed resistance, Emmanuel Ringelblum, *Oneg Shabbat* Archive, psychological resistance, and religious resistance.

Armed Resistance

In practically every ghetto, labor camp and concentration camp and with limited resources, under horrific conditions, and unspeakable terror, underground groups committed acts of sabotage, organized escapes, collected arms, and plotted revolts. Two of the most notoriously horrific death camps, Sobibor and Treblinka, were put out of operation partly as a result of revolts carried out by Jewish underground resistance fighters. While other **armed resistance** efforts may not have been as "successful" as those at Sobibor and Treblinka, they are nonetheless heroic. While the Warsaw ghetto fighters manufactured and smuggled weapons into the ghetto, the underground movement in the Lachwa ghetto was unable to obtain even a single revolver. Nonetheless, the Jews of Lachwa staged a revolt by fighting with knives, cleavers and their bare hands. The following section focuses on three examples of armed resistance: the partisan movement, the parachutists from Palestine, and the Warsaw Ghetto Uprising.

Abba Kovner is perhaps the best-known partisan leader, yet there were thousands of other partisans as well. Frank Blaichman[103] was 16 years old when the German army invaded his small Polish town in September 1939. Prior to the invasion, Blaichman had lived a carefree life, experiencing few incidents of anti-semitism. Within months of the invasion, though, German officials issued a host of administrative decrees and regulations intended to isolate Jews, deprive them of their livelihoods, and dispossess them of their property. By 1942, the situation was dire: Blaichman and his neighbors suffered from hunger and disease; were terrorized by harassment, raids and random shootings; and heard more and more frequent rumors of mass killings and deportations to death camps. One of Blaichman's uncles was shot when the Germans searched his house and discovered fresh meat there.

In October 1942, as his family and neighbors were being forced onto trains with destinations unknown to them, Blaichman slipped away, hiding just outside of town. Hearing that there were Jews in a nearby forest, Blaichman made his way there where he found an encampment of more than a hundred Jews living in primitive conditions, sheltered in small bunkers that they had dug into the ground and padded with straw.

Soon after arriving at the encampment, Blaichman encouraged his comrades in the forest to fight against the Germans. "We had no firearms," says Blaichman, explaining, "The only thing we had was the will and the courage." Blaichman heard that there was a local farmer bragging that he had a hidden cache of guns. He went to the farmer's house accompanied by a companion who looked Russian. Wearing a Soviet paratrooper jacket he had found, Blaichman told the farmer he had just arrived from Moscow and they were there to organize a Polish partisan group. He asked the farmer to hand over his guns voluntarily, saying he and his companion would use force to get them if necessary. The farmer relinquished his hidden firearms and told Blaichman about a neighbor who also had a hidden cache of weapons. By night's end, Blaichman and his companion had obtained six rifles, ammunition, and a handgun. Blaichman eventually became the platoon commander of 100 young Jewish resistance fighters.

---

[103]The story about Frank Blaichman is excerpted in part from *Frank Blaichman: Jewish Platoon Commander, Study Guide* (San Francisco: Jewish Partisan Educational Foundation, 2003). Used with permission.

Blaichman's partisan group committed many acts of sabotage against the Germans. They dynamited bridges and railroad tracks, made hit-and-run attacks on trains carrying military supplies and soldiers to the front. They ambushed German trucks and military cars, and bombed the German headquarters in several towns in the area. Blaichman takes pride in the contribution his Jewish partisan unit made in the effort to defeat the Nazi war machine. When he reflects on the years spent as a resistance fighter, he says he is still astonished at how his small group of frightened and terrorized Jews became such a disciplined and courageous force. "I'm very proud of what I did all those years," he says. "The reality was we had nothing to lose, and our way to survive was to fight."

Blaichman was just one of 20,000 to 30,000[104] Jewish **partisans** in Europe who fought against the German military and its collaborators in World War II. Comprised mostly of teenagers and young adults, the partisans organized guerilla warfare inside occupied enemy territory. Strategically utilizing the dense woods to hide their encampments, they existed on meager food rations and built dugouts for shelter. They were constantly at risk of being discovered and killed, not only by Nazis and their sympathizers, but even by non-Jewish partisans, next to whom they fought. The partisan groups operated primarily in Eastern Europe and in the Balkan states, which had wide expanses of forests and swamps ideal for guerrilla warfare. There were also large numbers of Jews in partisan groups in France, Greece, and Italy.

It was extraordinarily difficult for most Jews to escape into the forest to become partisans in the first place. While approximately 10 percent of the entire partisan population was Jewish, the majority of partisan fighters were former Red Army soldiers who became partisans after the Germans attacked the Soviet Union. Most Jews were in partisan groups that were therefore a mix of Jews and non-Jewish Red Army soldiers. Many Jewish partisans in these groups were the victims of violent anti-Semitic harassment by their non-Jewish comrades whose primary goal was not to aid European Jews, but to free their countries from German rule. Blaichman's group was thus unusual in having been an all-Jewish group specifically formed to avoid such problems. It was also, therefore, able to protect hundreds of other Jews who hid in the forest and villages.

While partisans were relatively few in number, and most often vastly outnumbered and outgunned, they staged important resistance efforts by interfering with enemy communications, by cutting telephone, telegraph, and electrical lines, and by destroying power stations. They sabotaged transportation links by

---

[104]The U.S. Holocaust Museum website estimates that there were between 20,000 and 30,000 Jewish partisans, while historian, Ruben Ainsztein, in *Jewish Resistance in Nazi-Occupied Europe* (New York: Barnes and Noble, 1974) puts the number at 30,000.

blowing up bridges, roads, and railway equipment and destroyed factories that produced materials for the German war effort.

While these partisans fought the Nazis on the ground, other resistance fighters left the relative safety of Palestine and parachuted inside enemy lines to assist them. **Hannah Szenes** (pronounced Senesh) is the most famous of these **parachutists from Palestine**. Szenes was not only a fighter but a poet. Nearly every Jew in Israel can recite the four simple lines of the poem, *Blessed is the Match* that Szenes wrote shortly before she was executed. At nearly every Jewish summer camp and Jewish youth group, children sing *Eli Eli*, a song composed from one of Szenes' poems. As a young woman, as a fighter and as a Jew, Szenes has become a symbol of heroism and dedication for generations of young people.

Szenes was born in Budapest, Hungary, in 1921. Her parents, the playwright Bela Szenes and his wife Katherine, raised Szenes in a middle class, assimilated household. Though her father died when she was only six-years-old, Szenes inherited his literary talent and wrote plays performed at her school. At age 13, she began writing a diary about her daily life, her desire to become a professional writer, and her dreams of joining young Jewish pioneers in Palestine. In 1939, shortly after the outbreak of war in Europe, Szenes followed her dreams, leaving Hungary for Palestine.

After arriving in Haifa, Szenes studied at the Nahalal Agricultural School and continued her literary pursuits in Hebrew. In 1941, she joined *Kibbutz Sdot Yam*. Her diary from that time chronicles life in Palestine: the joy and hardships of living on a farming *kibbutz* and the influx of refugees under the British Mandate.

As troubling reports from war-torn Europe made their way to Palestine, Szenes grew increasingly concerned for the fate of the Jewish people. Determined to save her mother and other Jews in Eastern Europe, Szenes joined the Women's Auxiliary Air Force of the British Army in 1943. The British Army had decided to permit a limited number of Jewish volunteers to depart from Palestine and be dropped behind enemy lines in occupied Europe. Szenes was one of 37 Jewish volunteers chosen for the job. She entrusted her poems to a friend on the *kibbutz*, donned the code name "Hagar," and set out for training in Cairo.

The parachutists' mission was twofold, to notify the British of the placement of enemy camps in the Balkans and to rescue Jews from southeastern Europe by evacuating them into territories already liberated by the partisans. The British Army allowed Jewish partisans to parachute behind enemy lines because as émigrés from Europe they were familiar with the language and landscape of the countries into which they were being sent. As a paratrooper for the British

Special Operations Executive, in March 1944, Szenes flew with other paratroopers to Bari, Italy, and then parachuted into Slovenia. It is here that she wrote *Blessed is the Match* that memorializes her idealism and commitment. She spent three months with a partisan group, and then gave the poem to a fellow paratrooper before crossing into Hungary.

On June 7, 1944, at the height of the deportation of Hungarian Jews, Szenes entered Hungary. She was denounced the following day by an informer and taken to a Gestapo prison in Budapest. After four months of imprisonment and torture, she was executed, at the age of 23, shot by a firing squad.

Fellow prisoners and parachutists who survived report that while in captivity, Szenes refused to reveal any information about the resistance efforts. Defiant to the end, she chose to stare at her executors rather than be blindfolded. Out of a group of 37, she was one of seven parachutists killed.

Szenes was buried in the Martyr's Section of the Jewish Cemetery in Budapest. In 1950, hers and the other paratroopers' remains were transferred to the Israeli National Military Cemetery on Mt. Herzl near Jerusalem. Several monuments in her memory have since been erected throughout Israel, and numerous streets, settlements, a forest, and even a species of flower bear her name. A museum devoted to her memory was built at her former home on *Kibbutz Sdot Yam*.

Szenes' literary legacy far outlives her short military career. Her writing, diary, poetry and plays have been translated into several languages, and many of her poems, including *Eli Eli,* have been set to music. Her writings also provide primary source materials about Jewish life in Budapest during the rise of Nazism in Europe and the work of early Zionists in Palestine. She remains an inspiration to young writers and idealists, ensuring her place as an international heroine.

While the partisans and parachutists hid their whereabouts in order to fight, other Jews staged resistance efforts from inside ghetto walls. Between 1941 and 1943, about 100 Jewish groups formed underground, armed resistance movements in the Jewish ghettos throughout Eastern Europe. The most famous revolt staged by one of these groups is the **Warsaw Ghetto Uprising**, which has become a universal symbol for the invincibility of the human spirit.

The Warsaw Ghetto Uprising holds this distinct place in Holocaust history for three main reasons. It was the first major, urban revolt against German forces in all of occupied Europe. Second, despite the considerable odds against them, a bedraggled group of Jews fought off well-trained German troops and police for nearly a month, which was a longer period of time than it took the entire Polish army to be defeated by the Germans when they invaded Poland in 1939. In addition, the uprising was led mostly by a group of teenagers and young adults. Though tragic, their story is inspiring.

In the summer of 1942, the Germans deported at least 300,000 people from the Warsaw ghetto to Treblinka concentration camp. When reports of mass murder trickled back to the ghetto inhabitants, eventual deportation and inevitable death seemed a certainty for the 60,000 Jews who remained. In response, a group of young people formed an underground self-defense unit known as the Jewish Fighting Organization (in Polish, the *Zydowska Organizacja Bojowa* or Z.O.B). Led by 23-year-old **Mordecai Anielewicz**, the Z.O.B. issued a proclamation calling for the people in the ghetto to resist deportation.

In January 1943, the Germans tried to resume deporting Jews from the Warsaw ghetto. However, a group of Jewish fighters succeeded in thwarting the transport, forcing the Germans to suspend further round ups. Encouraged by their success, members of the Z.O.B. began to construct subterranean bunkers and shelters in preparation for an all-out uprising.

Equipped with extensive weaponry, German troops and police entered the ghetto on April 19, 1943 —the eve of Passover—with orders to rid the ghetto of all of its remaining Jews. To the Germans' shock, though, they were met by Jewish resistance fighters armed with Molotov cocktails, hand grenades, bombs, rifles, and pistols. Hiding behind windows, balconies, and in attics, the Jewish resistance fighters bombarded the German forces as they entered the ghetto, seeming to attack from all angles by quickly repositioning themselves via the underground tunnels. Despite their inadequate weapons and scarce ammunition, the Jewish fighters utterly stunned the German military, and at the end of the first day of the uprising, jubilant Jewish fighters celebrated the first night of Passover.

The Nazi command had presumed that the 'liquidation' of the Warsaw ghetto would last no more than three days; in the end, it took nearly a month and significantly more force and resources than planned. In the end, the Nazi forces 'won' not by superior fighting force, but by razing the ghetto, building by building. On May 16, 1943, the Germans destroyed the Great Synagogue on Tlomacki Street in Warsaw, leveling it to the ground. Though the ghetto was eventually fully destroyed and the few remaining Jews who were not burned along with the buildings were routed out of hiding, word of the Warsaw Ghetto Uprising spread to other ghettos and to the partisans in the forest, providing inspiration and encouragement.

Unarmed Resistance

While perhaps not nearly as tangible as acts of armed resistance, **unarmed resistance** is equally dramatic, inspirational and heroic. Unarmed resistance efforts spanned a gamut from devising and implementing escape plans and spreading information about the death camps, to subtle and symbolic acts like observing Jewish rituals in secrecy or outright acts of martyrdom. Countless Jews, starved to the point of near death, chose to fast on *Yom Kippur* rather than eat the morsels of stale bread offered to them. Legend has it that the Jewish slaves forced to erect the infamous sign above the gates of Auschwitz that reads, *"ARBEIT MACHT FREI"*—work sets you free—inverted the capital letter B as a (literal) sign of resistance, testament to the lie inherent in the Nazi slogan. Jews also created vast, underground economies in resistance to Nazi regulations. Illegal mills and workshops served clandestine marketplaces, and ghetto inhabitants smuggled food and other goods into and out of ghetto walls. Sometimes Jewish slave laborers worked slowly or purposely damaged equipment at their factories.

Some argue, and we agree, that the very attempt to remain humane while surrounded by inhumanity is a powerful act of resistance itself. For many Jews living in Nazi occupied Europe during these years, holding onto their dignity and respect for humanity was their only available means of resistance, no matter how temporary or even illusory.

By 1933 in Germany, it was dangerous to be a member of an opposition party or even to speak out against Nazism. By mid-July of that year, all opposition parties had either been outlawed or had been harassed so much that they dissolved themselves. Only a handful of opposition groups continued to operate clandestinely, transforming themselves into underground resistance organizations that provided food, received and transmitted news and information. While opposition newspapers were forbidden, almost every underground party published one. And while the penalty for possession of a radio was death, in the Lodz Ghetto, an underground group successfully operated a radio listening post for years. Fearing that the world would never know about the atrocities inflicted by the Third *Reich*, countless Jews managed to chronicle the events they witnessed and experienced to serve as testimony for future generations.

Emmanuel Ringelblum, a Jewish historian and resistance fighter who perished during the Warsaw Ghetto Uprising, chronicled the lives of Jews in Warsaw before his death. Combined in a diary called the **Oneg Shabbat** Archive (Delight of the Sabbath Archive), Ringelblum and other underground activists collected testimonies from Jews and reported on the actions of the Nazis. Towards the end of the Warsaw ghetto's existence, Ringelblum and his comrades had the Polish underground workers smuggle into London evidence that documented Jewish deportations and murder. Some say that this was how London, the whole of England and the rest of the world first learned about the Chelmno extermination camp, having seen a detailed report on the deportation of 300,000 Jews from Warsaw. Ringelblum was executed by the Nazis at the end of the Warsaw Ghetto Uprising. Before his death, he buried three milk cans containing the *Oneg Shabbat* Archive, hoping they would be recovered when the war ended. Two of the milk cans were unearthed post-war, providing firsthand accounts and primary source documentation of life in the ghetto. The third milk can was never found.

Before dying of starvation in the Terezin Concentration Camp in Czechoslovakia, Mina Pachter compiled a handwritten book of recipes and entrusted it to a friend, imploring him, if he survived, to deliver it to her daughter, Anny, in Palestine. Pachter had earlier refused to escape with Anny, believing that the Nazis would never hurt an old woman. Once imprisoned in the camp, Pachter and other older Jews suffered intensely as they were given less food than younger Jews because the Nazis considered them to be closer to death and not worth feeding. The man to whom Pachter entrusted her collection survived and settled in Czechoslovakia. Sadly, after the war he was unable to locate Anny. He kept the manuscript for 15 years, and when a cousin mentioned that she was headed to Israel, he gave it to her. She took it with her, only to learn that Anny had moved to New York. Another 10 years passed before Anny was found. Twenty-five years after her mother died of starvation at Terezin, Anny got a phone call from a stranger, saying, "Hello. Is this Anny Stern? I've got a package for you from your mother." The collection of recipes was published as the book, *In Memory's Kitchen: A Legacy from the Women of Terezin*. The collection of recipes was heralded as a profound act of **psychological resistance**. A way for the older women to remember their past lives, a time when they fed others and fed themselves, the cookbook became a way for them to perpetuate their traditions even as they themselves were murdered.

Other Jews resisted by observing their religious traditions in secret. Individual praying, collective worship and religious study continued clandestinely throughout Nazi occupied Europe. One form of **religious resistance** has since been incorporated into the literary genre of Hasidic tales that grew out of the movement in the early 1800s.

Hasidic tales flourished in this era, the stories emerging from the ghettos, forests and camps. In the aftermath of the Holocaust, author Yaffa Eliach interviewed survivors, turning their stories into original Hasidic tales, many of which provide illuminating examples of religious resistance. In one story, for example, *The First Hanukah Light in Bergen Belsen*, Eliach retells a story of the Grand Rabbi of Bluzhov when he was a prisoner in that camp. The German commandants had just committed a brutal massacre, leaving behind piles of dead bodies. That evening was the first night of *Hanukkah*. With no oil, no candles, and no *hanukkiah*, Rabbi Bluzhov used shoes as containers, strings from a concentration camp uniform as a wick, and camp shoe polish as oil. He proceeded to lead his fellow inmates in reciting the blessings in celebration of *Hanukkah*.

Rabbi Ephraim Oshry was a young rabbinical scholar in Kaunas (also known as Kovno), the second largest city in Lithuania, when the Germans invaded in 1941. The Nazis forced Rabbi Oshry to work as the custodian of a warehouse where Jewish books and objects were being stored for a planned exhibit on 'artifacts of the extinct Jewish race.' Rabbi Oshry surreptitiously used the books to render interpretations of religious law for the town's ghettoized Jewish community. He carefully recorded the questions posed to him and his responses, writing them on bits of paper torn from cement sacks he was forced to carry. He buried these scraps in tin cans. After the war, the **responsas** were dug up and compiled into five volumes, two of which later won the National Jewish Book Award. Rabbi Oshry firmly believed that the persistence of Jewish life amidst the Holocaust represented the most important kind of resistance against the Nazis. Many Jews might not survive, he said, but Judaism would.

Teaching Ideas

1. **Poetry of Hannah Szenes:** Hannah Szenes' poems are filled with hope for the future and optimism for humanity. Read some of her poems, in particular *Blessed is the Match* and *Eli Eli* and have your students interpret and discuss their meanings. How might the same words, written under different circumstances, have been meaningful in the same way? Szenes' literary work can be accessed via the **Hannah Senesh Legacy Foundation** website.

2. **Discussion Prompts**: The history of the Holocaust, particularly resistance efforts, raises many important ethical questions that pose no easy answers. The following questions are intended to challenge beliefs and assumptions, to deepen and broaden learning, and to personalize the topic. You can

adapt the following ethical questions to the age of your students and you can deepen their learning by connecting the ethical dilemmas to religious sources on the topic.

a. The Jewish partisans struggled daily to survive, which meant making difficult choices on a constant basis. For instance, in the face of possible starvation, many partisans stole food or other supplies necessary for their survival. Is breaking national laws or breaking one of the Ten Commandments justified in this kind of scenario? Is there a difference between breaking a secular law and a Jewish law? Why/why not?

b. All of the Jewish resistance fighters took tremendous risks in order to survive. Have your students describe a situation in their lives in which they took risks for a cause they believe in. In what ways are the situations comparable and incomparable? What do those similarities and differences tell us about understanding people who lived in the past?

c. Parachutists came out of relative safety in Palestine and entered the war zone. Why do you think they risked their lives to save others? Was it right to do so? Why and why not?

d. In the aftermath of the Holocaust, unarmed resistance efforts were not as celebrated or as well documented as armed resistance efforts. Many Orthodox Jews opposed the use of physical force and viewed prayer and religious observances as the best form of resistance, while others believed that the only way to resist was to fight back. Do you think that one form of resistance should be valued over another or even compared to another? Why/why not?

3. ***Oneg Shabbat* Archive:** Read and discuss excerpts from Emmanuel Ringelblum's *Oneg Shabbat* Archive. You may choose to give different excerpts to different small groups, making sure they understand when it was written, what it describes, and what it means about life in the Warsaw ghetto. When all the students feel they have mastered their excerpt, have the students jigsaw so that one member from each document group is a member of a new group. Ask these new groups to share their documents and to see what the array of documents indicates about the life of the ghetto as a whole. Ask your students to ponder why they think the underground activists called the collection the *Oneg Shabbat* (Delight of the Sabbath) Archive. You can access the Archive at the **U.S. Holocaust Memorial Museum** website and at the **Ghetto Fighters House** website.

4. **Art Exploration:** Study Holocaust-era art as a form of spiritual resistance. You may then ask your students to create art responsas of their own. **Spiritual Resistance: Art from Concentration Camps** is a moving collection of drawings and paintings that serve as powerful examples of spiritual resistance. Another resource for this activity is **Learning about the Holocaust through Art**, an extensive on-line collection of Holocaust-era art that includes high-quality images and full documentation-artist biographies, articles on the camps and ghettos, and educational resources.

5. **Books and Films:** Based on the real life stories of resistance fighters, **Uncle Misha's Partisans** by Yuri Suhl is a fictional account of a 12-year-old Ukrainian boy who joins the partisan movement. The story is suspenseful and historically accurate, yet Suhl avoids disturbing details making it an appropriate read for elementary school students. Most of the folktales in **Hasidic Tales of the Holocaust** by Yaffa Eliach can be read as portraits of acts of unarmed resistance. While the collection is not specifically written for children, the tales are short, often only a page or two, and are not overly graphic. They therefore lend themselves easily to classroom reading and discussion. Similarly, **In Memory's Kitchen** can be read in short sections and is appropriate for middle and high school students. There are some good videos that tell the story of the partisan movement including: **Come and See** about Russian partisans, **The Partisans of Vilna**, and **Resistance: Untold Stories of Jewish Partisans.** Finally, if you would like your students to look at a variety of brief partisans' stories and video clips, see the **Jewish Partisan Educational Foundation** website.

Resources for Teaching

Come and See. Directed by Elem Klimov and released by Kino Video, 1985, 78 minutes. *A good film about the Russian partisan movement, in Russian with English subtitles.*

Hannah Senesh Legacy Foundation. Website: www.hannahsenesh.org.il. *Includes Hannah's literary work and information about* Beit Hannah, *a culture center established in her memory by members of* Kibbutz Sdot Yam.

Hasidic Tales of the Holocaust. Retold by Yaffa Eliach and published by Vintage Books, New York, 1982. *A collection of 89 short folktales that provide inspirational glimpses into the Hasidic experience during the Holocaust era.*

In Memory's Kitchen: A Legacy from the Women of Terezin. Edited by Cara Desilva, translated by Bianca Steiner Brown and published by Jason

Aronson Inc., New York, 1996. *A collection of recipes created out of the memories of women imprisoned in the Terezin Concentration Camp in Czechoslovakia.*

Jewish Partisan Educational Foundation (JPEF). Website: www.jewishpartisans.org. *JPEF provides an in-depth, on-line educational resource of the Jewish partisan movement. The website includes study guides, discussion questions and activities, along with videos of original interviews with partisans including Frank Blaichman. JPEF can also assist educators with arranging for partisans or educators to speak at your school.*

Learning about the Holocaust through Art. Website: http://art.holocaust-education.net. *Produced by World ORT in conjunction with Beit Lohamei Haghetaot. An extensive online collection of Holocaust-era art that includes high-quality images and full documentation including artist biographies, articles on the camps and ghettos, and educational resources.*

***Oneg Shabbat* Archive.** Websites: U.S. Holocaust Memorial Museum, www.ushmm.org and Ghetto Fighters' House, http://english.gfh.org.il/. *Includes excerpts of the* Oneg Shabbat *Archive and photographs of the milk jugs where they were hidden, Emmanuel Ringelblumand other underground activists.*

Resistance: Untold Stories of Jewish Partisans. PBS Home Video, 2002, 60 minutes. *Interviews with former partisans and survivors. The clips of Frank Blaichman are particularly moving.*

Spiritual Resistance: Art from Concentration Camps. From the collection of *Kibbutz Lohamei Haghetaot*, Israel, with essays by Miriam Novitch, Lucy Dawidowicz and Tom L. Freudenheim and published by the Jewish Publication Society of America, Philadelphia, 1981. *A moving collection of drawings and paintings that serve as powerful examples of spiritual resistance.*

The Partisans of Vilna. National Center for Jewish Film, 1986, 130 minutes. *Includes interviews with survivors. Especially poignant is clip of partisan leader, Abba Kovner telling his story. A shorter, edited school version of the video is also available.*

Uncle Misha's Partisans. Written by Yuri Suhl and published by Four Winds Press, New York, 1973. *A suspenseful and historically accurate fictional account of a 12-year-old Ukrainian boy who joins the partisan movement.*

Resources for Further Learning

Blessed is the Match: The story of Jewish Resistance. Written by Marie Syrkin and published by The Jewish Publication Society of America, Philadelphia, 1980. *First published in 1947,* Blessed is the Match *is a compilation of interviews with partisan leaders, ghetto fighters and parachutists from Palestine.*

The Defiant. Written by Shalom Yaron and published by Square One Publishers, Garden City Park, NY, 2003. *When Shalom Yaron was 17-years-old, his parents were* *killed by the Nazis. For the next three years he fought as a partisan along with his brother, Musio. The Defiant is his personal memoir chronicling their experiences as resistance fighters.*

Fighters Among the Ruins: The Story of Jewish Heroism During World War II. Written by Yisrael Gutman and published by B'nai B'rith Books, Washington, D.C., 1988. *Highlights the stories of Jewish heroism during World War II.*

They Fought Back: The story of the Jewish Resistance in Nazi Europe. Edited by Yuri Suhl and published by Schocken Books, New York, 1975. *One of the foremost anthologies detailing the various forms of Jewish resistance during World War II.*

RESCUE

Danish-Jewish children in a Swedish children's home, after their escape from Denmark, Oesterskar, Sweden, 1943–1944. USHMM, courtesy of Frihedsmuseet.

Much of Holocaust study is devoted to the horrors of the Holocaust—the crimes of the Nazis and their collaborators, the treatment of the victims who suffered mercilessly. This chapter is devoted to another aspect of the Holocaust: the stories of rescuers.

Rescuers were men, women, and even children, laborers, farmers, intellectuals, and diplomats. For the most part, rescuers did not regard their actions as heroic. On the contrary, they were faced with unexpected situations that demanded immediate action, and they felt compelled to assist. Rescue during the Holocaust was a humane response to inhumane times. However, like most things in life, the issue of rescue is complicated, messy, and even controversial.

Non-Jews who saved Jewish lives during the Holocaust are called in Hebrew, *hasidei umot haolam*—**Righteous Among the Nations** (sometimes referred to as Righteous Gentiles). In English, the word righteous implies acting in a morally upright or just way. However, the Hebrew word *hasidei* comes from the root *hesed* meaning goodness or kindness. Predating the Holocaust, the term, *hasidei umot haolam,* originally referred to certain non-Israelite tribes whose members treated Israelites with kindness in Biblical times. Implied in this choice of terminology, then, is the idea that rescuers aided Jews out of the goodness of their hearts, out of a generalized sense of human kindness. In actuality, the intentions of rescuers spanned a huge range of human feelings.

Some rescuers helped Jews because they believed in equality for all humanity; some, though, were antisemitic, assisting Jews simply as a means to oppose German goals. While some rescuers saved Jews out of the goodness of their hearts, others saved Jews to in order to charge money. Consider Oskar Schindler, who, thanks to Steven Spielberg, is now the most famous rescuer. Schindler initially was motivated to rescue Jews not because of a sense of morality, but out of sheer greed. Even those who rescued Jews because they believed it was good did not necessarily act in ways we would consider good. Corrie ten Boom's evangelical Christian family hid Jews in their watch shop and home in the Netherlands in order to 'save' them, that is, in order to convert them to Christianity. As a young girl during the war years, Debbie's aunt Fanny was hidden in a Belgian convent. Rather than preserving Fanny's Jewish identity, the nuns raised her as a Catholic, preparing her to become a nun as well. When the war ended, one of Fanny's uncles who had survived came to find her. The nuns refused to hand Fanny over to him, however, and went so far as to file a custody lawsuit. Eventually, the nuns lost, and Fanny was rejoined with the few surviving members of her original family.

Despite this range of motivations, rescuers who helped Jews in Nazi-occupied Europe did so under the threat of persecution themselves and under the constant danger of informers betraying them. In most cases, rescue efforts involved providing a hiding place for Jews, whether temporarily or long-term. In some cases, though, individuals aided Jews already in hiding by bringing them food, supplies and information. Other rescuers helped by providing forged documents, enabling members of targeted populations to live under false identities. Rescuers and resistance members also smuggled people across national borders to neutral countries or simply safer locales.

Tragically, the number of people who tried to save Jews during the Holocaust is remarkably small. Moreover, the number of lives they saved is tiny when compared to the millions who were murdered. However, according to Jewish tradition, acts of rescue are indeed acts of righteousness. As the Talmud teaches, "Whoever destroys a soul, it is considered as if he destroyed an entire world. And whoever saves a life, it is considered as if he saved an entire world."[105] Because, according to the Biblical account in Genesis, the entire world was created from a first human being, each human being contains an entire world. While each life rescued during the Holocaust thus marks a tremendous accomplishment, it's hard not to ask how many more might have been saved if more people tried to help. The question is important to ask as it intensifies the reverence afforded to those who did help, at great risk to themselves and their families.

Historian Henry R. Huttenbach implores us to remember that amidst the sea of non-Jewish neighbors who turned against their Jewish friends or turned in their Jewish acquaintances, "in this morally depraved Europe, there were islands of exceptions."[106] This chapter focuses on those islands of exceptions. As with the other chapters in this book, we urge educators to portray rescue honestly, that is, not as merely good or bad, but rather in all of its heartwarming and heartbreaking shades of grey.

The big ideas of this chapter are that:

- Although the number of non-Jews who saved Jews during the Holocaust is small, according to Jewish tradition, their acts of bravery are akin to saving all of humanity.

- Rescue efforts shouldn't be judged by their outcomes. In other words, in historical perspective, the very act of attempting to rescue is admirable in and of itself.

- Rescue efforts were big and small, planned and unplanned. In a few cases, entire communities worked together to rescue Jews. In other cases, the minor remark of one individual meant the difference between life and death for another.

- Rescue wasn't always selfless, moral or good.

Key terms of this chapter include: *hasidei umot haolam*—Righteous Among the Nations, Le Chambon-Sur Lignon, Danish resistance, *Kindertransport,* and Raoul Wallenberg.

---

[105]Jerusalem Talmud, Sanhedrin 4:1 (22a)

[106]Henry R. Huttenbach, *Destruction of the Jewish Community of Worms, 1933-1945: A Study of the Holocaust Experience in Germany,* (Memorial Committee of Jewish Victims of Nazism from Worms, 1982), 69.

Rescue Efforts and Operations

Most rescue efforts involved many people working together within a network to save Jewish lives. In rare instances, though, these networks involved the populations of entire villages, towns or in one case, almost the entire country. The townspeople of **Le Chambon-Sur Lignon** in Southern France, for example, rescued some 3,000–5,000 Jews, both those from their own and neighboring towns and those who came seeking refuge. Le Chambon's Protestant pastor Andre Trocme and his wife Magda encouraged their congregants to hide Jews in their homes, farms and public institutions. They themselves were Hugenots, a Protestant sect that had endured persecution. The tight-knit community followed the Trocme's moral leadership, taking in Jewish adults, families and children and hiding them, in some cases, for years. Volunteers from Le Chambon risked their own lives on dangerous journeys through the French countryside to smuggle Le Chambon's Jews into neutral Switzerland. Pastor Trocme's cousin, Daniel, ran a home in which he hid Jewish children, was found out and deported with the children to Buchenwald concentration camp. After the war, 32 people from Le Chambon, including Pastor Trocme, his wife, Magda, and their cousin, Daniel, were honored by *Yad Vashem* as Righteous Among the Nations.

The degree of Nazi control in various European countries was a significant factor in how Jews were treated by their fellow countrymen. When the German army occupied Denmark on April 9, 1940, for example, the Danes agreed to surrender peaceably on the condition that they be allowed to continue running their own government and army and that Danish Jews would be protected from discrimination. Moreover, **Danish resistance** organizations avowed their commitment to protect Danish Jews. For the next few years, Denmark's 7,800 Jews remained relatively safe from their Nazi enemies.

By the spring of 1943, however, the situation was deteriorating. By August of that year, the Danish government could no longer meet the Nazis' legislative demands, such as the requirement that any Dane found to be involved in resistance work be put to death. As a result, the Danish government resigned, the king was placed under house arrest, and the Nazis declared martial law. By October, the German police secretly laid out plans to deport Denmark's Jews. Just days before the deportations were to begin, Georg Ferdinand Duckwitz, a German delegation attaché, leaked word of the impending roundup to a few key Danish politicians who, in turn, warned the Jewish community.

The Danes reacted quickly on all fronts. Neighbors hid Jews in their homes. Doctors falsified documents and hid Jews in hospitals. Clergy sheltered Jews in churches. Under cover of darkness, Danish resistance groups and fishermen ferried Jews into neutral Sweden where the Swedish government announced it would welcome all Danish refugees. Within three weeks, in fact, some 7,200 Danish Jews and about 700 of their non-Jewish relatives made it safely to Sweden. Even after the daring rescue, Danish political parties publicly denounced the Nazi campaign and underground newspapers encouraged the Danes to stand in solidarity with their Jewish countrymen. The bishop of Copenhagen prepared a document denouncing the persecution of Jews, which was sent to Nazi officials and read aloud from church pulpits during services.

Although some 500 Danish Jews were arrested by the Nazis and sent to Theresienstadt, as a direct result of the Danish government's unrelenting pressure and public protest, most of those arrested eventually made it to Sweden. After the war, too, the Jewish Danes who returned to Denmark received a warm welcome. In contrast to all other Nazi-occupied countries, Denmark's citizens had cared for their Jewish neighbors' homes, kept their belongings intact and allowed them to return to their previously held jobs. As a result of Denmark's exceptional response to its Jewish brethren, *Yad Vashem* declared the entire country's people to be Righteous Among the Nations.

The **_Kindertransport_** (children's transport) was the informal name of a rescue effort that brought thousands of Jewish children to Great Britain between 1938 and 1940. Soon after *Kristallnacht*, the British government eased its immigration restrictions for children only and allowed an unspecified number of children under the age of 17 to enter the country from Germany and Nazi-occupied territories. Parents or guardians were not allowed to accompany their children, and the British government permitted the temporary immigration only on the condition that all costs related to their care, education, and eventual emigration from Great Britain would be fully paid for. Jewish organizations and individuals guaranteed to cover the costs, and the children's parents made the agonizing decision to send their children away, fully expecting that they would be reunited soon. Most of the children, of course, never saw their families again.

The majority of the *Kindertransports* departed by train from Berlin, Vienna, Prague, and other major cities in central Europe and stopped in Belgium and the Netherlands. From there, the children sailed to Harwich, England, where about half went to live in London with sponsors who served as their foster families. The others were housed in summer camp facilities or lived in group homes. After the war, many children from the *Kindertransport* operation became British citizens or immigrated to Israel, the United States, Canada, or Australia. The operation rescued nearly 10,000 children.

The *Kindertransport* operation, the rescue efforts of Denmark and Le Chambon illustrate large-scale operations involving many individuals working in solidarity to save Jews. Other rescue efforts were smaller in scale, though they still carried great impacts.

Raoul Wallenberg was a Swedish diplomat assigned as first secretary to the Swedish legation in Budapest, Hungary. He is credited with protecting tens of thousands of Hungarian Jews from deportation to the Auschwitz-Birkenau extermination camp. He did so by issuing Swedish protective passports to Budapest's Jews and by personally removing Jews already on the trains bound for Auschwitz. He also established protective hospitals, nurseries, and a soup kitchen, and he set up more than 30 safe houses for Jews. In time, other diplomats joined Wallenberg's rescue efforts. Swiss diplomat, Carl Lutz issued emigration certificates so that nearly 50,000 Jews in Budapest were under Swiss protection. Giorgio Perlasca, an Italian businessman, posed as a Spanish diplomat and issued forged Spanish visas for Jews. Wallenberg vanished in January 1945 after being summoned by Soviet officials. A month after his disappearance, Soviet forces liberated Budapest, where more than 100,000 Jews remained, mostly due to the efforts of Wallenberg and his colleagues. While Wallenberg's fate was unknown for a long time, the opening of Soviet archives in 1989 revealed that he died in a Soviet prison.

While Wallenberg was able to save thousands of Jews by utilizing his political clout, most rescuers had fewer resources available to them. Varian Fry was an American journalist sent to France by the Emergency Rescue Committee. While there he worked tirelessly, forging documents for refugees and setting up the American Relief Center, which aided approximately 2,000 Jews and non-Jews to escape. Among those Fry helped rescue are Marc Chagall, Heinrich Mann and Max Ernst. Anna Borkowska was the mother superior of a small cloister of Dominican sisters in Lithuania. In 1941, Borkowska agreed to hide 17 Jewish Zionist youth in her convent. She also helped smuggle weapons into the Vilna ghetto. Abraham Sutzkever, the Yiddish poet, recounted that the first four grenades received in the Vilna ghetto were a gift from this mother superior. Borkowska was arrested in September 1943 by the German police and eventually released. The convent was subsequently closed, and the sisters, dispersed. Jean Kowalyk Berger and her family hid 14 Jews in an attic concealed behind a false wall that Berger and her mother had built for that purpose in their home in the Ukraine. They hid the group for two long years. After the war ended, Berger married one of the Jews she had helped rescue. Fearing the antisemitism they would continue to face there, they left the Ukraine and moved to the U.S.A.

Teaching Ideas

1. **Definition of Rescuers:** Some historians limit the definition of rescuers to non-Jews, while others include Jewish rescuers. The following section details the controversy.

   Yad Vashem,[107] the organization and site in Jerusalem that commemorate victims of the Holocaust, has recognized more than 19,000 men and women as rescuers. The Holocaust and Heroism Memorial Act enacted by the Israeli parliament in 1953, established *Yad Vashem* as the official, state memorial to the Holocaust. In so doing, the Israeli parliament stipulated that *Yad Vashem* honor the Righteous Among the Nations, whom it defined as non-Jews who risked their lives, freedom, and safety in order to rescue one or several Jews from the threat of death or deportation to death camps, without exacting monetary compensation.

   These criteria are somewhat controversial for at least three reasons. First, they limit those who may be considered Righteous Among the Nations to those who risked their lives in their rescue efforts. However, as Holocaust historian Martin Gilbert argues, "a single act, even a single remark could save a life—as when a Polish peasant woman, hearing her fellow villagers say, of four- or five-year old Renee Lindenberg, 'throw her into the well', replied: 'She's not a dog after all', and Renee was saved."[108]

   Second, *Yad Vashem*'s criteria limit the possible title of Righteous Among the Nations to non-Jews. Marion P. van Binsbergen Pritchard, who was honored by *Yad Vashem* as a Righteous person, argues that limiting the definition this way perpetuates the notion of Jews as victims only. She says, "There were many Jews who found a way to save other people's lives for whom it would have been much safer to maintain a low profile, and yet that is not what they chose to do. Many Jews were courageous rescuers, and many did not survive just because they decided to try to save other Jews. I

---

[107]*Yad Vashem*—literally means a hand and a name; figuratively, a monument and a memorial. The words are taken from the book of Isaiah (56:5): "I will give them, in My House and within My walls, a monument and a name better than sons and daughters. I will give them an everlasting name which shall not perish." In his book, *The Israelis and the Holocaust,* Thomas Segev notes that it is a problematic verse, since it argues that the "everlasting name" will be "better than sons and daughters"—that is, better than life itself. The verse is carved in the yard of *Yad Vashem* in huge stone letters, but instead of the words "better than sons and daughters" there is a discreet ellipsis.

[108]Martin Gilbert, *The Righteous: The Unsung Heroes of the Holocaust* (New York: Henry Holt and Company, 2003), xvi-xvii.

believe they should be honored the same as a non-Jew who tried to rescue Jews."[109] Simone's grandmother, Dora, a wealthy woman who owned a successful rag business in Strasbourg, handed out money to Jewish refugees streaming into Marseilles in hopes of leaving Europe. She also bribed an official, paying him to release a group of Jews from a French transit camp. While she was thus able to save most of her nephews who had been rounded up, she was also able to save Jews she had never met and didn't know.

Third, *Yad Vashem* limits the definition of rescuers to those working inside enemy territory as efforts to rescue Jews from outside Nazi-occupied Europe were few and far between.

Ask your students to debate the merits of these criteria and to argue for a different definition of rescue during the Holocaust. Should both Jews and non-Jews be considered Righteous Among the Nations? Why or why not? Should those who charged money to rescue be considered Righteous? Should those who risked nothing but saved lives?

2. **Jewish Rescuers:** When the Holocaust began, Alicia Appleman Jurman was a nine-year-old Jewish girl growing up in the southeastern Polish city of Buczacz. Alicia fled the Nazis through the forests and wheat fields and saved other Jews along the way. At the end of the war, at age 15, she went on to risk her life again by leading Jews along an underground route from Poland to Palestine. Her autobiography, **Alicia: My Story**, is an engaging read for teenagers and portrays first-hand the story of a Jewish rescuer. Use a brief excerpt from the book to discuss the perils of both being rescued and acting as a rescuer.

3. **Ethical Dilemmas**: The following three stories raise ethical questions that challenge our assumptions and broaden our understandings of the complexities of rescue during the Holocaust. Ask your students to explore the ethical issues raised by these stories. You can deepen the Jewish learning by connecting these ethical dilemmas to Jewish sources related to the topic. (See the Resources for Teaching section below for a complete list of books and websites that include testimonies, artifacts and photos connected to these rescuers.)

   • **Irene Opdyke** is a Polish Catholic who was honored by *Yad Vashem* as a Righteous Among the Nations for saving Jews when she was a young nursing student. Opdyke hid 12 Jews in the Ukrainian villa of Eduard Rugemer, an elderly SS officer who employed her as his

---

[109]The Simon Wiesenthal Center, website: http://motlc.wiesenthal.org/text/x00/xm0027.html, Los Angeles, 1997.

housekeeper. The Jews hid in the attic when Rugemer was downstairs and in the cellar when he was upstairs, until one day they were accidentally discovered. Opdyke pleaded with Rugemer not to turn them in to the Gestapo. He agreed, on the condition that Opdyke become his mistress. In order to save them, she acquiesced.

Why do you think Opdyke agreed to become Rugemer's mistress? On what basis was the trade-off worthwhile? Have your students describe a situation in their lives where they took a risk for a particular cause in which they believed. What was the result? What was the trade-off? How is it comparable and incomparable to Opdyke's situation?

- **Marion P. van Binsbergen Pritchard** was born in Amsterdam in 1920. When she was 22 years old she was asked by friends in the resistance movement to help hide Freddie Pollak and his three small children. She arranged for them to hide in a house in the country and brought them food and supplies on the weekends. A year later, she moved into the house to better care for them. The family hid in a basement crawlspace underneath the floorboards. One night four Germans and a Dutch policeman searched the house, but didn't find them. However, a short time later the local policeman returned alone. He knew that if you returned a short time after a raid, you might catch those hiding in the house. When the policeman came back, the family was indeed already outside their hiding place. Certain of the fate that awaited the Pollak family, Pritchard shot and killed the policeman. An undertaker helped her by concealing the body in the coffin of someone who had just died. After the war, Pritchard moved to the U.S.A., and in 1983, she was honored by *Yad Vashem* as a Righteous Among the Nations.

Did Pritchard commit murder? Is breaking the law or breaking one of the Ten Commandments ever justified? Is there a difference between breaking a secular law and a Jewish law? Why/why not?

- Holocaust survivor, **Abraham Foxman** was born in 1940, in Baranowicz, Poland. Shortly after his birth his parents fled to Lithuania, only to be forced into the Vilnius ghetto in 1941. His Polish-Catholic nanny, Bronislawa Kurpi, offered to keep him safe until his parents could return. Kurpi had Foxman baptized and raised him for four years as a Catholic named Henryk Stanislas Kurpi. Miraculously, Foxman's parents survived and returned to Lithuania to find him. However,

Kurpi refused to give the boy back and Foxman had no memories of his birth parents. After several custody battles between Foxman's parents and his nanny, the boy fled with his parents from then Soviet controlled Lithuania to the American Zone in Austria. They lived in a Displaced Persons camp until 1950 when they were granted visas to the U.S.A. After the war, Foxman visited the Vatican, and asked the Pope to pray for the soul of his nanny. Of the visit, Foxman said, "For the first 50 years after the Holocaust, survivors bore witness to evil, brutality and bestiality. Now is the time for us, for our generation, to bear witness to goodness. For each one of us is living proof that even in hell, even in that hell called the Holocaust, there was goodness, there was kindness, and there was love and compassion."[110]

Do you think Foxman's nanny was justified in fighting for his custody? Why/why not? Why do you think Foxman asked the Pope to pray for his nanny's soul? What does Judaism have to say about forgiveness? Do you think that the rescue efforts of Opdyke and Pritchard should be valued more than those of Foxman's nanny? Why/why not?

4. **Films:** There are lots of good films to help teach about rescue during the Holocaust. **My Knees Were Jumping: Remembering the *Kindertransport*s** is a documentary by filmmaker Melissa Hacker whose mother was one of the 10,000 children saved in the *Kindertransport* movement. The film includes interviews with Hacker's mother as well as other now adult children of the *Kindertransport*. *Au Revoir, Les Enfants* (Goodbye, Children) tells the story of Jewish children hiding in France. Based on the book of the same name, **Courage to Care** includes interviews of survivors including Magda and Nelly Trocme, Marion P. Pritchard, and Irene Opdyke. Another video, **They Risked Their Lives: Rescuers of the Holocaust**, includes interviews of rescuers from Hungary, the Netherlands, Belgium, Poland, Germany, France, Czechoslovakia, and the Ukraine who were honored by *Yad Vashem* as Righteous Among the Nations. *God Afton, Herr Wallenberg* (Good Evening, Mr. Wallenberg) is a dramatic recreation of the Swiss diplomats' rescue efforts. In **Weapons of the Spirit,** Pierre Sauvage returns to Le Chambon-Sur Lignon, where he and his parents were sheltered by Pastor Trocme. While not specifically related to rescue in the Holocaust, **The Hangman** is a retelling of Maurice Ogden's classic

---

[110]Remarks by Abraham Foxman, Hidden Child conference, Jerusalem, notes of the proceedings, July 14, 1993, in *The Righteous: The Unsung Heroes of the Holocaust,* Martin Gilbert, p. xvii, Henry Holt and Company, New York, NY, 2003.

poem. The graphics in the video are simple and dated; however, the video is still a good trigger film for discussions about bystanders and rescuers.

Resources for Teaching

Alicia: My Story. Written by Alicia Appleman-Jurman and published by Bantam Books, New York, 1988. *Autobiography of a Jewish girl who risked her life to rescue other Jews.*

Anti-Defamation League. Website: www.adl.org. *Teacher's guides, lesson plans, first-hand accounts, photos and artifacts for teaching about the* Kindertransport *and hidden children of the Holocaust.*

Au Revoir Les Enfants (Goodbye Children). Released by Orion Home Video, 1987, 103 minutes. *Tells the story of Jewish children hiding in France.*

Courage to Care. The book is edited by Carol Rittner and Sondra Myers and published by New York University Press, NY, 1986, and the film is produced by Carol Rittner and Sondra Myers, 1986, 29 minutes. *Both the book and film feature first-person accounts of rescuers including Irene Opdyke, Marion P. Pritchard, and Andre Trocme's wife, Magda from Le Chambon.*

God Afton, Herr Wallenberg (Good Evening, Mr. Wallenberg). Released by Fox Lorber Home Video, 1990, 115 minutes. *A dramatic recreation of the Swiss diplomats' rescue efforts in Swedish, German and Hungarian with English subtitles.*

The Hangman. Released by McGraw-Hill Films, 1964, 12 minutes. *A retelling of Maurice Ogden's classic poem. Even though the graphics in the video are simple and dated, the video is a good trigger film for discussions about bystanders and rescuers.*

My Knees Were Jumping: Remembering the *Kindertransport*s. Produced by IFC, 1995, 77 minutes. *Nominated for a Grand Jury Prize at the Sundance Film Festival, filmmaker Melissa Hacker tells the story of the* Kindertransport *through the voices of those who lived through it, including her own mother.*

Rescuers: Portraits of Moral Courage in the Holocaust. Written by Gay Block and Malka Drucker and published by Holmes & Meier Publishers, New York, 1992. *First-hand accounts of rescuers with color photographs including Marion P. Pritchard, Irene Opdyke and Jean Kowalyk Berger.*

A Teacher's Guide to the Holocaust. Web site: http://fcit.coedu.usf.edu/holocaust. A project of the Florida Center for Instructional Technology, College of Education, University of South Florida. *Web links to stories of rescuers, a photo of a group of children who were sheltered in Le Chambon, a map showing the rescue of Danish Jews, and lesson plans.*

They Risked Their Lives: Rescuers of the Holocaust. Released by Ergo Home Video, 1992, 12 minutes. *Includes interviews of rescuers from Hungary, the*

Netherlands, Belgium, Poland, Germany, France, Czechoslovakia, and the Ukraine who were honored by Yad Vashem *as Righteous Among the Nations.*

U.S. Holocaust Memorial Museum. Website: www.ushmm.org. *Web links to photos of André Trocme's family Bible containing annotations he made in preparation for his sermons, and artifacts and photos of Raul Wallenberg, Oskar Schindler, and children of the* Kindertransport.

Weapons of the Spirit. Distributed by the Anti-Defamation League, 1989, 35 minutes. *This classroom version is adapted from Pierre Sauvage's award winning feature-length documentary. Sauvage returns to Le Chambon where he and is parents were sheltered by the townspeople.*

Resources for Further Learning

Into the Arms of Strangers: Stories of the *Kindertransport*. Written by Mark Jonathan Harris and Deborah Oppenheimer and published by Bloomsbury Publishing, New York, 2000. *The story of the* Kindertransport *told in the words of the child survivors, rescuers, parents and foster parents and includes photos and artifacts.*

Righteous Gentile. Written by John Bierman and published by The Viking Press, New York, 1981. *The story of Raul Wallenberg's rescue efforts.*

The Righteous: The Unsung Heroes of the Holocaust. Written by Martin Gilbert and published by Henry Holt and Company, New York, 2003. *A comprehensive description of rescue efforts by country and includes narratives about Le Chambon, Denmark, Raul Wallenberg, and Irene Opdyke.*

Saving the Jews: Amazing Stories of Men and Women Who Defied the "Final Solution". Written by Mordecai Paldiel and published by Schreiber Publishing, Rockville, MD, 2000. *Stories of rescuers divided by types of rescue efforts (e.g. escape and visas, sheltering and hiding, sheltering children, etc.).*

THE WAR

Smoke billowing from U.S. ships hit during the Japanese air attack on Pearl Harbor, Honolulu, Hawaii, Dec. 7, 1941. USHMM, courtesy of National Archives and Records Administration, College Park.

In the years leading up to World War II, German domestic and foreign policies came to serve the same goal. That is, to make Nazi Germany a great nation by 'restoring' the German peoples' strength through 'racial purity' and by expanding the country's borders, especially regaining the territory lost in World War I, that had become Poland, and annexing Austria whose population was mostly German-speaking. To accomplish these goals, the Nazi Party promulgated the ideals of the German peoples' 'racial supremacy' and set in place the machinery to rid itself of its 'internal enemies'—Jews and others who did not fit the Nazi ideal. The Nazi Party also built up its national armed forces, in the hope of positioning Nazi Germany as an unrelenting opponent of anyone or any country that got in its way, thereby setting the stage for World War II.

The big ideas of this chapter are that:

- Nazi Germany's aggressive domestic and foreign policies were aligned to create a German nation that would conquer all of Europe.

- Hitler began an aggressive campaign to dominate all of Europe through militaristic acquisition, which many conquered countries' people enthusiastically welcomed.

- Nazi Germany instigated the outbreak of World War II by attacking Poland in 1939.

- Nazi Germany made (and then violated) non-aggression pacts with several countries during the war years.

Key terms of this chapter include: *lebensraum*, Treaty of Versailles, *Anschluss*, Munich Conference, German-Soviet Pact, *blitzkrieg*, Vichy government, 'round-up', Battle of Britain, 'Axis of Power', Tripartite Pact, Pearl Harbor, Siege of Stalingrad, U.S. General Dwight D. Eisenhower, beaches of Normandy, France, D-Day, Battle of the Bulge, atomic bombs, and Hiroshima and Nagasaki, Japan.

Instigating World War II

Soon after taking office, Hitler began aggressively implementing his plan to expand Germany's borders through militaristic acquisition. Hitler referred to this plan as **lebensraum** (more living space), the goal of which was to literally create a larger country so that the expected influx of 'racially pure Aryans' would have ample space to live. To achieve this goal, Nazi Germany needed to increase the size of its military; however doing so was in direct violation of the **Treaty of Versailles**, the peace treaty the Germany signed after losing World War I. The treaty limited the number of German soldiers to 100,000, prohibited the institution of military draft, and demarcated that the Rhineland area in Western Germany near the French border as a demilitarized area (an area free of military presence). In violation of the treaty, Nazi Germany began drafting men into the armed forces beginning in 1935 and sent troops to the Rhineland the following year. Neither Britain nor France intervened to stop Germany from violating the Treaty of Versailles.

In March 1938, after building up its armed forces, German troops annexed Austria with the overwhelming support of the Austrian people in a process called **Anschluss** meaning union or joining. Nazi Germany then sought to take over the Sudetenland region of western Czechoslovakia, claiming that Czechoslovakia was mistreating the large number of German-speaking residents who lived there. In September 1938, Hitler convened a meeting in Munich, Germany, known as the **Munich Conference**, with leaders from Britain and France (Czechoslovakia's allies) and Italy's dictator, Benito Mussolini, who was Hitler's ally. Hitler assured the British and French representatives that if they agreed to allow Nazi Germany to annex the Sudetenland, Germany would not seek to expand its borders any further. They agreed not to intervene with the planned takeover and by March 1939, the last two provinces of Czechoslovakia, Bohemia and Moravia, were annexed by German troops.

Nazi Germany had long desired to attack Poland; it had been articulated as far back as 1922, when General von Seeckt said:

> Poland's existence is intolerable and incompatible with the essential conditions of Germany's life. Poland must go and will go—as a result of her own internal weaknesses and of action by Russia—with our aid…. The obliteration of Poland must be one of the fundamental drives of German policy…[and] is attainable by means of, and with the help of, Russia.[111]

However, before it could invade Poland, Germany had to ensure that the Russians would not get in its way. Nazi Germany and the Soviet Union agreed to sign a non-aggression pact in August 1939 called the **German-Soviet Pact**, also known as the Ribbentrop-Molotov Pact after the two foreign ministers who negotiated its terms. The pact consisted of two parts: an economic agreement that stipulated that Germany would exchange manufactured goods in exchange for Soviet raw materials and a 10-year agreement in which each signatory promised not to attack the other. The pact also contained a secret protocol for the partition of Poland and the rest of Eastern Europe into Soviet and German spheres of influence.

With the Soviet Union's neutrality secured, Germany then sought to ensure the passive compliance of Poland's allies, Britain and France, who Hitler had assured at the Munich Conference that Germany would not expand its borders any further. The Nazis created a series of provocations and propaganda myths to bolster its justification for attacking Poland. The myths implied that the Polish cavalry charged against German tanks, thereby provoking the Polish invasion. Nazi leaders surmised that the British and French would back down if Germany attacked Poland. It was a calculated error: on September 1, 1939 Germany set

---

[111]In William L. Shirer, *The Rise and Fall of the Third Reich* (New York: Simon and Schuster, 1960), 458.

World War II into motion when it attacked Poland; two days later Britain and France declared war on Germany.

Engaging in a new military campaign called *blitzkrieg*—lighting attack—the German military employed successive bombings along narrow fronts in Poland from the ground and air. Within a month, Poland was defeated and divided as conquered territory by German and Soviet forces according to the terms for partition established in the German-Soviet Pact. After conquering Poland, the Nazis immediately began establishing ghettos within the former Polish territories and deporting Jews to them.

Encouraged by its early military success in Poland, throughout the spring and summer of 1940, Germany attacked and conquered Denmark, Norway, Belgium, the Netherlands, Luxembourg and France. As part of the armistice agreement that France signed with Germany, Northern France came under German control while Southern France remained unoccupied. A new French government was established in the town of Vichy, called the **Vichy government,** which declared neutrality in the war between Germany and Great Britain, while promising to cooperate with Germany. In Northern France, the French police assisted the Germans in rounding up Jews. In Vichy, however, the French police themselves arrested Jews. In one so-called **'round-up,'** 4,000 children, were arrested without their parents and brought to Drancy, a transit camp that delivered people to Auschwitz. The few adults already arrested there tried to assist them, but they were sorely outnumbered, had few supplies and in the end, could only make marginal improvements in the filthy children's short lives. One of the adults, Odette Daltroff-Baticle, remembered the day before the children were shipped east:

> We lied to them. We told them that you're going to see your parents, you're going to find your parents again, and of course they didn't believe us. They curiously suspected what was going to happen. A lot of them said to my friends or to, to myself, 'Madame, adopt me, adopt me' because they wanted to, to stay at the camp. Even though it was very bad there, [filthy, insect-ridden], they didn't want to go any further. So the morning before the departure, we, we dressed them the best we could, most of them couldn't even carry their little sack....[112]

Though immediately after the war, the French would consider the Vichy government as having heroically resisted the Nazis, a symbol of French courage,

---

[112]Auschwitz, (British Broadcasting Company, London, England in conjunction with KCET, Los Angeles, 2005) from the transcript of Programme 3.

their elegant collaboration tells a dramatically different story of their rightful place in Holocaust memory.

'Axis of Power'

Nazi Germany also waged a brief military strike on Britain. For three months beginning in July 1940 German forces bombed English ports, shipping, air-fields, factories, and cities. Hitler's attempt to invade Britain was met with strong reluctance from German military leaders who did not think they had the forces necessary to mount a large-scale land campaign nor the ability to effectively cross the English Channel. Although Hitler continued to attack Britain by air for another seven months, the **Battle of Britain** (as it was called) was essentially over by October and further plans to attack Great Britain were put on indefinite hold by the German army. Many historians have doubted that an invasion of Britain was ever a real threat. General von Rundstedt, who was in charge of the invasion, told Allied investigators in 1945:

> The proposed invasion of England was nonsense, because adequate ships were not available.... We looked upon the whole thing as a sort of game because it was obvious that no invasion was possible when our Navy was not in a position to cover a crossing of the Channel or carry reinforcements. Nor was the German Air Force capable of tak-ing on these functions if the Navy failed.... I was always very skeptical about the whole affair.... I have a feeling that the Fuehrer never really wanted to invade England. He never had sufficient courage....[113]

Although Nazi Germany had signed the non-aggression German-Soviet Pact with the Soviet Union, Nazi Germany wanted to expand its borders into the Soviet Union to claim all of Communist-controlled Russia. On June 22, 1941, less than two years after signing a non-aggression pact with the Soviet Union, German forces launched an attack against the Soviet Union. More than three million German soldiers attacked, reinforced by nearly a half million of its allied troops from Finland, Romania, Hungary, Italy, Spain, Slovakia, Croatia and Spain. German troops advanced deep into the Soviet Union, inciting ire among the Russian populace. In the first few months, the Nazis advanced so quickly that hundreds of thousands of Russian POW's were arrested. Those who were military officers were often shot outright; the rest were purposefully starved, mass starvation being thought of as an appropriate tool to deal not only with the military, but with all of the Soviet communists. Strong resistance among

---

[113]In William L. Shirer, *The Rise and Fall of the Third Reich* (New York: Simon and Schuster, 1960), 761.

the Soviets arose, preventing the Nazis from capturing Leningrad and Moscow. While the Soviet army officially fought off the German invasion, many individuals welcomed the German troops, this was especially true in Ukraine and the Baltic states which were independent countries that had been taken over the year before by the Soviet Union.

Nazi Germany made and broke several military alliances with various countries throughout war. Known as the **'Axis of Power,'** these allied countries included Italy and Japan, and to a lesser extent, Hungary, Romania, Slovakia and Bulgaria. Aligned with the Axis nations, in late spring 1941, German forces next invaded Yugoslavia and Greece. British troops sent to defend Greece were quickly forced to withdraw.

The U.S.A. Enters the War

Hitler was aware of the danger of engaging in war with the Soviet Union and Britain. He knew that if Germany attacked Britain, the U.S.A. and Soviet Union might enter the war to Britain's defense. To avoid that possibility, in 1940, Hitler decided to offer Japan a place in the German and Italian Axis. Japan, Italy and Germany were natural allies because all three nations were ruled by undemocratic dictatorships. On September 27, 1940 the three countries signed the **Tripartite Pact** which provided for mutual assistance should any of the three countries fall under attack. Such an alliance would provide the added bonus of weakening the Soviet Union's military strength in Europe by forcing them to maintain sizeable military forces close to Japan. Germany, Italy and Japan also wanted to send the message to America that it would be at war with Germany, Italy and Japan if the United States entered the war on Britain's side.

Germany was also using Japan as a pawn to attack Britain's colonies in Asia on its behalf. In April 1941, Hitler met with Japanese Foreign Minister Yosuke Matsuoka in Berlin and urged the Japanese to attack Britain's military base at Singapore. Hitler then made a fateful blunder. To encourage Japan to attack Singapore, Hitler assured Matsuoka that Germany would assist Japan if it attacked the United States. The minutes from the meeting note Hitler's words, "If Japan got into a conflict with the United States, Germany on her part would take the necessary steps at once. Germany...would promptly take part in case of a conflict between Japan and America."[114] Just months later, on December 7, 1941, the Japanese bombed **Pearl Harbor**, Hawaii, and the U.S.A. declared war on Japan.

---

[114]William L. Shirer, *The Rise and Fall of the Third Reich* (New York: Simon and Schuster, 1960), 876.

Within days, Germany and Italy declared war on the United States. The Soviet Union and the U.S.A. thus became officially allied with Britain.

When the Wannsee Conference was held in January 1942, Hitler's war had been ravaging Europe for two and a half years. Germany and the Axis nations had attacked and/or occupied nearly all of Eastern Europe and much of Western Europe including Austria, Czechoslovakia (Bohemia and Moravia), Poland, Belgium, Denmark, Estonia, Finland, Greece, Latvia, Lithuania, Luxembourg, the Netherlands, France, Norway, Tunisia, Yugoslavia, and had attacked the Soviet Union. Although the U.S.A., Great Britain and the Soviet Union were allied against Germany, they had achieved minimal offensive success. The Nazis had set up concentration camps in the former Polish territory with others scattered throughout Europe. The *Einsatzgruppen* extermination squads were conducting regular mass shootings. The 'Final Solution' was in full swing.

In the months following the Wannsee Conference, the Nazi regime stepped up its efforts to carry out the planned 'Final Solution.' The Nazis began the systematic deportation of Jews from all over Europe to six extermination camps established in former Polish territory—Chelmno, Belzec, Sobibor, Treblinka, Auschwitz-Birkenau, and Majdanek. Special trains were employed to deport Jews from already established ghettos and from locations throughout Europe. Jewish men, women and children were sometimes even forced to pay their passage on the trains that transported them in sardine-like freight cars. The railway system was an integral tool in implementing for the 'Final Solution.' Even when railroad cars were desperately needed for Nazi military war aims to be accomplished, the Nazi genocidal war against the Jews trumped those needs. It was deemed more important to murder Jews than to send German soldiers to fight on the Eastern front. By war's end, the European railway system had carried nearly three million victims to the death camps.

Beginning in 1943 the military war began to turn against Germany and the Axis nations. In January, the Soviets pushed back the German forces in Stalingrad. The **Siege of Stalingrad** was a decisive battle of World War II because it ended the German offensive. The German troops surrendered there within weeks, marking the first big defeat of the German military since the outbreak of the war. That same month, U.S. troops bombed German soil for the first time. Though Germany was suffering significant military defeats, the Nazi Party was unrelenting in its attack on European Jewry. In the spring of 1943, the Nazis liquidated the Warsaw ghetto, deporting 60,000 Jews to the Treblinka death camp. Early that summer, Himmler ordered the liquidation of all Jewish ghettos in Poland. Germany was beginning to lose the war, Italy signed an armistice agreement with the Allied nations in September 1943, but the Holocaust continued for two more years.

By the following year, on June 6, 1944, more than 150,000 Allied soldiers, under the command of **U.S. General Dwight D. Eisenhower**, landed on the **beaches of Normandy, France,** known as **D-Day**, and within months entered Paris. By August, the Allied troops had liberated most of France. Around the same time, Soviet forces launched an offensive along the entire eastern front, pushing German troops nearly back to Warsaw. By the end of the summer, Germany's allies Romania, Bulgaria, and Finland had left the war. In September the first U.S. troops crossed into Germany. A few months later, German troops launched a counter attack through the Belgium forests, but the Allied air forces blocked the advance, winning a decisive victory in what has come to be known as the **Battle of the Bulge**. The Allied air forces also attacked several Nazi industrial plants, including the plant at the Auschwitz camp for nearly a month in the summer of 1944, though the gas chambers were never targeted.

The following spring, U.S. and Soviet troops together launched a powerful attack. Soviet forces liberated Western Poland in January 1945, forcing Hungary to surrender. By mid-February, the Allies bombed Dresden, Germany, killing approximately 35,000 civilians. U.S. troops crossed the Rhine River in early March and an offensive in mid-April enabled Soviet troops to surround Berlin. Hitler committed suicide on April 20, 1945 as Soviet forces neared his command bunker in central Berlin. And within days, Germany surrendered unconditionally. The Second World War continued for four more months until the war in the Pacific ended after the U.S. military dropped the first **atomic bombs** to be used in history on **Hiroshima and Nagasaki, Japan,** and killing 120,000 civilians.

Germany surrendered unconditionally to the Allies in May 1945, Japan surrendered the following September. Six years after it had begun, World War II officially came to an end.

Teaching Ideas

1. **Board Game:** The board game **Axis & Allies, Spring 1942: The World at War**[115] is a historically accurate world-map that effectively portrays the military and economic aspects of the countries at war. Players work as a team to challenge the expansion of the either the Axis nations of Germany

---

[115] Thanks to Debbie's WWII history buff, nephew, Elias Stahl, for alerting us to this game and testing it out with her.

and Japan or the Allied nations of the United Kingdom, the Soviet Union and the United States. The game illustrates the military strategies of the war including the weaponry involved, and the roles, placement and combat movement of each (infantry, fighter planes, industrial complex, aircraft carriers, transport ships, submarines, battleships, antiaircraft guns, armored tanks, and bombers). While the game does not necessarily represent an accurate portrayal of the war's outcome (i.e. each time the game is played, a different country could theoretically "win" the war); it is very effective at visually and kinesthetically representing the geography, and military and economic strengths and weaknesses of each of the countries involved in the war in the spring of 1942.

2. **Mapping Exercise:** Using a blank world map, with only the outlines of countries demarcated (and their names if your students don't know them), have your students simply color in those countries that were Axis powers, that were Allied nations, and those that were neutral. While this may seem like a childish activity (since you can have them use crayons), it's actually helpful in providing them with an understanding of how much of the world was involved in the war. You might want to have students do this mapping exercise three times: once to represent the year 1933, once for 1942, and once for 1946.

3. **Perspective Play:** Studs Terkel's book, **The Good War: An Oral History of World**, consists almost entirely of interview transcripts from people involved in the war from all walks of life, all careers, and many different experiences. The interview excerpts are mostly short and often powerful. Compile a collection of excerpts from the book, and stage them with your students, presenting them, collage-like, as multiple experiences during the same, 'Good War.' If you are truly brave, put on the show, and when the lights go up in the theatre, ask if there are any veterans from the war in the house, any refugees, any survivors, any descendants of those categories. In a small theatre venue, you can ask those who raise their hands to share their experiences briefly.

4. **Oral History:** Following what Terkel did, (see above,) assign each of your students to find someone who lived through World War II or their direct descendant. Your student's job is to record a story from that time. Put all the stories together, asking the students to visually represent them, and offer your local library the option of displaying them. Ceremoniously, contribute your students' research to the local library as well.

5. **American Memory and the War:** Many students (or their parents) have both historic World War II artifacts (flags, trunks, pins) and/or post war souvenir-type memorabilia (American hero army collectibles, posters) in their homes. Ask your students to bring their artifacts and memorabilia to class as a sort of "show and tell." Engage your students in a discussion about the differences between historical artifacts and souvenir memorabilia. In what ways does each of these represent a different memory of the war? What role do these artifacts and memorabilia play in shaping memory of World War II? What do the artifacts and memorabilia teach us about American memory of the so-called 'Good War'? How are these artifacts and memorabilia similar to or different from other memory keepsakes such as family heirlooms?

6. **Films:** There are a couple of good films specifically on the topic of the war years, many of which include archival footage. **The Holocaust: In Memory of Millions** is as a good introduction to the Holocaust era, tracing the gradual escalation of the 'Final Solution'. It includes interviews with survivors and soldiers who liberated the camps. **Hitler: The Whole Story** is a three-part documentary about Adolf Hitler. The last film in the series, *The War Years*, focuses on Hitler's leadership of the Third *Reich* during the war effort.

Resources for Teaching

Axis & Allies, Spring 1942: The World at War. Distributed by Milton Bradley Co., MB Gamemaster Series, Springfield, MA, 1986. *An engaging way for students to learn about the military aspects of the war. The game is a bit costly, however, at approximately $40.*

The Good War: An Oral History of World War II. Written by Studs Terkel and published New Press, New York, reprint edition, 1997. *Consists almost entirely of interview transcripts from people involved in the war from all walks of life, all careers, and many, many different experiences. The interview excerpts are mostly short and often powerful.*

Hitler: The Whole Story. Distributed by Social Studies School Service, 1989, 50 minutes each. *A three-part documentary on Adolf Hitler. The last film in the series,* The War Years, *focuses on Hitler's leadership of the Third* Reich *during the war effort.*

The Holocaust: In Memory of Millions. Distributed by Social Studies School Service, 1993, 90 minutes. *This film is a good introduction to the Holocaust era, tracing the gradual escalation of the 'Final Solution'. It includes interviews with survivors and soldiers who liberated the camps.*

Resources for Further Learning

The Rise and Fall of the Third Reich. Written by William L. Shirer and published by Simon and Schuster, New York, 1960. *While we don't recommend this for students because of its sheer density, this book provides a comprehensive, detailed analysis of the military aspects and political decisions involved in the war.*

The War Against the Jews: 1933–1945. Written by Lucy Dawidowicz and published by Holt, Rinehart and Winston, New York, 1975. *Several chapters provide comprehensive overviews of the war years.*

Witness to the Holocaust. Edited by Michael Berenbaum and published by Harper Collins, New York, 1997. *An illustrated volume on the Holocaust that presents primary source material including testimonies, letters, government documents, newspaper reports, and diary entries.*

THE WORLD'S RESPONSE

Members of the Dublon family pose on the deck of the S.S. St. Louis en route to Cuba, May 22, 1939.
USHMM, courtesy of Peter S. Heiman.

A cartoon that appeared in an American newspaper during the Holocaust era depicts the Statue of Liberty with the New York skyline in the distance. At the statue's base are the words, "Give me your tired, your poor, [Your huddled masses yearning to breathe free], The wretched refuse of your teeming shore. Send me those, the homeless, the tempest-tossed to me. [I lift my lamp beside the golden door.]" A Jewish refugee ship passes by, but cannot rest on U.S. shores. With her arm stretched to the sky, Lady Liberty holds a sign that reads, "KEEP OUT" as she shields her face in embarrassment. Drawn by an unknown artist, the cartoon is symbolic of world-wide politics and public opinion in the years leading up to and during the war. The genocide of European Jewry was largely ignored by most Western countries including the United States, Canada and Great Britain. This chapter explores both the actions and inaction of the world, particularly of the United States, in regard to the plight of European Jewry.

The lack of any significant response to their plight has been the focus of enormous scholarly discourse, with little agreement on the impact of American quiescence. The ultimate responsibility for the annihilation of European Jewry clearly rests on the shoulders of the Nazi regime. However, some historians have accused the United States and other Western nations of being accomplices to this genocide through their callous indifference and failure to intervene. In his highly acclaimed and controversial book, *The Abandonment of the Jews*, historian David Wyman claims that thousands of European Jews might have been saved if the world had intervened earlier and more aggressively. Historian Deborah Lipstadt agrees. She writes, "During the 1930s and 1940s America could have saved thousands and maybe even hundreds of thousands of Jews but did not do so."[116] Other historians question the validity of such claims. Martin Gilbert, author of *Auschwitz and the Allies,* believes it is unlikely that the Allied nations could have saved any Jews from the death camps.

Despite such arguments, there is some agreement on the complicated social and political factors that led to the so-called abandonment of the Jews. These include restrictive prewar immigration policies, world-wide antisemitism, and political maneuvering that stifled opportunities to rescue Europe's Jews.

The big ideas of this chapter are that:

- The persecution of European Jewry was largely ignored outside of Europe.
- The so-called abandonment of the Jews can be attributed to several factors, including: restrictive prewar immigration policies in the United States and elsewhere, world-wide antisemitism, and political maneuvering.

Key terms of this chapter include: restrictive immigration policies, Immigration Act of 1924, Evian Conference, S.S. St. Louis, antisemitism, Catholic Church, Pius XII, and the Roosevelt administration.

Immigration Restrictions

Up until 1941 the Nazis encouraged Jews to emigrate from Europe. Nonetheless, relatively few got out because most countries were unwilling to provide refuge. Historian David Wyman writes, "The aim of the persecution was to make life for Jews in Germany so difficult that they would emigrate. By the end of 1937, however, only 135,000—about 25 percent—had left. The doors of the outside world were not open to very many Jewish immigrants."[117] **Restrictive immi-**

---

[116]Deborah Lipstadt, *Beyond Belief* (New York: The Free Press, 1986), 1.

[117]David S. Wyman, "The United States," in *The World Reacts to the Holocaust*, David S. Wyman, editor (Baltimore: The John Hopkins University Press, 1996), 701.

gration policies throughout the world severely limited Jewish emigration from Nazi-occupied Europe. Great Britain limited the number of Jews allowed to enter British-controlled Palestine to 15,000 annually. In America, the passage of the **Immigration Act of 1924** limited the total number of immigrants from any country admitted to the United States to 165,000 annually, and within three years, that number was reduced to 150,000.

In July 1938, delegates from 32 countries met at the French resort of *Evian-les-Bains* on Lake Geneva, near the Swiss border. The **Evian Conference**, as it was known, was called by President Franklin D. Roosevelt to discuss the plight of European Jewry; the conference, however, failed to organize any rescue programs for Europe's threatened Jews. During the meeting, each of the delegates expressed sympathy for the Jewish refugees, but most, including those of the U.S.A. and Great Britain, refused to loosen their immigration quotas. Australia's delegate, T. W. White, Minister for Trade and Customs, expressed the most shameful sentiment at the conference: "As we have no real racial problem, we are not desirous of importing one."[118]

The Nazi regime took great pleasure in the irony of the outcome of the Evian Conference. While a number of countries readily criticized Germany for its treatment of Jews, none wanted to allow those same Jews entry into their countries. Reporting on the Evian Conference, a German newspaper ran the headline, "JEWS FOR SALE—WHO WANTS THEM? NO ONE!"[119]

If at Evian, it became apparent that no one would come to the aid of German Jews, just a few months later *Kristallnacht* signaled just how desperately such aid was needed. Dr. Chaim Weizmann, who later became Israel's first president, said of the time, "The world seemed to be divided into two parts—those places where the Jews could not live and those where they could not enter."[120]

Weizmann's words became more poignant the following May 1939, when a transatlantic cruise liner named the **S.S. St. Louis** left Hamburg, Germany for Havana, Cuba, carrying more than 900 passengers. Nearly all of the passengers had purchased landing papers to disembark in Cuba, hoping to obtain visas to emigrate to the U.S.A. However, unbeknownst to the passengers, eight days before the St. Louis even set sail, their landing permits had been retroactively invalidated by the corrupt Cuban director-general of immigration. Unaware of

---

[118]Arthur R. Morse, *While Six Million Died: A Chronicle of American Apathy* (New York: Random House, 1967), 212.

[119]Helen Waterford, *Commitment to the Dead: One Woman's Journey Toward Understanding* (Frederick, CO: Renaissance House Publishers, 1987,) 23.

[120]Manchester Guardian, 23rd May 1936, cited A.J. Sherman, *Island Refuge, Britain and the Refugees from the Third Reich, 1933-1939* (London: Elek Books Limited, 1973), 112.

the passengers' fate, the captain of the St. Louis, Gustav Shroder, penned in his diary optimistic notes about the departure:

> There is a somewhat nervous disposition among the passengers. Despite this, everyone seems convinced they will never see Germany again. Touching departure scenes have taken place. Many seem light of heart, having left their homes. Others take it heavily. But beautiful weather, pure sea air, good food, and attentive service will soon provide the usual worry-free atmosphere of long sea voyages. Painful impressions on land disappear quickly at sea and soon seem merely like dreams.[121]

Unfortunately, the nightmares of life in Germany would resurface for the passengers of the St. Louis. After *Kristallnacht*, the Nazi regime had accelerated Jewish emigration, which it hoped would both rid Germany of its Jewish population and force other nations to refuse admittance to Jews, furthering their anti-Jewish propaganda efforts. The fate of the St. Louis accomplished the latter goal. When the ship docked at the Havana port, Cuban authorities revoked the passengers' visas, permitting only 22 Jewish passengers to disembark. The ship docked there for nearly a week, the providence of its passengers in limbo, until it was ordered out of Cuban waters.

The St. Louis sailed toward Florida, in the hopes that the United States would grant emergency entry status to the Jewish refugees. When the ship neared Miami's coast, the passengers sent a cable to President Roosevelt, pleading for sanctuary on U.S. soil. The cable went unanswered. The 1924 U.S. Immigration Act limited the number of immigrants from each country who could enter the United States. In 1939, the quota of people allowed in from Germany had already been met. Allowing the passengers on the St. Louis to enter the United States would have meant denying entrance to passengers who had been on the waiting list for years. Allowing the St. Louis passengers' entry would also have been met with protests from the American public, which was still largely isolationist and approved of immigration restrictions. As a result, the U.S. State Department refused to allow the St. Louis to dock at *any* American port, claiming it did not wish to intervene in Cuban affairs. Instead, U.S. diplomats asked Cuba to admit the passengers as a humanitarian effort. The Cuban government refused, and the St. Louis was sent back to Europe. Great Britain agreed to take nearly one-fourth of the passengers, while Belgium, France and Holland allowed the remaining 600 temporary refuge. Tragically, approximately 250 of the ship's passengers

---

[121]Gustav Schroeder as quoted in Thomas, Gordon and Max Morgan Witts, *Voyage of the Damned* (New York: Stein and Day, 1974), 64.

were subsequently killed by the Nazis. If the Evian Conference proved that the nations of the world would not allow legal immigration to solve the Nazis' 'Jewish problem,' so the voyage of the St. Louis highlighted the fact that even under exceptional circumstances, exceptions would not be made.

By 1941, America's gates were nearly completely closed to Europe's Jews. In the spring of that year, Debbie's father and two uncles were among the fortunate few granted entry visas into the United States. They set sail from a Portuguese port along with hundreds of other Jewish refugee children aboard a rickety ship named the Serpa Pinto, which would turn out to be one of the last ships allowed to enter U.S. waters during the war years.

Antisemitism

While the United States' restrictive immigration policies were determined by Congress and the Roosevelt administration, they were shaped by public opinion. U.S. opinion polls in the late 1930s consistently revealed that up to 85 percent of Americans opposed increasing immigration quotas for all groups. Millions were unemployed as a result of the Great Depression and, as a result, Americans didn't want Jewish refugees from Europe to compete for jobs that they thought rightfully belonged to unemployed Americans. Wyman and others have argued, though, that the economy was not the only factor influencing American opinion about Jewish immigration. Wyman writes, "The plain truth is that many Americans were prejudiced against Jews and were unlikely to support measures to help them."[122] The antisemitic views of several highly placed civil servants in Canada were also instrumental in keeping that country's doors virtually closed to European Jewish refugees. World-wide **antisemitism** increased steadily in the 1930s, reaching a peak in the United States during the war years.

Much criticism has been levied against the **Catholic Church** for its silence during the Holocaust. John Cornwell, author of *Hitler's Pope: The Secret History of Pius XII*, indicts Eugenio Pacelli, **Pius XII**, of antipathy towards Jews, which helped the Nazis' unimpeded rise to power. In the early 1930s, Pius XII made a treaty with Hitler that authorized the papacy to impose new Church law on German Catholics. By agreeing to the treaty, the Catholic Church validated the legitimacy of the Nazi government. Moreover, the treaty sent a message to German Catholics that it was possible to remain a good Catholic *and* support the Nazi Party. Cornwell explains, "In exchange, the Catholic Church in Germany agreed to completely withdraw from German social and political action. [This]

---

[122]David S. Wyman, *The Abandonment of the Jews: American and the Holocaust 1941-1945* (New York: Pantheon Books, 1984), 9.

ensured that Nazism could rise unopposed by the most powerful Catholic community in the world.... As Hitler himself boasted in a cabinet meeting on July 14, 1933, Pacelli's guarantee of nonintervention left the regime free to resolve the Jewish question. ...The perception of papal endorsement of Nazism, in Germany and abroad, helped seal the fate of Europe."[123] The Catholic Church's apparent endorsement of the Nazi regime also sent a powerful message to Catholics around the world that legitimized antisemitic sentiments.

Whether Americans at that time were passively or actively antisemitic continues to be hotly debated. While reports of Nazi atrocities were widely reported in the U.S. press, many Americans were simply indifferent to the plight of Jews. In her Pulitzer Prize winning book, *A Problem From Hell: America and the Age of Genocide*, Samantha Power writes, "It is not that readers' prejudice against Jews necessarily made them happy to hear reports of Hitler's monstrosity. Rather, their indifference to the fate of Jews likely caused them to skim the stories and to focus on other aspects of the war."[124] While Power describes America's antisemitism at the time as passive indifference, Wyman describes it as an acute epidemic. He writes:

> Most often, youth gangs were the perpetrators. Jewish ceremonies were vandalized, synagogues were damaged as well as defaced with swastikas and antisemitic slogans, anti-Jewish markings were scrawled on sidewalks and Jewish stores, and antisemitic literature was widely distributed. Most upsetting of all, in scores of instances, bands of teenagers beat Jewish school-children—sometimes severely, as when three Jewish boys in Boston were attacked by 20 of their classmates. In another incident, in a Midwestern city, young hoodlums stripped a 12-year-old Jewish boy to the waist and painted a Star of David and the word *Jude* on his chest.[125]

Whether Power or Wyman are correct, that is whether Americans were passively indifferent or actively antisemitic or some combination thereof, the Jews of Europe were persecuted while America did very little to intervene on their behalf. Not all of America's indifference toward the plight of European Jewry can be blamed on immigration restrictions and antisemitism, though.

---

[123]John Cornwell, *Hitler's Pope: The Secret History of Pius XII* (New York: Penguin Books, 1999), 7.

[124]Samantha Power, *A Problem From Hell: America and the Age of Genocide* (New York: HarperCollins, 2002), 35.

[125]David S. Wyman, *The Abandonment of the Jews: American and the Holocaust 1941-1945* (New York: Pantheon Books, 1984), 10.

Disbelief and Information

In the years following the Holocaust, much scholarship has been devoted to the questions of how much and when the Roosevelt administration and the American public came to know about the fate of European Jewry under Nazism. Power argues that the United States and Great Britain had collected a significant amount of information about the Nazis' plans and activities:

> Intelligence on Hitler's extermination was plentiful in both classified and open sources. The Untied States maintained embassies in Berlin until December 1941, in Budapest and Bucharest until January 1942, and in Vichy France until late 1942. The British used sophisticated decryption technology to intercept German communications. The major Jewish organizations had representatives in Geneva who relayed vivid and numerous refugee reports through Stephen Wise, the president of the World Jewish Congress and others.[126]

Moreover, this information was not kept secret from the American and world publics. Lipstadt writes, "An astonishing amount of information was available long before the end of the war. There was practically no aspect of the Nazi horrors which was not publicly known in some detail long before the camps were opened in 1945."[127] Both Power and Lipstadt note, however, that the information was often played down because officials and journalists were skeptical about its veracity. The stories sounded too gruesome to be true, too unprecedented to be believed. Power writes, "In 1944, when John Pehle, the director of Roosevelt's War Refugee Board, wanted to publish the report of two Auschwitz escapees, Elmer Davis, the head of the U.S. Office of War Information, turned down his request. The American public would not believe such wild stories, he said, and Europeans would be so demoralized by them that their resistance would crumble."[128]

When the Nazi regime came to power in the early 1930s, most Americans were aware of its antisemitic platform. The anti-Jewish legislation in Germany in the early 1930s, the Nuremberg Laws of 1935, and the events of *Kristallnacht* in 1938 were all widely reported in the American and world presses. However, at the time, no one could anticipate the extent of the Nazis' antisemitic activities or their gruesome end results. Moreover, Power explains, "The vast majority of people simply did not believe what they read; the notion of getting attacked for

---

[126]Samantha Power, *A Problem From Hell: America and the Age of Genocide* (New York: HarperCollins, 2002), 34.

[127]Deborah Lipstadt, *Beyond Belief* (New York: The Free Press, 1986), 2.

128 Samantha Power, *A Problem From Hell: America and the Age of Genocide* (New York: HarperCollins, 2002), 35.

being (rather than for doing) was too discomforting and too foreign to process readily. A plot for outright annihilation had never been seen before and therefore could not be imagined. The tales of German cremation factories and gas chambers sounded far fetched."[129] As a result, American discourse was focused on the course of the war, not on the plight of the Jews. The dramatic dispatches from the battlefields were simply more engaging to the American public than the stories of Jewish persecution. Consequently, coverage of the desperate situation of Jews was pushed off the front pages of newspapers, buried instead in their middle sections and dropped out of public consciousness.

Furthermore, newspapers, radio broadcasts and movies in the United States positioned Japan as the primary enemy. The United States entered the war because Germany had allied itself with the Japanese who had attacked America at Pearl Harbor. For Americans of the period, Germany had not, in fact, attacked—the Japanese had. Indeed, Germany was considered a distant enemy; revenge was slated for Japan. Exacerbating the issue, American Jews did not want to be seen as dragging the United States into the war. Insecure about their place in society and facing antisemitism at home, American Jews wanted to be perceived as patriotic rather than parochial. For a variety of reasons, then, the importance of European Jewish persecution during the war was downplayed in the United States.

Political Maneuvering

In the years following the war, other questions arose as to why the **Roosevelt administration** neglected various rescue opportunities. The suggestion that the American military bomb the rail lines leading to the gas chambers or bomb the camps directly has become symbolic of all missed rescue opportunities. Many survivors and historians have wondered how many lives might have been saved if only one rail line or gas chamber would have been put out of commission, however temporarily. Peter Novick contends that U.S. troops never attempted to bomb the rail lines because it would not have been effective at saving lives or wining the war. He writes, "Railways might be bombed in support of tactical operations—to prevent the enemy from moving troops and material for several hours, perhaps a day or two. Beyond that, the method was nearly useless."[130] He likewise dismisses the tactic of bombing the camps because too many innocent civilians would have become casualties. "There were more than 100,000 Jewish prisoners at Auschwitz. How would they have fared in the event of an aerial

129 Ibid, p. 36.

130 Peter Novick, *The Holocaust in American Life* (New York: Houghton Mifflin Company, 1999), 54-55.

assault on the killing facilities?"[131] Novick suggests that rather than focus on the unknown outcome of specific rescue events, "Roosevelt had to convince the public at large, and in particular nativists and isolationists, that the greater involvement he sought in the European conflict was in the American national interest—a matter of self defense, not some globalist do-gooding; he was not letting Jewish interests determine American policy."[132] While Novick's claims are compelling, it is hard not to wonder what more could have been done.

Power's analysis of America's failure to save European Jewry is more critical than Novick's. By comparing America's response during the Holocaust to subsequent genocides in Cambodia, Bosnia, Rwanda, Srebrenica, Kosovo and Iraq, Power concludes that American politics consistently prevent the United States from intervening. As she concludes:

> American policymakers, journalists, and citizens are extremely slow to muster the imagination needed to reckon with evil. Ahead of the killings, they assume rational actors will not inflict seemingly gratuitous violence. They trust in good-faith negotiations and traditional diplomacy. Once the killings start, they assume that civilians who keep their heads down will be left alone. They urge ceasefires and donate humanitarian aid.[133]

Furthermore, she argues that American political leaders interpret societal silence as an indicator of public indifference, and, as a result, there is insufficient political pressure forcing them to act. Many historians have argued that this indifference was perceived by the Nazis as a sign of complicity, thereby encouraging their murderous acts. In looking at U.S. responses to genocides throughout history, Power adds that the U.S. government has consistently neglected to deter genocide. Instead, American officials argue that, "any proposed U.S. response will be futile. Indeed, it may even do more harm than good, bringing perverse consequences to the victims and jeopardizing other precious American moral or strategic interests."[134]

In the years leading up to and during World War II, most countries outside of Europe contained citizens whose attitudes ranged from passive indifference to active and violent antisemitism towards the plight of European Jewry. Whether Wyman, Novick, Lipstadt or Power is correct, we'd argue that every point along this continuum played a role in sealing the fate of European Jewry.

---

[131]Ibid, p. 55.

[132]Ibid, p. 51.

[133]Samantha Power, *A Problem From Hell: America and the Age of Genocide* (New York: HarperCollins, 2002), xvii.

[134]Ibid, p. xviii.

Teaching Ideas

1. **Am I My Brother's Keeper?:** The Biblical story of Cain and Abel (Genesis 4) conveys a quintessential moral lesson about our responsibility to care for each other. In the story, Cain murders his brother, Abel. When God probes Cain about Abel's whereabouts, Cain responds with a lie and a question, "I know not; am I my brother's keeper?" (Genesis 4: 9) The resounding message of this story is that, yes, indeed we are (or at least should be) our brothers' and fellow humans' keepers. Ask your students to read the Cain and Abel story and to discuss in what ways its teachings were followed or ignored by various religious communities during the Holocaust. Include the Catholic Church and American Jews in your discussion. In what ways did religious communities lie to God and to others? In what ways was the Pope's decision not to intervene with the politics of the Nazi regime an abnegation of this Biblical teaching? In what ways was the American Jewish community culpable by not vigorously pressuring the Roosevelt administration to act on behalf of its Jewish brethren in Europe?

    Ask your students to consider current events and the ways in which people stand up for or take risks to save others. Don Pagis, an Israeli poet, wrote a short and chilling poem about Cain and Abel that ends with a thunderous silence. Ask your students to read and consider the questions that are raised in the poem entitled, *Written in pencil in a sealed box car:*

    Here in this transport/ I am Eve/ with Abel my son/ if you see my older son/ Cain son of Adam/ tell him that I

    If your students know even basic Hebrew, have them read the poem in its original, since some of the nuance is lost in translation. "Son of Adam," for instance, in Hebrew, is *"ben Adam,"* which also means, simply, human being.

2. A useful resource to help students explore the role of the Catholic Church during the Holocaust era is the play, **The Deputy**, written by Rolf Hochhuth, translated by Richard and Clara Winston. The play, which was considered highly controversial when it premiered in Berlin in 1963, examines the relationship of the Catholic Church to Nazi Germany and raises important questions about authority and the courage to stand up for others—questions which are still powerfully relevant today. Ask your students to read and act out sections of the play, followed by discussions of the characters' roles and responsibilities. Ask them to consider why they think the play created such a firestorm when it opened in Berlin. Do they think

it would still be considered controversial by Germans or Catholics today? Why or why not?

3. **Music**: A quick search through just about any music store or online music collection will reveal a surprising number of compilations by various artists with titles like, "Songs That Got Us Through WW2," and "Those Were Our Songs: Music of World War II," and "G.I. Jukebox: Songs from World War II." Jazz, swing and big band were all popular in the United States and throughout Europe during the war. Select a few songs for your students to listen to. Ask your students to explore and comment on the contrast between the upbeat music and the fate of European Jewry, particularly the ways that the music of the time may have served as sign of indifference and/or as a release and escape from the war. Select songs that serve as a cultural commentary of the era, songs that question the war, songs that seem to completely ignore the struggles of the time, and those that seem to be written for young men in the armed forces or for the young women at home or serving.

Then ask your students to listen to some European Jewish music that emerged during the same time period. Suggested compilations include: **Songs Never Silenced**, a book and accompanying CD of songs of the Holocaust performed by various musicians; **Yes, We Sang!: Songs of the Ghettos and Concentration Camps**, a good book of songs with English translations; **Ghetto Tango: Wartime Yiddish Theater**, a CD of cabaret music from the Jewish ghettos of Poland and Lithuania; and **Partisans of Vilna: Songs of World War II Jewish Resistance**, the soundtrack CD to the film of the same name. Ask your students to consider what the words and music convey about the Jewish experience during the war. How are the themes, beats, words, messages and meanings similar to or different from American popular music at the time? What can we learn about World War II through an exploration of its music? How does it compare and contrast to current events and pop music in history (e.g. music of the Vietnam era) and today?

4. **The News Unfolded:** Have your students investigate what Americans knew about the fate of European Jewry and when. Have students research the information that was on the front pages of American newspapers as the Holocaust was unfolding. What stories were featured on which pages and when? How much information was the American public getting about the events in Europe? Pick one event such as *Kristallnacht*, the Berlin Olympics,

or the Warsaw Ghetto Uprising and ask them to research how that event was reported in the American press. Or, ask your students to create an entire historical timeline of newsworthy Holocaust-related events and then compare those with when and how the same events were covered in the American press or even in their local paper. Did the stories appear on the front page or were they buried on subsequent pages? Ask them to consider why various editorial decisions were made. A great resource for this teaching idea is **Page One: The Front Page History of World War II as Presented in the New York Times,** which chronicles front page headlines and stories that appeared in the paper between September 1, 1939, when Germany attacked Poland, and September 2, 1945, when Japan surrendered to the Allies.

You might also ask your students to scour current newspapers and bring in articles that relate to Holocaust themes or ongoing genocides. Are there noticeable trends in the ways that the American press and public opinion respond to these issues today? For sophisticated students, you may want to compare magazines from various political positions (*The Progressive* vs. *The National Review* or *The Nation* vs. *The National Standard*, for example.) Ask your students to use that coverage in order to debate Samantha Power's thesis that American policymakers, journalists and citizens are incapable of responding justly to genocides. Can they find evidence to support or counter her argument? In what ways do particular political orientations support or resist intervening in possible genocides?

5. **Compare and Discuss U.S. Immigration Policies and Public Opinion:** In the 1930s many Americans feared that immigrants would compete for scarce jobs. Ask your students to research the economic situation in their city or town during the 1930s. In what ways were the anti-immigration attitudes understandable or reprehensible? Discuss the economic situation today and research current immigration policies and quotas. How do Americans feel about immigrants today? Compare and discuss.

6. **Analysis of Editorial Cartoons:** Since the advent of the printing press, cartoonists have engaged in political commentary and debate, oftentimes overtly and at other times, subversively. The power of political cartoons to sway public opinion as events are unfolding is well known. In the U.S. press, cartoonists depicted and challenged political maneuverings, public opinions and cultural shifts during the Holocaust era. Ask your students

to investigate the United States' indifference and inaction to the plight of European Jewry through the lens of cartoons. A good resource is **Cartoonists Against the Holocaust,** an online exhibit of the David S. Wyman Institute for Holocaust Studies. Have your students analyze what event or policy each cartoon was commenting on and how. Ask them to locate cartoons that editorialize on specific policies such as immigration restrictions or anti-Semitic attitudes. Do different cartoonists have particular political slants? As a further extension, ask your students to locate current political cartoons that relate to Holocaust themes such as prejudice, hatred, antisemitism, resistance and rescue and/or to create their own.

7. **Films:** There are a few good films on the subject of the world's response during the Holocaust. The best is **The Double Crossing: The Voyage of the St. Louis**, which blends interviews with passengers of the St. Louis with archival footage to depict the issues raised by the ship's voyage that are still relevant today, including U.S. immigration quotas and policies. **America and the Holocaust: Deceit and Indifference** is a bit dry, but does a decent job of conveying the complicated social and political factors that shaped American responses to the Holocaust. The film is told through the story of Kurt Klein, who immigrated to the United States from Germany in 1937. **Who Shall Live and Who Shall Die?** examines American responses to the Holocaust and has a particular focus on American Jewish leaders.

Resources for Teaching

America and the Holocaust: Deceit and Indifference. Produced by PBS Video, Alexandria, VA, 1993, 60 minutes. *Conveys the complicated social and political factors that shaped American responses to the Holocaust. The film is told through the lens of Kurt Klein, who immigrated to the United States from Germany in 1937.*

Cartoonists Against the Holocaust. Website: www.wymaninstitute.org. *An online exhibit of Holocaust related political cartoons, which is a project of the David S. Wyman Institute for Holocaust Studies.*

The Deputy. By Rolf Hochhuth, translated by Richard and Clara Winston and published by Grove Press, New York, 1964. *This play examines the relationship of the Catholic Church with Nazi Germany and raises important questions about authority and the courage to stand up for others—questions which still powerfully relevant today.*

Ghetto Tango: Wartime Yiddish Theater. Performed by Adrienne Cooper with Zalmen Mlotek and produced by Harold G. Hagopian. *Cabaret music thrived in the Jewish ghettos of Poland and Lithuania during World War II. Jewish audi-*

ences gathered in makeshift clubs and theaters to hear newly created Yiddish songs, rooted in Jewish folk and liturgical music as well as European operetta, American ragtime and Argentine tango. Some of the songs have English translations incorporated into the songs themselves, making them good for classroom use.

Page One: The Front Page History of World War II as Presented in the New York Times. Published by Galahad Books, New York, 1996. *Copies of front page headlines and stories that appeared in* The New York Times *between September 1, 1939, when Germany attacked Poland, and September 2, 1945, when Japan surrendered to the Allies.*

Partisans of Vilna: Songs of World War II Jewish Resistance. Produced by Flying Fish Records, Chicago, IL, 1992. *The soundtrack CD to the film of the same name, it is a good collection of partisan and ghetto songs.*

Songs Never Silenced. By Velvel Pasternak and produced by Tara Publications. *In l948, Shmerke Kaczerginsky, a Holocaust survivor, wrote down the songs that he remembered from the Holocaust. Years later, Velvel Pasternak discovered this forgotten book and compiled it together along with an accompanying CD performed by various artists.*

The Double Crossing: The Voyage of the St. Louis. Distributed by Zenger Video, 1992, 29 minutes. *Incorporates interviews with passengers of the St. Louis with archival footage to depict the issues raised by the ship's voyage that are still relevant today including U.S. immigration quotas and policies.*

Who Shall Live and Who Shall Die? Produced by Kino International, 1982, 90 minutes. *Examines American responses to the Holocaust with particular focus on American Jewish leaders.*

Yes, We Sang!: Songs of the Ghettos and Concentration Camps. Compiled by Shoshana Kalisch with Barbara Meister and published by Harper & Row, New York, 1985. *A good book of songs with English translations, although it does not have an accompanying CD.*

Resources for Further Learning

The Abandonment of the Jews: America and the Holocaust 1941-1845. Written by David S. Wyman and published by Pantheon Books, New York, 1984. *The definitive work on the actions and inaction of the United States during the Holocaust and its impact on the fate of European Jewry.*

"A Problem From Hell": America and the Age of Genocide Written by Samantha Power and published by HarperCollins, New York, 2002. *Comparing the Holocaust to other genocides, Power asks the question: Why do American leaders who vow "never again" repeatedly fail to stop genocide?*

Hitler's Pope: The Secret History of Pius XII. Written by John Cornwell and published by Penguin Books, New York, 1999. *Drawing on Vatican and Jesuit archives, journalist John Cornwell shows that Pope Pius XII was instrumental in negotiating an accord with Hitler that helped the Nazis rise to unhindered power. The book explores the role of the Catholic Church in the Holocaust years and its lingering consequences today.*

The Holocaust in American Life. Written by Peter Novick and published by Houghton Mifflin Company, Boston, 1999. *A controversial and compelling account of America's actions and inaction during the Holocaust years.*

The World Reacts to the Holocaust. Edited by David S. Wyman and published by The John Hopkins University Press, Baltimore, 1996. *A comprehensive anthology of the unique historical circumstances that affected each country's behavior during the Holocaust including Western Europe, Eastern Europe, the Soviet Bloc, the Axis nations (Germany, Austria, Italy and Japan), Great Britain, and North America.*

WHERE WAS GOD?

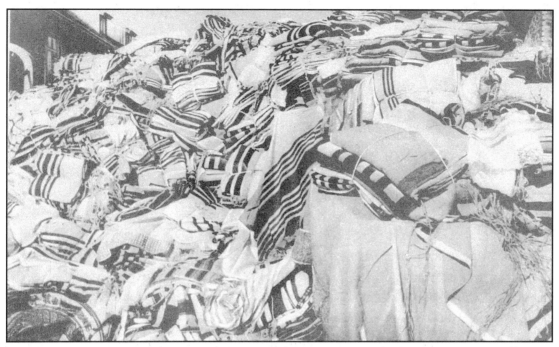

A pile of talitot (prayer shawls) confiscated from prisoners arriving at Auschwitz. USHMM, courtesy of National Archives and Records Administration, College Park.

In the aftermath of the Holocaust, theologians grappled with the question of God's place during the Holocaust. Jewish theologians have approached this question from a variety of perspectives, but most of their theories reflect a distinctly Jewish understanding of God. That is, to wrestle with the concept of God is a core Jewish precept. Aside from a sacrosanct belief in monotheism, Judaism has no doctrinal statement about the definition or conception of God. Instead, a core feature of the Jewish relationship to God is that it is engaged, even confrontational, rather than submissive. References to this kind of relationship with God can be found in Biblical, Talmudic, Kabbalistic, Hasidic and modern sources.

Questioning God has been a consistent guidepost through Jewish history: Abraham argued with God over the fate of Sodom and Gomorrah; Job wrestled with God over his misfortune; Moses questioned God at the burning bush; and Jacob wrestled with an angel then received a new name from God. "No more shall you be called Jacob, but Israel," declared the angel, "for you have wrestled with God and with men, and have prevailed" (Genesis 32: 29). As a result, the name Israel has come to mean "one who wrestles with God" and "one who is direct and honest with God." **Wrestling with God**, which the rabbis called *hutspah kelapei shmaya,* can take different forms, from arguing over the meaning of a sacred text to trying to understand the Holocaust.

The Biblical references to arguing with God presuppose God's existence and power in the world. Put simply, the existence of God was indisputable. However, in post-Holocaust writings, there is a dramatic shift from arguing *with* God to questioning where God was during the Holocaust, whether God exists at all. This shift has its roots in the post-Enlightenment era, where during the 18th century in Western Europe, reason was advanced as the culmination of faith. Rabbi Anson Laytner explains, "For many of us today, the argument is no longer rooted in faith; it is rooted in doubt. Where previous generations affirmed their belief in God's justice by expecting and demanding it, today's generation asserts its doubts about God's existence by questioning the lack of justice in Jewish history and the lack of meaning in Jewish suffering."[135] While the agnostic represents a questioner who is actively engaged in a relationship with God, the atheist proclaims simply that God does not exist at all. Therefore, for the atheist, the question of God and the Holocaust is moot.

Teaching about God and the Holocaust inevitably raises ethical and moral questions like these for both students and teachers. Some of us are firm in our theological beliefs, while others of us have unresolved or evolving understandings. Moreover, there is no definitive answer to the question of God and the Holocaust—perhaps there aren't even any adequate responses. While teaching about God is fraught with uncertainty, we hope you won't avoid the subject. Research consistently shows that children of all ages have questions about God and want a safe forum to wrestle with them. We hope that you will make your classroom that kind of space. Remember that when you engage in discussions about God:

- Don't confuse doubt with disrespect or avowed atheism with adolescent confrontationalism. Allow your students to try on positions and discard them if they so choose.

- Do encourage inquiry. Educators have an important role to play in nurturing faith. You don't need to have the answers in order to raise the questions.

---

[135]Anson Laytner, *Arguing With God: A Jewish Tradition* (Northvale, NJ: Jason Aronson Inc., Northvale, 1990), 236.

- Finally, there is no age too young and no student too old to consider the questions involved. The most appropriate age to broach the topic of God and the Holocaust is when your students raise the questions.

This chapter is intended as a launching board for discussion. While we explore numerous theological questions and responses, including critiques of each, this chapter is not an exhaustive survey of the topic.

The big ideas of this chapter are that:

- Struggling with God is a core concept of Jewish identity.

- There are many responses to the question of God and the Holocaust.

- Each person must find his/her own understanding of God and the Holocaust.

Key terms of this chapter include: *hutspah kelapei shmaya* —wrestling with God, free will, Hiding of the Face, 614th Commandment, and 'God is dead'.

Punishment

One strand of ultra-Orthodox Jewish theology justifies the Holocaust via a particular understanding of Jewish history and memory, namely, that Jewish history is made up of a series of persecutions with God as an eventual savior. A passage from the Passover *Haggadah* describing the Exodus from Egypt can be interpreted to support this claim. "It is this promise that has sustained our ancestors and us, for not just one enemy has arisen to destroy us; rather in every generation there are those who seek our destruction, but the Holy One, praised by He, saves us from their hands."[136] In this worldview, Jewish suffering results from God's chastising us for our sins or testing our love.

Critique: Most Jews, even most ultra-Orthodox Jews, however, reject this approach because it contradicts many other Jewish teachings. Not only does this approach suggest that all human decisions reflect God's will, but in this view, protest, doubt, and arguing with God are viewed as rebellions rather than engagements. Moreover, the depiction of God is one who is mostly wrathful and punishing. In addition, this approach implies that six million people were massacred because God was either testing or punishing us—a dangerous and problematic message. Would God need to test the faith of the newborn or punish the misdeeds of the young? (Both groups of course were murdered.)

---

[136]Ron Wolfson, Passover: *The Family Guide to Spiritual Celebration* (Woodstock, VT: Jewish Lights Publishing, 2003), 138.

Free Will

Arthur A. Cohen and Rabbi Joseph D. Soloveichik turn this strand of ultra-Orthodox reasoning on its head by asking not where God was during the Holocaust, but where was humanity. The infamous Biblical concept that we have been given **free will** or *bechira*—choice—is often used as a proof text for this philosophy. Tradition teaches that on the last day of his life, Moses gathered the Israelites together for a final initiation into the covenant. Moses said, "Surely this instruction which I command upon you this day is not too baffling for you, nor is it beyond reach. It is not in the heavens…neither is it beyond the sea…. No, the thing is very close to you, in your mouth and in your heart, to observe it. See, I have set before you this day, life and prosperity, death and adversity. …I have put before you life and death, blessing and curse. Choose life…" (Deuteronomy 30: 11-19). Many interpret this passage to mean that every individual in every generation has the freedom to choose whether or not to keep God's commandments and to work towards *tikkun olam* (repairing the world) or not. God gave each of us the power to enable or stop wrongdoing, to work for or against justice. The choice is ours to make. According to this philosophy, then, human beings are ultimately responsible for the atrocities of the Holocaust and, though God is important, God does not determine the course of history. In accordance with this view, it is a mistake to hold God responsible for the actions of humans.

Critique: The central problem with this interpretation concerns the notion of God as detached. According to traditional Judaism, God is omnipotent and compassionate. While the notion of free will supports the claim that humans created the Holocaust, it does not explain why God did not intervene to stop it. The Hebrew Bible is replete with references to God's benevolent intervention, the most obvious example being that God brought about the plagues to free the Hebrew slaves from Egyptian bondage. The depiction of a non-intervening God abnegates the Biblical and rabbinic conception of God as all-powerful and all-loving.

Hiding of the Face

Orthodox theologian Rabbi Eliezer Berkovitz finds meaning in the very contradiction between the notion of free will and God's presence. Berkovitz argues that in order for humanity to be free, God must not intervene. Berkovitz maintains that the history of the Jewish people has been continuously punctuated by a portrayal of God as either present or distant, with God nonetheless present even in silences. That is, God is both present and absent concurrently. When

God's face is hidden, it is not due to indifference, but reverence; God withdraws in order to create the space for human free will. In doing so, humans have the freedom to act in both good and evil ways. Berkovitz writes, "Because of the necessity of [God's] absence, there is the **'Hiding of the Face'** and the suffering of the innocent; because of the necessity of [God's] presence, evil will not ultimately triumph; because of it, there is hope for man."[137]

Critique: There are several problems with Berkovitz's interpretation. As with the problems with the free will approach, the portrayal of God as one who sits back and silently watches human suffering or who chooses to ignore it contradicts the depiction of God as savior, an image that appears throughout Biblical and rabbinic literature. In addition, the view that God must be hidden to enable humans to have free will is problematic. If God is omnipotent and benevolent, then God could have created a world where humans possess free will, but also possess an inclination for good over evil. Third, it could be argued that limiting human free will in order to prevent the Holocaust and other human atrocities would have been justified.

614th Commandment

Holocaust survivor and philosopher, Rabbi Emil Fackenheim claims that God was indeed present during the Holocaust, commanding the Jewish people to survive. Fackenheim proposed a 614th commandment, one beyond the 613 commandments that the medieval philosopher Moses Maimonides found in the Torah. Fackenheim famously claimed that Jews are forbidden to give Hitler a posthumous victory, by which he meant that Jews are commanded to survive and to remember the victims of the Holocaust so that Hitler does not 'win' again. Fackenheim argues that God mandated the **614th Commandment**, which obligates every Jew to ensure that Judaism survives and, by extension, that Jewish belief in God survives.

Critique: This argument is problematic for Jews who lack religious belief in the first place. For these Jews especially, it is highly unlikely that a divine commandment will persuade them to believe in God and observe Jewish ritual. However, the central difficulty with Fackenheim's position is that it offers no solution to the issue of human suffering. While Fackenheim depicts God as a commanding presence, not as a savior, the question left unanswered by Soloveichik, Cohen, Berkovitz and others remains unsolved by Fackenheim as well: Why didn't God intervene to stop the Holocaust?

---

[137] Anson Laytner, *Arguing With God: A Jewish Tradition* (Northvale, NJ: Jason Aronson Inc., Northvale, 1990), 60.

Death of God

Theologian and rabbi Richard Rubenstein's answer is that God did not intervene because '**God is dead**.' According to Rubenstein, God is now entirely absent from the Jewish people. Rubenstein asserts that since God did not intervene to stop the Holocaust, the traditional Jewish view of God must be untrue. While Rubenstein rejects the Biblical and rabbinic understandings of God, he insists that his position is not atheistic. Rather, he argues, the thread that once united God and humanity has been broken. In rejecting the traditional concept of God, Rubenstein maintains that although there can be no hope for a supernatural deity, spiritual subsistence can be found in traditional Jewish observances like *kashrut* and liturgy. Rubenstein later redefined his notion of God as a mystical expression akin to Buddhist theology.

Critique: A central problem with Rubenstein's theory is that it denies God's existence entirely. The statement that 'God is dead' offers no hope or comfort in religious terms and is contradictory to the understanding of God as infinite and eternal. Furthermore, Rubenstein's notion of an immanent rather than transcendent deity is far removed from the Jewish tradition of God.

Teaching Ideas

1. **Debate:** Ask your students to select one of the theological approaches from this chapter that they disagree with and to critique the approach. Then ask them to formulate an argument in favor of the approach. Students can learn a great deal by creating an argument in favor of something they disagree with. At the conclusion, explore whether their opinions about the approach have changed or shifted in any way.

2. **Talmudic Responsa:** Ask your students to develop their own response to God and the Holocaust, based in Jewish sources and building upon the work of other philosophers and theologians. Then ask them to engage in Talmudic discussion and debate. Ask them to write their argument on a sheet of paper leaving plenty of margins on all sides, then respond to and critique each other's arguments by writing responsas in the margins. Students can respond both to the original argument and to the added responsas so that each argument builds on the preceding ones.

3. **Spiritual Interview:** Ask your students to make a collective list of questions they have about God and the Holocaust. Then send them out to conduct interviews with their parents, friends, clergy, educators, and Holocaust survivors to find out what others think about God and the Holocaust. Come

back together to share the results: Are the responses similar to or different from the approaches described in this chapter? Were any of the responses surprising? What, if any, critiques do they have of the responses? Do any of the responses help answer their questions about God and the Holocaust? Do they present any new questions? What questions remain?

4. **Poetry:** Poetry naturally lends itself to exploring philosophical and theological issues. Holocaust survivor, Elie Wiesel is perhaps the best known poet and writer on the Holocaust; however, there are many others. Primo Levi's poetry is compelling and interesting. His two books of poetry are compiled together and translated into English in **Collected Poems**. Israeli poet, Dan Pagis questions whether Nazi persecutors were created in the image of God in his poem, *Testimony*. The poem is included in **The Selected Poetry of Dan Pagis** and in **Beyond Lament: Poets of the World Bearing Witness to the Holocaust.** Yala Korwin struggles with praying to God during the Holocaust in her poem, *A Prayer,* also published in Beyond Lament. R. Gabrielle S. Silten wrestles with God's role in the Holocaust in her poems, *Survivor's Shema* and *Where Were You, Adonai?*, both published in **High Tower Crumbling. And the World Stood Silent** is a collection of Sephardic poetry and **Blood to Remember** is a collection of Holocaust poetry written by American poets. Both books include poetry specifically related to God and the Holocaust. Finally, H. Leivick holds God directly responsible for the atrocities of the Holocaust in his poem, *The Accounting is Still Yours, Creator.* The poem, published in 1945, is not widely available; therefore we have reprinted it here.

> The accounting is still Yours, Creator,
> Even if it be true that You're not there.
> And however much people may have denied You—
> You are still there for the reckoning,
> To ask and to demand of You
> In our days which are dimmed over with death.
> —The final reckoning is still Yours, O Creator!…
>
> Even more than it is with him—Your own creation.
>
> The accounting is still Yours, Creator,
>
> Even though no one is demanding payment—
> A pile of ashes, however, is clear evidence…

That from Mount Moriah to Maidanek
It is no more than a leap of Isaac.
Judgment is still Yours, O Creator.[138]

Select various poems for your students to interpret. Then ask your students to write poetry of their own.

5. **Books and Films:** A handful of good books and films deal with the question of God and the Holocaust in a way that is appropriate for young people. **Hasidic Tales of the Holocaust** includes 89 original tales in the traditional Hasidic idiom. The tales are generally short and illuminate the issue of faith and the Holocaust. **I Have Some Questions About God** is a collection of 12 questions about God with responses from leading rabbis. The book is appropriate for elementary and middle schools students and does a fairly good job of answering questions about God head on. However, the chapter focusing on why there is evil in the world is a bit watered down, responding simply by saying that God gave people free will and is unable to intervene. Also geared for elementary and middle school students, **Tough Questions Jews Ask,** includes a chapter on why God lets terrible things happen, entitled, "How Can Anyone Believe in God After the Holocaust?" The answer given is that since all of us were created in God's image and given free will, God put us on the earth to intervene. Two good videos include: **The Quarrel**, based on a short story by Chaim Grade. The film, appropriate for high school age students, follows two Holocaust survivors as they discuss their painful wartime experiences and the religious questions they struggle with in its aftermath. **Questions of Faith: What's God Got to Do With Evil?** presents interviews with several Jewish and Christian thinkers on the notion of God and evil.

Resources for Teaching

And the World Stood Silent. Translated by Isaac Jack Levy and published by University of Illinois Press, Urbana, Chicago, 2000. *A collection of Sephardic poetry about the Holocaust.*

Beyond Lament: Poets of the World Bearing Witness to the Holocaust. Edited by Marguerite M. Striar and published by Northwestern University Press, Evanston, IL, 1998. *A collection of poems about the Holocaust including* Testimony *and other poems by Dan Pagis and several poems by Yala Korwin.*

---

[138]H. Leivick, H., "The Accounting is Still Yours, Creator, in *Arguing With God: A Jewish Tradition* (Northvale, NJ: Jason Aronson Inc., 1990), 201.

Blood to Remember. Edited by Charles Fishman and published by Texas Tech University Press, Lubbock, 1991. *A collection of poetry responding to the Holocaust written by American poets.*

Collected Poems. Written by Primo Levi, translated by Ruth Feldman and Brian Swann and published by Faber and Faber, Boston, 1988. *A collection of Levi's poetry from his two books,* Shema *and* Ad ora incerta.

Hasidic Tales of the Holocaust. Retold by Yaffa Eliach and published by Vintage Books, New York, 1982. *A collection of 89 original Hasidic tales about the Holocaust.*

High Tower Crumbling. Written by R. Gabriele S. Silten and published by Fithian Press, Santa Barbara, 1991. *A collection of Silten's poems dealing with the Holocaust.*

I Have Some Questions About God. Edited by Joel Lurie Grishaver and published by Torah Aura Productions, Los Angeles, 2002. *Designed for children in upper elementary, the book is a collection of 12 questions about God with responses from leading rabbis of various denominations including Bradley Shavit Artson and Elyse Frishman.*

The Quarrel. Produced by David Brandes and Kim Todd, 1990, 90 minutes. *Two Holocaust survivors meet again unexpectedly after the war. One has become an Orthodox rabbi and the other an avowedly secular intellectual. The film follows the two as they discuss their painful wartime experiences and the religious questions they struggle with in its aftermath.*

Questions of Faith, Part 3: What's God Got to Do With Evil? Distributed by UMCOM, 1988, 20 minutes. *Interviews with several Jewish and Christian clergy, theologians and writers including Rabbi Harold Kushner and Rabbi Susan Schnur on the notion of God and evil.*

The Selected Poetry of Dan Pagis. Written by Dan Pagis, translated by Stephen Mitchell and published by University of California Press, Berkeley, 1996. *A collection of Pagis' Hebrew poetry translated into English.*

Tough Questions Jews Ask. Written by Rabbi Edward Feinstein and published by Jewish Lights Publishing, Woodstock, VT, 2003. *Honest answers to some complicated theological questions about God and Judaism, with a chapter entitled, "Why Does God Let Terrible Things Happen?"*

Resources for Further Learning

After Tragedy and Triumph: Modern Jewish Thought and the American Experience. Written by Michael Berenbaum and published by Cambridge University Press, Cambridge, 1990. *A collection of essays exploring post-Holocaust*

Jewish identity in America. Includes references to Arthur A. Cohen, Joseph D. Soloveichik, Eliezer Berkovitz, Emil Fackenheim, and Richard Rubenstein.

Arguing With God: A Jewish Tradition. Written by Anson Laytner and published by Jason Aronson Inc., Northvale, NJ, 1990. *A comprehensive, user-friendly survey of the Jewish tradition of arguing with God.*

Hasidic Responses to the Holocaust in the Light of Hasidic Thought. Written by Pesach Schindler and published by Ktav Publishing House, Inc., Hoboken, NJ, 1990. *Explores the various trends within Hasidic thought in terms of spirituality and the Holocaust.*

Holocaust Theology. Written by Dan Cohn-Sherbok and published by Lamp Press, London, 1989. *Presents the arguments of various scholars concerning the Holocaust including Arthur A. Cohen, Eliezer Berkovitz, Emil Fackenheim, Richard Rubenstein, and Elie Wiesel.*

Man's Search For Meaning. Written by Viktor E. Frankl and published by Washington Square Press, New York, 1984. *Written by a Holocaust survivor and renowned psychiatrist who developed an approach to psychotherapy based on the theory that human's primary motivational force is our search for meaning.*

Stages of Faith: The Psychology of Human Development and the Quest for Meaning. Written by James W. Fowler and published by Harper & Row Publishers, San Francisco, 1981. *Considered the seminal theory on the stages of faith development.*

Teaching About God and Spirituality. Edited by Roberta Louis Goodman and Sherry H. Blumberg and published by A.R.E. Publishing, Inc., Denver, 2002. *A resource of various theories and techniques for teaching about God in a multitude of Jewish settings.*

AFTERMATH

Young children performing a dance in the Zeilsheim Displaced Person's' Camp, Germany, 1945.
USHMM, courtesy of Alice Lev.

In teaching about the aftermath of the war, there are three crucial and interlocked histories that deserve recognition: the plight of the survivors and remembrance of its victims, the trials of the perpetrators, and the destructions wrought by the war. This chapter concerns itself with the other two categories: the trials of the perpetrators immediately post-war and later, and the governmental responses post-war, including restitution payments and attempts at understanding.

Teaching about the trials of the perpetrators poses an interesting dilemma. On the one hand, it's important to humanize the perpetrators and to consider the ethical implications of the trials themselves. On the other hand, the very act of studying about people standing trial for war crimes can indict them in our imaginations. It is as hard for students as it is for jury members to bear in mind that those standing trial need their guilt to be proven rather than assumed.

Teaching about the aftermaths of the war also poses dilemmas of imagination and conscience. Whereas Germany, as a nation, clearly bore the guilt of having initiated a war of aggression, their country nonetheless lay in ruins at the close of the war. The German people were rightfully fully occupied; many were homeless; many more were starving. Should we sympathize with them or not? Should our disgust for the war, the atrocities and the Holocaust that were perpetrated mitigate that sympathy, erase it altogether or have no impact on it at all?

The big ideas of this chapter are that:

- The appropriateness of anger and disgust over the war and atrocities perpetrated by the German nation should not blind us to what the German people suffered.

- While some were brought to justice for the crimes they committed against humanity, many thousands never stood trial.

- Restitution payments were morally vexed ways for West Germany to atone for the atrocities of the Holocaust.

- The shifting political landscape of post-war Europe stunted the immediate possibilities for understanding the Holocaust.

Key terms of this chapter include: International Military Tribunal, Nuremberg Trials, crimes against humanity, bombing of Dresden, firestorm, *blitzkrieg*, Zones of Occupation, deNazification, Cold War, Conference on Jewish Material Claims against Germany, Konrad Adenauer, Adolf Eichmann, banality of evil, and reparations payments.

Nuremberg Trials

Long before the end of the war, the allies were already planning what to do in its aftermath, debating whether those responsible for the war should be summarily shot, brought before national tribunals or tried on the world's stage. Immediately after the surrender of Germany, the third option was taken. An **International Military Tribunal** was formed in the summer of 1945 under the direction of the United States, United Kingdom, the Soviet Union and France. Each country contributed a judge and a prosecution team. The presiding judge was Lord Justice Geoffrey Lawrence of Great Britain. While some in Germany objected, claiming that such a trial was simply another arena for the victors to triumph over the vanquished, many applauded the decision, claiming that the enormity of the crimes justified such an organization. Each country involved prepared for the trials; the Americans, for example, took responsibility for finding witnesses, gathering evidence, and rounding up some of the top-level officials who would be tried. In addition, the chief American prosecutor, Robert Jackson, drafted some of the laws that would serve as the basis for the trial. This, too, provoked controversy, as in most countries, trying someone for breaking a law that hasn't been drafted yet is regarded as unlawful. Jackson, however, argued carefully, that "what we propose is to punish acts which have been regarded as criminal since the time of Cain and have been so written in every civilized code."[139]

Rene Molho, an Auschwitz survivor from Greece whose brother died in his arms after being subjected to Nazi medical experiments, aided the Americans in rounding up Nazi bureaucrats. Molho told Simone a story about that phase of his life's work after the war. Having worked in Auschwitz for two and a half years, extracting gold teeth from the corpses of the gas chambers, Molho knew the SS in charge there personally and well. As he traveled with the American troops dedicated to capturing Nazi officials, he became friendly with them, trading jokes, sharing meals, and eventually telling them his story. It so happened that one of the men responsible for his brother's death was captured by the American squad. Recognizing both the special bond they had established with Molho and the complex emotions that Molho would have about this man, the Americans gave him a military-issued pistol and left him alone in the doctor's cell, licensing him to kill, even while it was explicitly against American orders. Molho didn't do it. "I couldn't do it," he told Simone, with a mixture of regret, disappointment and pride.

Once prepared, the Tribunal set the stage for the trials in Nuremberg (known as the **Nuremberg Trials**), site not only of massive Nazi propaganda rallies but also the place for which the detestable Nuremberg Laws were named. As a side note, Nuremberg was also chosen as the site of the trials since it was one of the few German cities left at that time with both a standing courthouse and a nice hotel. Twenty-one top-level Nazi officials stood trial. Among them were party leaders, state ministers, military leaders and propaganda ministers. While awaiting trial, each defendant's cell was guarded by a single guard whose job it was to make sure that the defendant didn't kill himself before he stood trial. Bolstered by an enormous amount of documentary evidence, careful witnesses and film footage, the prosecuting team accused the defendants of three types of crimes: crimes against peace (which included both the "conspiracy to wage an aggressive war" and the actual "waging of aggressive war"), war crimes (which included the murder of civilians, POW's, the use of slave labor, and the wanton destruc-

---

[139]International Military Tribunal, *Trial of the Major War Criminals*, 42 vols. (Nuremburg: Secretariat of the Tribunal, 1947-1949).

tion of property), and **crimes against humanity** (the deliberate murder of people on the basis of their religious, racial or political positions).

Jackson delivered an opening statement for the prosecution eloquently, saying in part, "The wrongs which we seek to condemn and punish have been so calculated, so malignant, and so devastating that civilization cannot tolerate their being ignored because it cannot survive their being repeated."[140] The defendants tended to argue that either they knew nothing about the mass exterminations or that they were following orders and performing their duties. Hermann Goering, who was second in command to Hitler, was unrepentant to the end, proclaiming that he was proud to have served "under the greatest son which my people produced in its thousand-year history."[141] Only a few of the defendants seemed to recognize the horrendousness of the atrocities they had perpetrated. Albert Speer, for example, who had served as the Minister of Armaments, said the following when called to the witness stand: "This war has brought an inconceivable catastrophe…. Therefore, it is my unquestionable duty to assume my share of responsibility for the disaster of the German people."[142] The few who did show remorse were given lighter sentences as a result.

In all, 18 of the defendants were found guilty of one or more of the counts, and three were not. The three were immediately arrested on the charges of breaking German laws. Of the other 18, eight were given ten years to life in prison, and the other ten were awarded the death sentence. All of those were publicly hung with the exception of Hermann Goering, who committed suicide by swallowing a cyanide capsule he had managed to smuggle into his cell. It's worth noting that of those who were condemned to death, each had a few weeks between the delivery of the verdict and their public hangings, weeks in which they could visit with family and friends and say their goodbyes: a marked contrast from the kinds of murders they inflicted on their victims.

Over the next four years, there were no fewer than 12 other trials held at Nuremberg. In addition to the trial of the famous war criminals, there were trials of doctors, members of the SS, judges, bureaucrats and industrialists. Lucille Eichengreen translated for the British troops as they prepared for the SS trials in Hamburg. Having survived the Lodz ghetto, Auschwitz and Bergen-Belsen concentration camps, upon liberation, Eichengreen helped the British round up members of the SS in what had been her pre-war hometown. Picked up from

---

[140]Trials of War Criminals before the Nuremberg Military Tribunals under Control Council Law No. 10. Nuremberg, October 1946—April 1949. Washington D.C.: U.S. G.P.O, 1949-1953.

[141]International Military Tribunal, *Trial of the Major War Criminals*, 42 vols. (Nuremburg: Secretariat of the Tribunal, 1947-1949).

[142]Albert Speer, *Inside the Third Reich*. (New York: Touchstone Books, 1997).

her barracks in the Bergen–Belsen DP camp, Eichengreen went with the British colonel from house to house, ringing the doorbells and asking in perfect German whether the SS inhabitants were home. In that capacity, she came face-to-face with the female SS who had beaten her at Bergen-Belsen. Eichengreen had to calmly translate the blatant lies the SS woman told about not having been involved. Eichengreen later testified as a witness at the trial, after which she received death threats, hastily scrawled on paper and shoved beneath the door of her barracks. The British colonel who had so valued her services helped arrange papers for her to leave the DP camp and Germany.[143]

Aftermaths

By the time of the first Nuremberg Trial, Germany and much of Europe lay in ruins. Because of the Allied practice of carpet bombing—dropping wave after wave of blankets of bombs on German cities—almost no German city remained unscathed. The **bombing of Dresden** was paradigmatic of the practice. In February of 1945, the British and Americans jointly bombed Dresden. In the first wave, the British bombed with 234 planes, and in the next wave, they bombed with 538 planes. Together, those two waves unleashed 2,656 tons of bombs, which by that point in the war, was routine. Also routine was the practice of targeting the lower-class neighborhoods of a city, as those tended to be places with higher concentrations of civilians. Ten hours later, the Americans bombed Dresden with 311 planes. Dresden went up in flames, generating a **firestorm**, where the thousands of small fires merged into a terrifying, howling hurricane of fire. The heat of the firestorm was so intense in Dresden that Germans taking refuge in their basements were literally baked alive. The fierceness of the firestorm earned Dresden initial reports of over 100,000 killed that single night. Though it turned out that fewer people had been killed in Dresden than in the similar bombing of Hamburg some months earlier, Dresden became the symbol of Allied attacks in Germany, deserved or not.

Such destruction characterized much of war-torn Europe and beyond. German *blitzkrieg* (lightning) warfare had decimated towns and cities throughout Europe and Britain. In fighting the war, the Americans' carpet bombing of Tokyo had razed that city. Indeed, in Tokyo, while the carpet bombing looked like that at Dresden, the American bombs had been laced with napalm. Hiroshima and Nagasaki were decimated by the atomic blasts. In China, the destruction wrought by the Japanese was large scale. In short, from Northern Africa to the edges of

---

[143]Lucille Eichengreen, *From Ashes to Life* (San Francisco: Mercury House, 1994), 130-159.

the Soviet Union, almost no country was unharmed by the massive destruction and carnage of the Second World War.

Not only did Germany lie in ruins structurally, but its people suffered at the end of the war. As the Russian armies liberated Germany from Nazism, many troops stole, pillaged and raped, an experience that German women tended not to discuss, having been part of the aggressor nation. (It's worth noting, too, that while the Russian liberators used rape as a kind of retribution, they often couldn't distinguish between German women and German Jewish women survivors.) Very few German families remained intact, having lost fathers and sons to the warfront, women and children to the bombings. The Germans were starving as well. And, because they were fully occupied by the French, British, Americans and Soviets, floods of refugees from Eastern Europe flowed into their borders, seeking aid and protection from the allied nations. Likewise, Germans from the Sudetenland were traveling back into Germany, having been ousted by the Czechs.

Divided into **Zones of Occupation**, Germany underwent **deNazification**, the attempt to root out all former Nazis from positions of power. The trials were one facet of deNazification. The process was uneven at best. In the French and British zones, former Nazis were sometimes allowed to remain in their positions since it was deemed important for someone who understood the regions' infrastructures to help in rebuilding them. In the American zones, the rules were stricter, though it was understood that lesser Nazis, whose trials would be simpler, were to be rounded up before Nazi higher-ups, a decision which allowed many Nazis to escape while they could. In the Russian zones, the screening process was the strictest. Property owners considered to be former Nazis had their land and businesses confiscated and were disbanded from their posts. Once they went through Soviet education efforts, however, they could be pardoned and rise to power again within the Soviet system. DeNazification also included the reinstatement of independent political parties and reeducation efforts among the populace at large.

Germany was aided in rebuilding its national infrastructures post-war through huge loans from the United States. In fact, while most Americans sought to "bring the boys home," the U.S. military kept a large presence in Germany and Japan, saving both countries the economic costs and possible excesses of rebuilding their armies. Almost immediately post-war, though, political tensions flared between Britain and the U.S.A. on one side and the Soviet Union on the other. Britain and the U.S.A. favored self-determination for the countries of Eastern

Europe, whereas the Soviet Union preferred Soviet allegiance. The Soviet Union wanted war reparations payments, given their enormous losses they had accrued in fighting the war. The **Cold War** that blossomed from this opposition transformed the world. In terms of Holocaust memory, the almost immediate realignment of West Germany as a close ally of the U.S.A. against the Soviet Union resulted in less concerted efforts to identify and prosecute war criminals and a kind of rejection or at least suppression of German wartime atrocities.

Ironically, perhaps, that suppression of German atrocities was aided by the eventual payment of reparations to Israel and to the **Conference on Jewish Material Claims against Germany**, which represented the interests of survivors outside of Israel. **Konrad Adenauer**, who became the first Chancellor of the newly established Federal Republic of Germany, West Germany, in 1949, famously accepted the guilt of the German people for the Holocaust, saying, "In our name, unspeakable crimes have been committed that demand compensation and restitution, both moral and material, for the persons and properties of the Jews who have been so seriously harmed…."[144] Thus, Adenauer agreed to make payments to both Israel and the Claims Conference for lost property, material claims and the restitution of the survivors. Importantly, the payments never attempted to compensate monetarily for the loss of life. No amount of money could do that. Thus, Adenauer's policy was laudable, and yet his promises to the German people left something to be desired. Not only did he stipulate that there was no legal basis to make reparations payments, but he seemed to consider the payments to stand in the place of a national dialogue about the atrocities. The payments were the precursor for West Germans to progress beyond the atrocities, to rebuild their lives and their country "normally." As a result, no national dialogue about the atrocities ensued until years later. That said, the reparations payments substantially aided both the survivors in Israel, a fledgling state in 1951, and in the U.S.A. and elsewhere. Reparations negotiations continued throughout the end of the century, determining who deserved restitution for what and what would be done with the Jewish assets with no surviving claimants.

Eichmann Trial

In 1960, the world was stunned by the capture of an infamous German war criminal, **Adolf Eichmann**. Israeli troops, in violation of Argentina's sovereignty, kidnapped Eichmann, who had been living in Argentina since the end of the war under an assumed name. During the war, Eichmann had been a lieutenant colonel of the SS and head of Jewish affairs for the German Gestapo. He had

---

[144]Nana Sagi, *German Reparations: A History of the Negotiations* (Jerusalem: Magnes, 1980).

participated in the Wannsee Conference as one of the 15 high-ranking German officers coordinating the extermination of the Jews, and he himself had coined the euphemistic term, the 'Final Solution.' It was his office that issued the orders for Jews to be rounded up in ghettos and mass murdered in the East. Moreover, he had served as supervisor of all four divisions of the *Einsatzgruppen*. Not surprisingly, though he was captured at the end of the war and put in an American camp for German POWs. He made sure to escape, knowing that if he were recognized, he would be put on trial. Using a variety of false names, Eichmann escaped to Argentina, where, he eventually felt comfortable enough to send for his wife and children.

A storm of controversy erupted after his capture, not disputing his status, but arguing over the legality of kidnapping him in order to stand trial. When at first, Argentines were unsure as to whether a group of furious survivors had kidnapped him or whether the Israeli Special Forces had, they protested to the United Nations, which subsequently held a special proceeding to discuss the case. International opinion was largely divided over whether fighting crime through lawless means violated the results. Israel's Prime Minister at the time, Golda Meir, apologized to the Argentine government, but was adamant that the ends justified the means. Most Israelis agreed, seeing themselves as the inheritors and defenders of the Holocaust's remnants. Dissatisfied with Meir's apology, Argentina returned Israel's ambassador, cutting off diplomatic relations, and yet they nonetheless never requested Eichmann's extradition.

A division of the Israeli police force prepared for the trial by living with Eichmann for almost a year. In a heavily guarded, secret location, they interviewed him daily, allowing him to check the transcripts of the interviews for errors. Eichmann cooperated fully. Eichmann himself chose his defense lawyer, Robert Servatius, a German lawyer whose fees were paid for by the Israeli government. The prosecution team was led by the Attorney General, Gideon Hausner. A panel of three judges presided over the hearings, all of its members native to Germany and fluent in German so that no translators were required. Eichmann stood trial in Jerusalem, encased in a bulletproof glass booth to prevent his assassination.

For every one of the 15 counts, Eichmann's defense team argued initially that the count itself was unlawful, for not only had the Israeli laws Eichmann supposedly violated not been in existence at the time of violation, but even the country of Israel had not existed. Moreover, Servatius argued for dismissal of the case given that Jewish judges couldn't possibly be impartial. For each count, the judges responded judiciously, allowing the trial to proceed by arguing, for example, that no one, Jew or non-Jew, should be impartial to mass murder. Once the proceedings continued, Eichmann's defense tended to be the same on all counts. While he admitted to his involvement in the murder of Jews, his defense team argued that he was powerless to prevent it, that he was a bureaucrat rather than an organizer, and that he had just been following orders. In these regards, Eichmann's defense was quite similar to many of the Nuremberg defendants'.

The entire trial was televised (with the permission of the Israeli government), and shown all over Europe and the United States. Hundreds of reporters covered the trial as well. In Israel, the public was glued to the television set for the entirety of the four-month trial. Many Holocaust survivors—most of whom had to be convinced to testify—provided their testimony as part of the trial, a feat which radically altered the place of survivors in Israeli society. Many thousands of letters reacting to the trial poured in as well: some of Holocaust survivors whose testimonies flooded out of them, released from a 15-year silence, others from Israeli youth who had literally never heard of the atrocities associated with the Holocaust, some from those who objected to the trial, some of which were antisemitic.

In December of 1961, four months after the end of the trial, the judges reconvened to render a verdict. Eichmann was found guilty on all counts. He was subsequently executed by hanging. His final words were unrepentant: "Long live Germany. Long live Austria. Long live Argentina. I owe a lot to these countries and I shall not forget them. I had to obey the rules of war and my flag."[145] His ashes were scattered in the Mediterranean to prevent his grave from becoming a pilgrimage site for neo-Nazis. He remains the only person ever to have received the death penalty in Israeli history.

Teaching Ideas

1. **Discussion Prompts**: Whereas Germany, as a nation, clearly bore the guilt of having initiated a war of aggression, their country nonetheless lay in ruins at the close of the war. The German people were fully occupied; many were homeless; many more were starving; some of the women had been raped by advancing Russian solders; many of the surviving children had lost their fathers and brothers, husbands and uncles. Should we sympathize with the Germans or not? Should our disgust for the war, the atrocities and the Holocaust that were perpetrated mitigate that sympathy, erase it altogether or have no impact on it at all?

[145]Peter Baehr (Ed), *The Portable Hannah Arendt,* (New York: Penguin Books, 2000), 365. (Originally appeared in Hannah Arendt's coverage of the trial that appeared in The New Yorker Magazine, March 16, 1963.)

When Heinrich Boll, the German writer, wrote his sons a final letter before his death, he told them that they would always be able to tell the difference between Germans by paying attention to their casual speech, specifically whether they referred to April, 1945 as "the liberation" or "the defeat." What do these two different terms reflect about their visions of Nazism? Are there parallels in our language today that position people politically? (How, for example, do your students' parents refer to the War in Iraq—as an invasion or liberation?) How do you suppose these different types of Germans responded to the verdicts at Nuremberg? How might such different Germans think about the telling of their stories after the war?

Compare dimensions of the Nuremberg and Eichmann trials. What are the advantages and disadvantages of an international military tribunal vs. a national (Israeli, German or otherwise) court deciding a case of war crimes? Why might some of the defendants in each case have cooperated? In the Eichmann Trial, for example, the defense team didn't try to delay the trial in any way, but cooperated with its proceedings fully, and Eichmann himself, in preparation for the trial, provided the prosecution with thousands of pages of transcribed interviews. Why? Was the Eichmann Trial itself legal?

One of the reporters who covered the Eichmann Trial for *The New Yorker Magazine* was the German Jewish émigré, Hannah Arendt. In discussing her impression of Eichmann, she coined a term that had tremendous currency for a long time. She described his smallness, his ordinariness as **"the banality of evil,"** its being utterly commonplace. Though Arendt mistakenly considered Eichmann not to be a raving antisemite, which later documentation proved him to be, her term was nonetheless intriguing. Ask your students whether they think evil really does come in banal packages, people, and events or whether evil is usually recognizable, obvious, blatant. How do your students imagine evil looks?

Among survivors, there have always been arguments over whether to accept or even to apply for **reparations payments** from the German government. At issue is not only the bureaucratic headache involved, (imagine trying to prove ownership of a bank account or personal property when none of the supporting documentation exists), but the moral issues at stake. Some survivors felt that they wanted nothing to do with Germany even after the end of the war; others felt that to grant reparations payments was the least that the German government could do and that the payments were well-deserved. Some survivors and their families refused to buy German goods in the post-war periods (Volkswagen cars, Krupps coffeemakers, etc.). Ask your students if, after learning about the Holocaust, they're inclined to privately boycott German-made products? Should Jewish descendents of survivors refrain from buying such products, and if so, until which generation, and more importantly, why?

2. **Simulating**: The Nuremberg Trials are a perfect venue for simulating, in part because of the wide availability of the courtroom transcripts and in part because of the appropriateness of the material. In having students role play the part of prosecution and defense attorneys, key witnesses and judges, your students will learn the very skills education is meant to foster: investigation, deliberation and judgment. For a pre-packaged simulation (which requires you only to pay), Social Studies School Service sells a product called **Nuremberg: A Simulation of the International Military Tribunal** for $28.00. For those willing to do a little footwork, however, there are many houses of digitized documents from the Nuremberg Trials, and they're easy enough to excerpt in order to prepare your students to play their roles in the courtroom. **The Nuremberg Mock Trials** website does that for you. Otherwise, for a complete archive of the Nuremberg Trials documents, see the website at **The Harvard Law School Library's Nuremberg Trials Project,** or, for an abridged set of documents, see the website at **The Nizkor Project.**

3. **Films**: If you do choose to enact a trial simulation, showing excerpts of the actual trial that the students have just enacted can be very powerful. Otherwise, fictionalized movies make for good viewing when excerpted, too. Once your students know something about the trial, they will be much more interested in these scenes and much more able to learn from them. A few good films include the following. The PBS produced documentary, **The Trial of Adolf Eichmann**: Though two hours long, this documentary provides excellent pieces for use in classrooms and it has an exceedingly rich accompanying website. We especially recommend the vignette in which Dr. Martin Foldi, survivor witness at the trial, described his selection at Auschwitz. The story provided the basis for Spielberg's piercing girl in the red coat in **Schindler's List**. The 1961 movie, **Judgment at Nuremberg**, is based on the judges' trials at Nuremberg. Though it's too long and too slow to watch in its entirety, it, too, has provocative clips for use in the classroom. (We don't suggest the part with Judy Garland as a *hausfrau* for classroom use, though it's interesting to see.)

4. **Play**: The text of Peter Weiss' play, **The Investigation**, is based almost wholly on the transcribed text of the Frankfurt War Crimes Trials. Peter Weiss rearranged the wording for dramatic effect, but he only actually wrote a few lines of the play. While the play in its entirety necessitates substantial discussion, for example, about where the Jewish victims of the Holocaust are. Nonetheless, the separate cantos work beautifully as classroom scripts.

5. **Document Analysis**: In studying the aftermath in Germany from an American perspective, there is a fabulous website that the American Historical Association posted called, **Constructing a Post-War World: The G.I. Roundtable Series in Context**. The website duplicates a series of pamphlets that the American Historical Association was drafted to write between 1942 and 1946. The pamphlets address such questions as "Do you want your wife to work after the war?" and "How did the Germans get that way?" The site includes discussion questions and fascinating analysis of the text of the pamphlets. For discussing the aftermath, we especially like "Can the Germans be reeducated?" which discusses the problem of teacher shortages in post-war Germany, the pros and cons of allowing pro-Nazi teachers to remain and the lack of textbooks.

6. **"Vicious Court"**: When the Jewish High Court, the *Sanhedrin*, had the power to assign capitol punishment; it never did, for a *Sanhedrin* that put a person to death once every seven years would be called a "vicious court," a court that didn't deserve to decide. Some sages considered that a *Sanhedrin* that put a person to death once every 70 years deserved the same derogatory title. Rabbi Akiva and Rabbi Tarfon, in fact, argued that had they served on the *Sanhedrin* when capitol punishment was allowed, they would have required such excruciating standards from witnesses, that, in effect, capitol punishment would never be employed. For example, two witnesses would have had to have overheard the murderer planning the act, warned him against it, seen him enact it, and agreed about not only the date, time, and place, but if such a murder had been committed beneath a tree, both witnesses would have to agree on the shape of the leaves of the tree above. In short, the death penalty was not to be invoked in the ancient, traditional Jewish court. Have your students do some research on the Talmudic Rabbis' positions on the question of the death penalty, then ask them to hypothesize what particular rabbis would have thought about Eichmann's punishment.

7. **Second Generation Issues**: Have your students research the psychological after-effects of surviving the Holocaust, asking them specifically to examine how survivors' behaviors and attitudes affected their children and grandchildren. How many generations do they suspect are affected when a single generation undergoes mass trauma? What's the difference between undergoing a collective trauma and an individual one? For advanced students, the following website may be a helpful launching point. It lists psychological studies that have been published about children of survivors, who are sometimes referred to as COS.

Resources for Teaching

Children of Survivors. Website: http://www.remember.org/children/children.html. *There are lots of websites dedicated to helping, researching and understanding children of survivors, often referred to as The Second Generation. This website is a good entryway to them. Maintained as a sub-site of the Cybrary, it has links to organizations to support second and third generations as well as studies and books about them.*

G.I Roundtable Series. Website: http://www.historians.org/projects/ GIRoundtable/GermanReEd/ GermanReEd_Intro.htm. *This website, produced by the American Historical Society, has fabulous documents as well as helpful guides to discussing them in class. Students love even just to see these reproduced as the content and the language both give them a sense of that time.*

The Harvard Law School Library's Nuremberg Trials Project. Website: http://www.law.harvard.edu/library/collections/digital/war_crime_trials_ nuremberg.php. *This website contains all of the Nuremberg Trials documents, which are in the process of being digitized so that they can be searched.*

The Investigation. Written by Peter Weiss and published by Marion Boyers Publishing, London, 2000. *Using almost wholly the text of the Frankfurt War Crimes Trials, this play is useful for having students examine the issues of justice, politics and memory that come into play.*

Judgment at Nuremberg. Directed by Stanley Kramer, 1961, 178 minutes. *Based on the actual Nuremberg Trials of war-time judges, this fictionalized version stars Spencer Tracy as the American judge who presides over the court and wrestles with his own notions of right and wrong. Maximillian Schell does a remarkable job of illuminating the role of the defense lawyer. The film is widely available and includes actual footage of the liberation of the camps.*

Nuremberg Mock Trials Website. Website: http://www.lib.uconn.edu/ online/research/speclib/ASC/Nuremberg/Mock_Trial.htm. *This website, based* on the archives of Senator Thomas Dodd, organizes excerpts from the Nuremberg Trials archives and sorts them into roles for students to read.

Nuremberg: A Simulation of the International Military Tribunal. Produced by Interact, http://www.interact-simulations.com, and available at www.socialstudies.com. *This simulation allows students to portray prosecution and defense attorneys, witnesses, and judges to re-create the Nuremberg Tribunal. The kit includes a student guide and a leader's guide. It's recommended for 25 players, but can be done with fewer.*

Tractate of Sanhedrin. Website: http://www.come-and-hear.com/sanhedrin/sanhedrin_40.html. *This translation of the Babylonian Talmud Tractate, Sanhedrin, can help students consider the war crimes trials from traditional, text-based, Jewish perspectives. The texts are annotated, though their language is still quite tricky, so you will need to guide them through it.*

The Trial of Adolf Eichmann. Produced by ABC News Productions for PBS, 1997, 120 minutes. *This documentary, available through PBS, uses heaps of film footage of the Eichmann Trial. It is well produced and excellent for classroom use. The accompanying website is easy to read and informative, excellent for classroom usage, too. It's located at:* http://www.pbs.org/eichmann/study4.htm

Resources for Further Learning

Fear and Hope: Three Generations of the Holocaust. Written by Dan Bar-On and published by Harvard University Press, Cambridge, 1995. *Through interviews with five families over three generations, Bar-On analyzes the ways in which each has dealt with the Holocaust, the stories that were told and weren't.*

From Ashes to Life. Written by Lucille Eichengreen with Harriet Hyman Chamberlain and published by Mercury House, San Francisco, 1994. *A lesser-known memoir with some appeal. The chapter entitled, "Displaced Persons Camp" describes her work with the British in preparation for the Hamburg Trials.*

Israel's Secret Wars: A history of Israel's Intelligence Services. Written by Ian Black and Benny Morris and published by Grove Press, New York, 1992. *A fascinating read, this book describes the intelligence machinery that allowed for the capture of Adolf Eichmann, among other events.*

While America Watches. Written by Jeffrey Shandler and published by Oxford University Press, Oxford, 2000. *This book is truly unique and fabulously interesting. Shandler documents how television, which was in the 1950s a powerful force in the American imagination, covered the Holocaust. His chapter on the Nuremberg Trials is thoroughly provocative, as is his coverage of the Sunday morning religious programming in which sermons dealt with the Holocaust.*

COMMEMORATION

Participants from around the world attended the annual March of the Living at Auschwitz May 2, 2000.
© Jacek Bednarczyk/CORBIS.

Given the enormous popularity of studying, commemorating and remembering the Holocaust now, it is important to acknowledge that Holocaust memory has not always been encouraged by either survivors them-selves or by the Jewish community at large. In the immediate aftermath of the Holocaust, many survivors simply wanted to forget their experiences and get on with their lives. They were absorbed with the challenges of raising young chil-dren in new lands, making a living, learning a new language, and acclimating to strange customs, neighborhoods, and political systems. Though they spoke of their experiences among themselves, they rarely spoke about the events of the Holocaust publicly. Publicly, they seemed to have 'forgotten' what they endured. In the United States and Israel, such forgetting was supported by the broader society.

Survivors who immigrated to the United States in the 1940s and 1950s were encouraged to assimilate into the Melting Pot of the American dream. However, in order to melt into the pot, it was necessary to forget one's past, or at least to hide it from public view. Like most immigrant groups in the first half of the 20th century, European Jews maintained some of the Old Country in their private homes, but publicly eschewed conspicuousness, preferring instead to blend into mainstream American culture. Alan Mintz explains the American Jewish psyche at the time. He writes that "overt identification with the Holocaust and memorialization of its victims would have drawn unwanted notice...."[146] Furthermore, survivors themselves were not held in high regard, but were often viewed as psychologically damaged by the ordeal of the Holocaust. In her memoir, Ruth Kluger explains that a fellow survivor, a young woman like she, had wanted to attend nursing school but was turned down for admission. Though the friend had stellar grades and great qualifications, she was assumed to be too damaged to be able to care for others.[147] The very term survivor with its intimation of heroism did not come into wide usage until decades later. At first, survivors were simply called refugees, a term that both minimized the severity of their experience and lumped them together with all other immigrants who sought refuge in America.

For somewhat similar reasons, the nascent State of Israel seemed to muzzle many survivors' stories. Israelis were occupied with establishing and constructing a new state, and while Israel recognized its perverse debt to the Holocaust, since nearly half its population was comprised of survivors, the newly emerging modern Israeli society opposed the very idea of victimhood. Anita Shapira juxtaposes Israelis' attitudes about the War of Independence and about the Holocaust. She writes:

> Compared with the heroics of the war, the ordeal of the Holocaust seemed miserable, even repulsive. One could talk endlessly about the war, tell stories, wax enthusiastic about acts of bravery. But it was difficult to talk about the Holocaust. People did not know how to handle the horror stories and did their best to avoid hearing them. The tendency of survivors to tell and retell what they had been through seemed masochistic, like refusing to let wounds heal. [148]

James E. Young elaborates that the Holocaust "seemed to prove the Zionist dictum that without a state and the power to defend themselves, Jews in exile would always be vulnerable to just this kind of destruction. As a result, the early

---

[146]Ian Mintz, *Popular Culture and the Shaping of Holocaust Memory in America* (Seattle: University of Washington Press, 2001), 6.

[147]Ruth Kluger, *Still Alive: A Holocaust Girlhood Remembered* (New York: Feminist Press, 2001).

[148]Anita Shapira, *The Holocaust and World War II as Elements of the Yishuv Psyche Until 1948*, in *Thinking About the Holocaust After Half a Century*, edited by Alvin H. Rosenfeld (Bloomington: Indiana University Press, 1997), 75.

leaders found little reason to recall the Holocaust beyond its direct link to the new state."[149]

It wasn't until the early 1960s with the trial of Adolf Eichmann in Israel and a cultural turn towards embracing the immigrant story in America that survivors' stories began to be heard in both places. The trial of Nazi SS Lieutenant Colonel Adolf Eichmann was the world's first televised trial. Israel's Prime Minister David Ben Gurion had agreed to let an American station televise the entirety of the trial in order to inform the world about the atrocities of the Holocaust. The trial revealed to a shocked audience the Nazi campaign to mass murder European Jewry. Haim Gouri explains, "The trial legitimized the disclosure of one's past. What had been silenced and suppressed gushed out and became common knowledge."[150] The trial captured the imaginations of viewers worldwide, shifting public interest from the abstractness of World War II to the personal, human stories of the Holocaust. Around the same time, the civil rights movement began to take shape in the United States, lifting the veil of suppression from all immigrants and oppressed groups' stories and inaugurating the beginnings of an era of diversity.

Over the next two decades, the status of survivors continued to improve, in part due to Elie Wiesel's rise to literary and political prominence in the United States. Mintz writes, "The stigma attached to survivors had gradually been removed, and in the meantime survivors had succeeded in the hard work of building families and businesses. Now that attitudes had shifted to make their stories sought after, survivors could afford, in several senses, to let memory-speak."[151]

Today, museums, monuments, and memorials to the past are being built in North and South America, Europe, and Israel at an unprecedented rate. In the United States alone, over 600 museums have been built since 1970, and the American Association of Museums estimates that another 150 will be constructed or expanded during the next few years, at a cost of some $4.3 billion. The U.S. Holocaust Memorial Museum in Washington, D.C. attracts over two million visitors per year. James Young explains that "as the last generation of survivors begins to pass on, many seem almost desperate to leave behind a place, an object around which Holocaust memory might live on. Moreover, as other forms of Jewish learning and traditional education wane among an ever more assimilated generation, the vicarious memory of past catastrophe serves increasingly

[149]James E. Young, *The Texture of Memory: Holocaust Memorials and Meaning* (New Haven: Yale University Press, 1993), 211.

[150]Haim Gouri, *Facing the Glass Booth in Holocaust Remembrance: The Shapes of Memory*, edited by Geoffrey H. Hartman (Oxford: Blackwell Publishers, Inc., 1995), 155.

[151]Alan Mintz, *Popular Culture and the Shaping of Holocaust Memory in America* (Seattle: University of Washington Press, 2001), 22.

as a center for Jewish identity and knowledge."[152] While today, the most widely observed form of Holocaust commemoration occurs once a year on Holocaust Remembrance Day, like most evolutionary processes, the development of Holocaust memory was and continues to be slow and oftentimes controversial.

This chapter describes the evolution of Holocaust memory and some of the challenges of commemoration.

The big ideas of this chapter are that:

- Memory is imbued with national myths, ideals and political needs.
- The Jewish notion of memory is rooted in the past and contains a focus on the future.
- Memory and commemoration of the Holocaust continue to evolve and change over time.

Key terms of this chapter include: *Yizkhor Bikher*—Memorial Books, *lizkhor*—to remember, *Yad Vashem*—Holocaust Memorial Museum in Israel, *Yom HaShoah VeHagvurah*—Day of Commemorating the Holocaust and Heroism (a.k.a. *Yom HaShoah*—Holocaust Remembrance Day), and *Yom HaZikaron*—Memorial Day.

The Evolution of Holocaust Commemoration

Any investigation of memory is a complex endeavor. Remembrance is vital in shaping our links to the past; the way we remember both defines us in the present, and orients us towards our futures. A society's memory is negotiated in beliefs and values, rituals and institutions, and by such public sites as museums, memorials, and monuments. Yet, memory is slippery and unstable, contingent on the rememberer to shape its destiny. Memory is caught in an extraordinarily complex web of ritual, historical, political, and psychological factors. Thus, commemorative sites and events exhibit a variety of national myths, ideals, and political needs and compromises. They are invested with a nation's rites or the objects of a people's pilgrimage; it could be said that commemoration is endowed with national soul and memory.

The nature of memory in Jewish thought is rooted in the Hebrew Bible. Yosef Hayim Yerushalmi emphasizes that "only in Israel and nowhere else is the injunction to remember felt as a religious imperative to an entire people."[153] Its echoes are everywhere in Jewish Scripture and reach a crescendo with the Jewish notion

---

[152]James E. Young, *The Texture of Memory: Holocaust Memorials and Meaning* (New Haven: Yale University Press, 1993), 19.

[153]Yosef Hayim Yerushalmi, *Zakhor: Jewish History and Jewish Memory* (New York: Schocken Books, 1989), 9.

of God. Ancient Israel knows God only insofar as God is revealed historically. God is referred to as "God of your fathers, the God of Abraham, Isaac, and Jacob" (Exodus 3: 16). Thus, the Jewish God is the God of history. When God is introduced directly to the entire people at Mt. Sinai, nothing is heard of God's essence or attributes, only, "I am God who brought you out of the land of Egypt, the house of bondage" (Exodus 20: 2). From here on, the people Israel know who God is from what God has done in history.

This command to remember history is extended not only to the ancient Israelites, but also to the generations of Jews who followed them. According to the Hebrew Bible, the covenant between God and the Jewish people is to endure forever. Consider the following Biblical text that serves as the master story of the Passover holiday: "I make this covenant with its sanctions, not with you alone, but with those who are standing here with us this day before the Lord our God and with those who are not with us here this day" (Deuteronomy 29: 13-14). Since future generations cannot literally return to Sinai, the covenant must take place along the conduits of memory, through the creation of commemorative stories, sites and rituals.

The roots of Holocaust memory in Israel took shape even before the creation of the state. In accordance with the erudite character of Jewish tradition, the first memorials and monuments to the Holocaust came not in stone, glass, or steel, but in narrative, in words on paper, as **Yizkhor Bikher** (memorial books). Written by hundreds of survivors, these books remembered Jewish communities obliterated during the Holocaust. Many scholars agree that the *Yizkhor Bikher* are the single most important act of commemorating the dead on the part of Jewish survivors. As James Young explains, "For a murdered people without graves, without even corpses to inter, these memorial books often came to serve as symbolic tombstones."[154] In need of a cathartic ceremony and in response to what Joost Merloo and others have called, "the missing gravestone syndrome," survivors created literary gravesites as the first memory work. Only later were physical Holocaust memory sites created in Israel and the Diaspora.

In Israel, policymakers, educators, Holocaust survivors, and the media argued for many years over methods for honoring survivors and commemorating victims. At the end of World War II, Jews living in what was then Palestine struggled to find appropriate forms of both private and public commemoration when they had little or no information about the fate of their loved ones. For most people, it was too early to commemorate their friends and family members as they still

---

[154]James E. Young, *The Texture of Memory: Holocaust Memorials and Meaning* (New Haven: Yale University Press, 1993), 7.

held out hope that they might be found alive. Well into the 1950s a special office of the Jewish Agency continued daily radio broadcasts of the names of people seeking information about their relatives.

Not surprisingly, it took decades before meaningful and agreed upon forms of Holocaust commemoration began to take shape in Israel. And many of those forms were at first highly symbolic because Israel chose to remember martyrs and heroes side-by-side, as though they were equivalent and equivalently redeemed by the creation of the state. This connection is exemplified by the Hebrew infinitive for remembering, *lizkhor,* (literally, to remember,) which carries a much larger significance in Hebrew than in English. In Hebrew, *lizkhor* means not only to remember, but to remember and to act. Yerushalmi emphasizes the uniquely selective nature of Hebrew memory, which calls for a particular kind of acting rather than simply holding a curiosity about the past. He writes, "Israel is told only that it must be a kingdom of priests and a holy people; nowhere is it suggested that it become a nation of historians."[155] In other words, Jewish tradition posits action to be the consequence and even the inheritance of memory. In Israel, as a result, memory of the Holocaust is directly linked to the act of creating the state.

When Tom Segev's book, *The Seventh Million,* was published in Israel in 1991, it was embraced and disdained by Israelis in equal numbers. Segev argued that the Zionist leaders and founders of the State of Israel were initially embarrassed by Holocaust victimhood. As an example, Segev reconstructs debates over where **Yad Vashem**, the commemorative site to the victims of the Holocaust in Israel, was to be situated. The central military cemetery in Jerusalem, honoring Israeli soldiers who fell in battle, is located on Mt. Herzl near the graves of Israel's national leaders and the fathers of Zionism. *Yad Vashem* is located on the slopes of the same mountain. The original planners of *Yad Vashem* wanted it to be situated on the highest point of the mountain to symbolize the immensity of the Holocaust. Instead, its chosen location is less assuming, as if there were reason to hide it.

The controversy over *Yad Vashem* was not limited to its geographic location. The memorial was originally conceived of in 1942 in what was then Palestine. The proposal lay dormant for years, however, until after the war when the plan was implemented, only to be interrupted again by the 1948 War of Independence. Due to pressure from the religious community and controversy over the best way to balance the symbols of victimization alongside acts of heroism, it wasn't until 1953 that a law was passed by the Israeli parliament establishing *Yad Vashem*

---

[155]Yosef Hayim Yerushalmi, *Zakhor: Jewish History and Jewish Memory* (New York: Schocken Books, 1989), xvi.

as the official, state memorial to the Holocaust, meant to serve as a national shrine to both Israeli pride in heroism and shame in victimization. The parliamentary bill for the establishment of *Yad Vashem* became the first remembrance law of the State of Israel. As such, it also established *Yad Vashem* as a secular institution and memorial. From the beginning, Holocaust memorial culture was thus considered an integral part of the secular national symbolism of the State of Israel. The education minister in Israel at the time that *Yad Vashem* was founded saw the War of Independence as a direct continuation of the war of the partisans and the underground fighters who fought the Nazis during World War II. The link between the victims of the Holocaust and the founding of the State of Israel became inextricably tied—symbolically rescuing Holocaust victimization through state heroism.

Today, *Yad Vashem* is one of the most visited modern sites in Jerusalem. Its library holds one of the world's most exhaustive archival and scholarly collections on the Holocaust; it is often the first site visited by foreign dignitaries; and it is considered by many to be second only to the Western Wall in its sacredness as a shrine of Israel's civil religion.

Concurrently, the religious community in Israel developed its own culture of memory, highlighting religious conceptions of the Holocaust that emphasized God's role and intervention. Although the religious conceptions differ from the secular versions, Holocaust commemoration amongst the religious community shares the secular ideology of heroism as opposed to victimization. In Israel, the Holocaust and heroism have become one for both the secular and the religious communities.

This link between the victimization of the Holocaust and the heroism of statehood can also be traced in the date chosen on the Hebrew calendar to commemorate the Holocaust. Like the creation and founding of *Yad Vashem,* the choice of a date to memorialize the Holocaust was fraught with controversy, this time over two major ideals: the desire to connect the holiday with resistance and heroism on the one hand, and the religious community's desire to associate the day with a traditional Jewish holy day on the other. Eventually, a resolution was passed by the Israeli parliament in 1951 which set a Holocaust remembrance day to coincide with the Warsaw Ghetto Uprising. The 27th day of the month of *Nisan* on the Hebrew calendar was to be known as **Yom HaShoah VeHagvurah**— Day of Commemorating the Holocaust *and* Heroism. (In the United States, the day is known as either *Yom HaShoah* or Holocaust Remembrance Day.) In 1961, an Israeli parliamentary amendment required that all places of entertainment be closed on the evening preceding the holiday. *Yad Vashem* also suggested that the siren, traditionally sounded for **Yom HaZikaron** (Memorial Day) and accompanying two minutes of silence, become part of the ritual observance of *Yom HaShoah VeHagvurah*, another move linking the martyrs of the Holocaust to the heroes who fell for the State.

Ritual observance of *Yom HaShoah* continues to evolve in Israel and the Diaspora. While there are clearly spiritual aspects to the day, there are no pre-scribed religious observances. Furthermore, unlike other Jewish holidays that dictate both public and private rituals, *Yom HaShoah* is largely observed in public forums. While many families light *yahrzeit* (memorial) candles in their homes to commemorate familial losses, most expressions of observance are community-based. Throughout Israel and the Diaspora synagogues, schools, community centers, federations, and other Jewish communal organizations hold *Yom HaShoah* observances with spiritual, community, and political leaders. These ceremonies sometimes include readings of names (of concentration camps or victims), silent remembrances, prayer vigils, sermons, singing the Israeli national anthem and other songs, readings of poetry, academic lectures, talks by survivors, candle lighting ceremonies, art exhibits or film screenings.

While Israel remembers victims (whom they call martyrs) and heroes side-by-side, in the United States, Holocaust memory tends to revolve around victims. Because Americans value individualism and a kind of can-do mentality, though, commemoration efforts in the United States have sometimes relied heavily on popular culture that exploits those orientations. When *Schindler's List* was released on video, for example, many synagogues across the country used the film in their annual commemorations. As Omer Bartov explains, *Schindler's List* sweetened the bitter pill of the Holocaust, softening its horrors for American audiences through American means. "The film actually distorts the 'reality' of the Holocaust, or at least leaves out too many other 'realities,' and especially that most common and typical reality of all, namely mass, industrial killing. Instead, the film caters to a certain kind of general post-Holocaust sensibility, as well as to a series of specific national and ideological biases."[156] The reasons that Anne Frank's story became so immensely popular in the U.S. foreground the same American ideals that made *Schindler's List* such a success. Anne's father edited the diary before its publication, deleting potentially controversial or unsavory details including references to Anne's emerging adolescent sexuality and the

---

[156]Omer Bartov, "Spielberg's Oskar: Hollywood tries evil" in Y. Loshitzky (ed) Spielberg's Holocaust: Critical perspectives on Schindler's List (pp. 41-60) (Bloomington: Indiana University Press, 1997), 46.

fights between Anne and her mother. Moreover and more importantly, in the initial play based on her diary, which became a Broadway hit in the 1950s, there is no mention of Anne's capture, deportation and murder. Anne's diary itself of course necessarily left that out. What resulted from the enormous popularization of the diary has been a sanitized version of the Holocaust, which ends with a message of faith and hope.

Research that Simone did has shown that, inadvertently, teachers in public schools sometimes shape their units or courses on the Holocaust in ways that highlight these American ideals, falling prey to the same impulses as the makers of popular culture. That is, when actually taught, Holocaust content is sometimes molded to fit particularly American cultural paradigms, even at the expense of its historical integrity. In one case, for example, a teacher taught the Holocaust as a story primarily about (rugged) individuals facing obstacles and overcoming adversity—the American mythos of individual agency—rather than as people constrained in their choices by the constellations of historical circumstance. In essence, though this teacher viewed the Holocaust as a mass phenomenon, understandable mainly in collective terms, his teaching funneled it into a cultural mold that emphasizes individualism, lauds heroism as individual accomplishment, requires redemption and supplies a happy ending. While it may be comforting for us to shape Holocaust memory, commemoration and education efforts around heroes, survivors, optimism and hope, ultimately the Holocaust must be remembered in all of its tragedy and in all of its complexity. Only then can dignified commemoration be offered in memory of the millions of voiceless victims whose stories never reached us.

Teaching Ideas

1. *Yizkhor Bikher*: Ask your students to interview family members, friends and survivors to gather personal stories of the Holocaust. Then publish them into *Yizkhor Bikher* to be distributed at school and in the community. Or, if you want to really challenge your students academically, consider having them research a single community for whom a *Yizkhor Bikher* hasn't been made. Have them do the work of tracking down survivors, their children, historical records, photographs and documents, etc. and make them into a meaningful memory book. If you'd like to show an example of a *Yizkhor* book, the **JewishGen** genealogy website has lots of different communities' books online.

2. **Is *Yom HaShoah* the Day to Rage Against God?:** In the Jewish calendar, there is a day for every purpose: a day for rest and a day for work, a day for parody, a day for penitence, a day for feasting and a day for fasting, a day for reenacting the Exodus and a day for reliving the Exile. In this regard, David Roskies asks:

> But where, in this orchestrated array of catharsis and commemoration, is there a day set aside for anger? How can we love God with all our heart and soul (Deuteronomy 10: 12) without a time for sanctioned rage? Can we rejoice before the Lord, affirm the covenant between the God of Israel and the people of Israel, if we cannot acknowledge the broken covenants? A marriage, no matter how solid, cannot be sustained without the ability to express one's disappointment, without a venue for one's sense of betrayal. So too the marriage promulgated at Sinai…. The destruction of European Jewry is the sign of God's betrayal of Israel. *Yom HaShoah* marks the day of broken covenants. It is the day of sanctioned rage against God.[157]

Ask your students to consider and debate Roskies' claims and questions. Is the Holocaust a sign of God's betrayal of Israel? Does *Yom HaShoah* mark the day of broken covenants? Do we need a day to rage against God? If so, do the current rituals and observances of *Yom HaShoah* (lighting candles, reading names, etc.) fulfill that need? If not, what sort of rituals do we need to create? And, what are the implications of this charge for interdenominational or interfaith commemorations? Ask your students to create new rituals for observing *Yom HaShoah*. Have them bring the suggestion before the ritual committee of their synagogue or the local organization that organizes Holocaust commemoration events.

3. **Ceremony:** Your students can host a meaningful *Yom HaShoah* ceremony (with the new rituals they created above) to commemorate the Holocaust. **Ritual Well** is a useful online resource for creating contemporary Jewish liturgy and rituals. **An Everlasting Name** by Rabbi Adam Fisher is a modern *makhzor* (holiday prayer book) for *Yom HaShoah* that incorporates poetry, reflections, and songs into the liberal evening and morning services. **Zakhor: Holocaust Remembrance** is an "instant lesson" and teacher's guide that presents the many ways in which Jews have remembered the Holocaust in the last several decades. **Teaching Jewish Holidays: History, Values, and Activities** by Rabbi Robert includes a chapter on *Yom HaShoah*. The 1980 act of Congress that created The United States

---

[157]David Roskies, *The Day of Broken Covenants*, (New York: JTS Magazine, Spring 1999), Forum Column.

Holocaust Memorial Council mandated that the museum lead the nation in civic commemorations and encourage appropriate remembrance observances throughout the country. As a result, the **U.S. Holocaust Memorial Museum** offers a comprehensive "how to" guide on its website for planning *Yom HaShoah* observances. You may want your students to critique this entry, asking what it suggests and avoids.

4. **The Nature of Memory in Jewish Thought**: Jewish Scripture contains hundreds of references to the nature of Jewish memory. We've listed just a few below to catalyze your students' thinking. Ask your students to study some of these Biblical passages in light of Holocaust memory:

- Remember the days of old, consider the years of ages past... (Deuteronomy 32: 7).
- Remember these things, O Jacob, for you, O Israel, are My servant: I have fashioned you, you are My servant, O Israel, never forget Me (Isaiah 44: 21).
- Remember what Amalek did to you... (Deuteronomy 25: 17).
- My people, remember what Balak king of Moab plotted against you... (Micah 6: 5).
- Remember this day, on which you went free from Egypt... (Exodus 13: 3).

After studying these passages in context, ask your students to consider:

- What do these passages teach us about the nature of Jewish memory?
- What do you think is the significance of the repetition of the word remember (*zakhor* in Hebrew) in each passage?
- Why do you think it is necessary for God to remind the Jewish people repeatedly to remember?
- What does it mean to remember? How do individuals and groups remember? Is there a difference between remembering people, events or things?
- What do these Biblical texts teach us about creating meaningful Holocaust commemoration (or commemorating any Jewish historical event)?

5. **Memorial Liturgy**: In the various Jewish denominational movements, several *minhagim* (customs) have emerged to mark and commemorate the victims of the Holocaust using traditional liturgy. Ask your students to study and learn to recite the following traditional forms of memorial liturgy.

- *Kaddish yitom*, the mourner's prayer that is recited at funerals and by mourners both praises God and expresses a yearning for the establishment of God's kingdom on earth. In many liberal synagogues, *Kaddish yitom* is recited by the entire congregation in remembrance of the six million Jews who perished in the Holocaust, thereby symbolizing that we are all in mourning.

- The period between Passover and *Shavuot* is called *Sefirah* (counting). The name is derived from the practice of counting the *Omer*, the days from the second night of Passover until the eve of *Shavuot*. The *Sefirah* period is a time of sadness for many reasons; most notably because according to the Talmud, 12,000 of Rabbi Akiva's disciples were massacred between Passover and *Shavuot*. Another reason for the sadness of *Sefirah* derives from modern times. Some notable Holocaust-era events took place during the *Sefirah* period including the Warsaw Ghetto Uprising. As a result, *Yom HaShoah* falls on the 27th of the Hebrew month of *Nisan* which occurs during the *Sefirah*. In traditional communities, the mourning period of *Sefirah* is observed by refraining from participating in joyous events including weddings, listening to or performing music, and dancing. It is also customary to adopt the traditional custom among mourners of refraining from having one's hair cut during the *Sefirah*.

- *El maleh rachamim* is a prayer for the dead with special reference to the deceased's *yahrzeit* (anniversary of death). While the prevalent custom is to chant *el maleh rachamim* on the *yahrzeit* of a family member, it has become customary in many circles to chant *el maleh rachamim* on *Yom HaShoah* as well since the *yahrzeit* of countless victims of the Holocaust is unknown and since many whole families were murdered, leaving no one to observe the rituals.

6. **Visit Local Monuments and Memorials:** While not every city is home to a Holocaust museum, many communities have monuments and memorials to the Holocaust in public civic spaces, in synagogues or community centers. Find out what sorts of Holocaust memorials exist in your community. Ask your students to research the artist, form, medium and history of the memorial and then visit it. As preparation, have your students design their own memorial. Ask whether they think its important to include Jewish as well as non-Jewish victims in the same memorial, how much space their memorial should occupy and why, where it should be located, what materials they would build it of (and why), etc.

7. *Bashert:* For a secular way to commemorate the Holocaust read aloud the first part of Irene Klepfisz's moving poem, *Bashert*. Make enough copies for everyone, but highlight only a few lines on each copy. Then ask your audience or students to read aloud the lines that are highlighted on their copy. This communal reading format creates a commemorative space, and the text of the poem itself commemorates the myriad ways to have survived (and not).

8. **Music and Film:** Ask students to free write, draw, or compose poetry while listening to Holocaust-era music. Jerry Silverman's acclaimed book, **Undying Flame: Ballads and Songs of the Holocaust** presents the story of the Holocaust through the music of the people who experienced it. The 100 songs in 16 languages are augmented with narrative stories and descriptions of the people who wrote them, how they came to be, and the specific events which surrounded the songs. The book includes a CD with 14 songs. **I Have Taken an Oath to Remember: Art Songs of the Holocaust** by soprano, Paulina Stark, is a CD that includes 17 songs written before or during the Holocaust. **Holocaust Remembrance Day** is a powerful one-minute silent film that suggests that if we observed one minute of silence for each of the six million Jewish victims of the Holocaust we would need to remain silent for more than 11 years.

Resources for Teaching

An Everlasting Name. Written by Rabbi Adam Fisher and published by Behrman House, West Orange, NJ, 1991. *A modern* makhzor *(holiday prayer book) for* Yom HaShoah *that incorporates poetry, reflections and songs into the liberal evening and morning services.*

JewishGen: The Home of Jewish Genealogy. Website: www.jewishgen. org/Yizkor. *JewishGen is an affiliate of the Museum of Jewish Heritage—A Living Memorial to the Holocaust and includes* Yizkhor Bikher *from several different Jewish communities.*

Holocaust Remembrance Day. Website: www.thejewishexchange.com. *This website is produced by The Jewish Exchange and the film, entitled Holocaust Remembrance Day, is powerful one minute silent film, viewable and downloadable for free, that suggests that if we observed one minute of silence for each of the six million Jewish victims of the Holocaust we would need to remain silent for more than 11 years.*

I Have Taken an Oath to Remember: Art Songs of the Holocaust. Performed by Paulina Stark and produced by UAHC Press, New York. *A CD that includes 17 songs written during or before the Holocaust.*

Ritual Well. Website site: www.ritualwell.org. *Produced by Kolot: The Center For Jewish Women's And Gender Studies and Ma'yan: The Jewish Women's Project, Ritual Well is a useful online resource for creating contemporary Jewish liturgy and rituals.*

Teaching Jewish Holidays: History, Values, and Activities. Written by Rabbi Robert Goodman and published by A.R.E. Publishing, Denver, 1997. *For teachers of elementary and high school students and includes a chapter on* Yom HaShoah.

Undying Flame: Ballads and Songs of the Holocaust. Composed by Jerry Silverman and published by Syracuse University Press, 2002. *Presents the story of the Holocaust through the music of the people who experienced it. The 100 songs in 16 languages are augmented with narrative stories and descriptions of the people who wrote them, how they came to be, and the Holocaust specific events which surrounded these songs. The book includes a CD with 14 songs.*

United States Holocaust Memorial Museum. Website: www.ushmm.org. *Offers a comprehensive "how to" guide for planning* Yom HaShoah *observances.*

Zakhor: Holocaust Remembrance. Written by David Bianco and published by Torah Aura Productions, Alef Design Group, Los Angeles, 2000. *An "Instant lesson" and teacher's guide that presents the many ways in which Jews have remembered the Holocaust in the last several decades and considers how to best keep the memory alive.*

Resources for Further Learning

The Jewish Way: Living the Holidays. Written by Rabbi Irving Greenberg and published by Simon and Schuster, New York, 1988. *The chapter entitled, "The Shattered Paradigm: Yom HaShoah" is an excellent resource on the evolution of Holocaust commemoration.*

Holocaust Remembrance: The Shapes of Memory. Written by Geoffrey H. Hartman and published by Blackwell Publishers, Cambridge, 1994. *In this collection, scholars, artists and writers consider the ways in which the events of the Holocaust have been, might be, and will be remembered.*

The Holocaust in American Life. Written by Peter Novick and published by Houghton Mifflin Company, Boston, 1999. *A survey of how the Holocaust became emblematic in American culture.*

The Seventh Million: The Israelis and the Holocaust. Written by Tom Segev, translated by Haim Watzman and published by Hill and Wang, New York, 1993. *A controversial account of the decisive impact of the Holocaust on the identity, ideology, and politics of Israel.*

The Texture of Memory: Holocaust Memorials and Meaning. Written by James E. Young and published by Yale University Press, New Haven, 1993. *Considered the premier text on Holocaust memory-work in Israel and the Diaspora.*

INDEX

Kovner, Abba, 89, 94, 114, 191, 201

Kovno, 18, 105, 111, 112, 114, 115, 198

Kristallnacht, 67, 69, 73, 75, 76, 77, 78, 82, 207, 229, 230, 233, 237

L

labor camps, 28, 119, 121, 123, 125, 131, 156

landsmanschaft, 89, 96

Law for the Protection of German Blood and Honor, 69, 74, 80

lebensraum, 69, 78, 216

Le Chambon-Sur Lignon, 205, 206, 212

Lemkin, Rafael, 24, 26

Levi, Primo, 4, 5, 117, 118, 124, 130, 136, 249, 251

Levin, Meyer, 99, 100

liberation, 2, 120, 121, 125, 131, 132, 134, 142, 189, 256, 262, 265

Liebster, Simone Arnold, 159, 164

Life within the Ghetto, 105

Lipstadt, Deborah, 63, 64, 228, 233

lizkhor, 270, 272

Louis de Groot, 139, 140

Lueger, Karl, 57

Luther, Martin, 63

M

MacDonald, Malcolm, 90

MacDonald White Paper, 90

Magnus Hirschfeld, 153

Majdanek, 120, 122, 221

March of the Living, 4, 7, 36, 267, 290

Marr, Wilhelm, 57

martyrs, 2, 153, 158, 272, 274

maskilim, 41

Master Race, 67

Maus, 127

Meir, Golda, 260

Memorial Books, 270

Mendelssohn, Moses, 37, 44, 48

Mengele, 155

Metaphors, 62

Milgram, Stanley, 170, 174, 186

Mintz, Alan, 268, 269

mischlinge, 153, 154

Modern Orthodox Movement, 37, 46

mohelim, 106

Molho, Rene, 255

monotheism, 243

Mossad, 89, 91, 92, 95

Mourner's Prayer, 16

Muller, Heinrich, 75

Munich Conference, 216, 217

Mussolini, Benito, 217

myth of the wandering Jew, 55

N

Nagasaki, 216, 222, 257

Nazi-Soviet Pact, 69, 78

Nazis, 2, 25, 26, 29, 32, 36, 43, 55, 67, 69, 71, 73, 74, 78, 89, 97, 102, 103, 108, 121, 137, 151, 152, 153, 154, 157, 158, 159, 160, 162, 164, 168, 169, 170, 178, 179, 181, 190, 192, 193, 197, 198, 202, 203, 206, 207, 210, 217, 218, 219, 220, 221, 228, 231, 233, 235, 241, 258, 261, 273

Night of the Long Knives, 157

Nobel Prize, 39

Normandy, beaches of, 216, 222

Novick, Peter, 1, 33, 234, 241, 280

Nuremberg Laws, 69, 73, 74, 80, 153, 233, 255

Nuremberg Trials, 26, 254, 255, 263, 265, 266

O

obedience to authority, 174

olah, 29

olim, 89

Olympics, 83, 85, 154, 237

Oneg Shabbat, 103, 106, 190, 196, 197, 199, 201

Oneg Shabbat Archive, 190, 196, 197, 199, 201

On the Jews and their Lies, 63

Oshry, Rabbi Ephraim, 198

OstJuden, 40

Oswiecim, 28, 49

P

Palestine, 2, 42, 78, 79, 87, 88, 89, 90, 91, 92, 93, 94, 95, 96, 97, 98, 99, 100, 139, 189, 190, 191, 193, 194, 197, 199, 201, 210, 229, 271, 272

Palestinians, 88

Palmach, 89, 93

parachutists from Palestine, 189, 190, 191, 193, 201

Paragraph 175, 156, 157

partisans, 94, 190, 191, 192, 193, 194, 195, 199, 200, 201, 273

Passover, 42, 82, 195, 245, 271, 278

Paul Schwarzbart, 137

Pearl Harbor, 215, 216, 220, 234

People for the Ethical Treatment of Animals, 32, 33

Pharisees, 54

Philip Zimbardo, 176, 184, 186

pink triangle, 153, 156

pogroms, 54, 55, 89, 93

Poland, 4, 7, 17, 26, 36, 37, 38, 39, 41, 42, 43, 44, 47, 48, 49, 50, 75, 78, 80, 89, 93, 98, 99, 103, 104, 111, 114, 121, 145, 147, 149, 170, 178, 179, 186, 187, 195, 210, 211, 212, 214, 215, 216, 217, 218, 221, 222, 237, 238, 239, 240, 290

Police Battalion 101, 170, 177, 178, 187

Police Battalion 309, 178

political prisoners, 69, 70, 152, 160

Pope Pius XII, 169, 241

Poreimas, 24, 30

Porraimos, 155, 162, 163

Power, Samantha, 33, 72, 187, 232, 233, 235, 238, 240

POWs, Soviet, 121, 123

Pre-Kindergarten, 14

Prison Experiment, 186

problem of moral culpability, 101, 102, 103

problem of overgeneralization, 101, 103

propaganda, 52, 69, 70, 71, 72, 74, 80, 81, 82, 83, 84, 85, 157, 178, 217, 230, 255

Protocols of the Elders of Zion, 63

Purim, 14

putsch, 153, 157

R

Rathenau, Walter, 63

Reform Movement, 37, 44, 45, 46, 49

Reich Labor Service, 68, 167

reparations payments, 254, 259, 262

resistance
    armed resistance, 190
    psychological resistance, 190, 197
    religious resistance, 190, 197, 198
    unarmed resistance, 190, 196, 199, 200

responsas, 198, 200, 248

Rhodes, Richard, 135, 171, 172, 186

Ribbentrop-Molotov Pact, 217

Righteous Among the Nations, 204, 205, 206, 207, 209, 210, 211, 212, 214

Righteous Gentiles, 204

Ringelblum, Emmanuel, 115, 190, 196, 199, 201

Rohm, Ernst, 157

Roma, 11, 26, 30, 33, 54, 55, 56, 70, 71, 131, 151, 152, 153, 154, 155, 156, 158, 162, 163, 172

Romania, 91, 92, 100, 155, 219, 220, 222

Roosevelt, Franklin D., 229

Roosevelt, Theodore, 56

Rothschild, Lord, 89

round-up, 216, 218

Rubenstein, Richard, 248, 252

Rumkowski, Chaim, 115

S

614th Commandment, 245, 247

S.S. St. Louis, 227, 228, 229

Sadducees, 54

Schindler, Oskar, 204, 214

Schwarzbart, Paul, 137

Schweber, Simone, i, ii, 118, 290

Segev, Tom, 272, 280

sekhel, 37

selection, 111, 121, 128, 135, 146, 263

Servatius, Robert, 260

She'erit HaPletah, 89, 95

Shoah, 23, 24, 30, 64, 65, 126, 133, 134, 136

shtetl, 15, 38, 39, 40, 42, 48, 49, 50

shtetlach, 38

Siege of Stalingrad, 216, 221

Simhat Torah, 14

Simon, Katherine, 3, 7

Sinti, 26, 30, 33, 56, 70, 71, 131, 151, 152, 153, 154, 155, 162, 163

slave labor, 18, 101, 109, 124, 255

Slovakia, 219, 220

Sobibor, 120, 122, 123, 181, 190, 221

Social Darwinists, 56

Soloveichik, Rabbi Joseph D., 246

Sosnowice-Bedzin, 102

Soviet Union, 18, 25, 70, 78, 120, 121, 145, 154, 170, 192, 217, 219, 220, 221, 223, 254, 258, 259

Spiegelman, Art, 127

Spielberg, Steven, 48, 49, 115, 204

spoon actions, 106

SS, 72, 75, 76, 85, 105, 107, 108, 122, 124, 125, 127, 132, 134, 135, 155, 157, 158, 161, 167, 170, 173, 182, 183, 210, 255, 256, 257, 259, 269

stabbed in the back, 54, 60

stereotypes
anti-Roma, 54, 55, 163
antisemitic, 39, 52, 56, 57, 62, 63, 64, 70, 71, 85, 89, 93, 178, 179, 204, 231, 232, 233, 261

sterilization, 56

Supercession, 61

survivors, 4, 5, 10, 28, 48, 49, 91, 92, 93, 94, 95, 96, 97, 99, 100, 114, 115, 126, 129, 132, 133, 134, 139, 143, 146, 163, 181, 198, 201, 212, 214, 223, 224, 234, 248, 250, 251, 253, 258, 259, 260, 261, 262, 263, 265, 267, 268, 269, 271, 274, 275

Szenes, Hannah, 190, 193, 198

T

ten Boom, Corrie, 204

Terezin, 114, 115, 135, 197, 200, 201

Tevet, 10th of, 14

"The 105", 42

The Great War, 59

Theology, 129, 252

the Struma, 89, 91, 92

Simone Schweber is the Goodman Professor of Education and Jewish Studies at the University of Wisconsin-Madison where she conducts research on how teachers in various school settings teach about the Holocaust and what students learn. Her last book, on Holocaust education in American public high schools, is entitled, *Making Sense of the Holocaust: Lessons from Classroom Practice* (published by Teachers College Press, New York, 2004).

For more than 10 years **Debbie Findling** led Holocaust-education pilgrimages to Poland and Israel on the March of the Living. Her doctoral dissertation investigated Holocaust education memory-work, and she also holds graduate degrees in education and literature in Hebrew letters from the University of Judaism in Los Angeles.